YESTERDAY'S NAVY

A Selection of Royal Navy Ship Histories of World War Two

By

Lt Cdr Ben Warlow RN

First published in the United Kingdom in 2009 by Maritime Books, Lodge Hill, Liskeard, Cornwall, PL14 4EL

CONTENTS

Introduction v

HMS *Iron Duke* 1

HMS *Warspite* 5

HMS *Malaya* 11

HMS *Repulse* 17

HMS *Renown* 23

HMS *Rodney* 27

HMS *Nelson* 35

HMS *Duke of York* 41

HMS *Indomitable* 47

HMS *Cumberland* 55

HMS *London* 63

HMS *Sussex* 67

HMS *Exeter* 71

HMS/HMNZS *Leander* 77

HMS/HMNZS *Achilles* 81

HMS *Orion* 85

HMS *Ajax* 91

HMS *Arethusa* 97

HMS *Aurora* 103

HMS *Newcastle* 113

HMS *Glasgow* 117

HMS *Liverpool* 123

HMS *Dido* 131

HMS *Phoebe* 135

HMS *Euryalus* 139

HMS *Cleopatra* 143

HMS *Argonaut* 147

HMS *Gambia* 153

HMS *Bermuda* 159

HMS *Newfoundland* 163

HMS *Ceylon* 169

HMS *Manxman* 175

HMS *Keppel* 181

HMS *Encounter* 185

HMS *Hero*/HMCS *Chaudiere* 191

HMS *Mohawk* 199

HMS *Tartar* 203

HM Ships *Lookout* & *Loyal* 207

HMS *Petard* 213

INTRODUCTION

These histories were originally prepared for publication individually in the magazine *Warship World* under my pen name Bill Johnson. There were about 60 of these histories so published. On reflection, it now seems appropriate to put some of them together in book form to provide a more permanent record of the work these ships carried out, often in the intense stress of continuous action. It becomes clear from just these few records that there was never a 'Phoney War' for the Royal Navy, with action in Norway, the North Sea, the Low Countries cumulating in bringing the troops clear from Dunkirk and other French ports. Nor was there a period of inaction after Dunkirk, when the Navy suffered heavy losses in recovering the troops from Holland, Dunkirk and the western ports of France. The Navy continued its action without respite in the Mediterranean (Greece, Crete, Tobruk, North Africa, Sicily, Salerno, Anzio and Aegean) and also in Home Waters with attacks at Dieppe, St. Nazaire, Norwegian coastal operations (attacks against *Tirpitz* etc) and later for the Normandy landings. Meanwhile the initial Japanese advances in the Far East were slowed and finally halted at high cost. All the while the Battle of the Atlantic was waged, bringing food, fuel and other materials to Britain, while other convoys were fought through to destinations in the Arctic, Mediterranean, the Middle East, Australia and southern ports. Nor did the action cease after V-E Day, as the Navy carried out the final actions in the Pacific and Indian Oceans.

Ben Warlow
2009

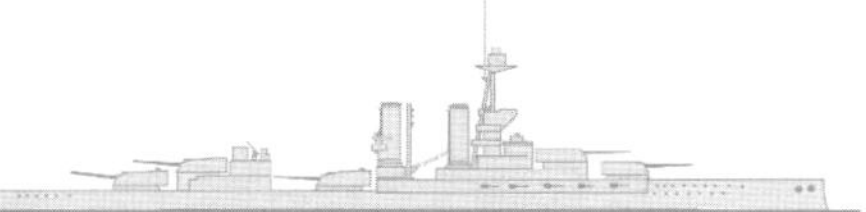

HMS IRON DUKE

HMS Iron Duke with anti-torpedo net fittings along her sides. *(Maritime Photo Library)*

The early 20th century saw an arms race develop between Great Britain and Germany. One major feature of this race was the construction of battleships. In this Britain led the way with the *Dreadnought*, introducing a powerful, uniform armament and turbine engines giving her a high speed. Various classes of battleships followed, with the Orion class introducing a larger, 13.5-inch gun, with all turrets mounted on the centre-line. There followed the King George V class of a slightly improved design. Next was the Iron Duke class. Two of this class of four ships were the last British battleships completed before the outbreak of the Great War, with the other two completing later in 1914. This class was 25.25-feet longer and a foot more in beam than the King George Vs. They reverted to carrying a more powerful secondary armament of 6-inch guns in place of the 4-inch in earlier Dreadnoughts. This allowed them to engage enemy torpedo boats without having to divert their main armament away from maintaining fire at an enemy battlefleet. *Iron Duke* was the first warship to carry an AA armament - of two 3-pounder guns, later replaced by two 3-inch.

At 25,000 tons displacement, *Iron Duke* was 622.75 feet long and had a beam of 90 feet. She carried five twin 13.5-inch guns, twelve 6-inch and two AA guns. She also had four submerged 21-inch torpedo tubes with 20 torpedoes. This was the last class of British battleships to be coal fired. Their 18 boilers fed two sets of turbines, developing 29,000 shaft horsepower giving them a speed of 21.25 knots. They had a radius of action of 7,780 miles at 10 knots, and 4,800 miles at full speed. Early experience showed that the two after 6-inch guns were too low down to be worked in a seaway, and they were removed. Extra 6-inch guns were fitted port and starboard forward one deck above the forward 6-inch battery. Although these ships proved steady gun platforms, their low freeboard made them very wet.

Iron Duke was laid down at Portsmouth Dockyard on 15 January 1912, and was launched just nine months later on 12 October by the wife of the

Fourth Duke of Wellington. She was completed on 9 March 1914. Her boilers were by Babcock and her machinery by Lairds. On trials her engines developed 30,040 shaft horsepower giving her a speed of 21.6 knots.

In 1914 she joined the Home Fleet and became the Flagship of Admiral Sir Geo. Callaghan, the Commander-in-Chief, Home Fleet. When war was declared in August 1914, she became the Flagship of Admiral Sir John Jellicoe, Commanding the newly titled Grand Fleet. She was the Flagship for the Battle of Jutland in May 1916, with Captain F C Dreyer CB as the Flag Captain. The co-ordination of the Fleet was conducted from the *Iron Duke*, sections of the Fleet sailing from Scapa Flow, Invergordon and Rosyth to take part in this major action between opposing battlefleets. During the battle she engaged the enemy and came under fire, but received no hits and had no casualties. Her sister ship *Marlborough*, was hit by a torpedo, but was still able to steam at 17 knots and could continue firing, maintaining her position in the line. This was a clear demonstration of the good design and construction of the class. From November 1916 to 1919 she was with the Second Battle Squadron. She was present at the surrender of the German High Seas Fleet off the Firth of Forth on 21 November 1918.

On 21 March 1919 she commissioned for the Fourth Battle Squadron in the Mediterranean, taking over from *Superb* as the Flagship in April. From April to June she took part in Black Sea operations supporting the White Russians against the Bolsheviks. In June and July 1920 she took part in operations against the Turkish Nationalists on the South Coast of the Sea of Marmara. In July she shelled Turkish Nationalist forces at Beicos. She re-commissioned at Portsmouth on 9 March 1921, again to serve as the Commander-in-Chief's flagship in the Mediterranean. She visited the Bosphorus in April 1922 with Admiral Sir John de Robeck on his farewell visit, and the next month was at Marseilles where Admiral Sir Osmond de B. Brock relieved Admiral Robeck. In September 1922 she was sent to Smyrna to protect British

HMS Iron Duke in dock. Note the sternwalk, a reflection of an earlier era of wooden ships. *(Syd Goodman Collection)*

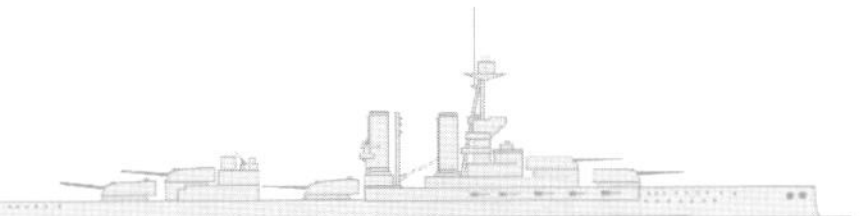

HMS Iron Duke as a training ship with B and Y turrets removed and AA guns aft. *(Syd Goodman Collection)*

interests during the rout of the Greek army, and helped to maintain order during the massacre and fire there. The next month she carried the Allied Representatives to the Mudania conference. In November she landed an armed guard at Constantinople to escort the deposed Sultan Mahommed VI to the battleship HMS *Malaya*, which took him to safety at Malta.

In October 1923 she called at Portsmouth to re-commission, again as Flagship in the Mediterranean.

In 1925 all four of the class were earmarked for a reduction in complement and to serve as training ships with the Atlantic Fleet. She returned to Portsmouth on 14 March 1926 and on 30 June1926 she commissioned at Portsmouth for the Atlantic Fleet. On 12 May she paid off, her crew exchanging with that of the *Benbow*, who took her to Devonport to pay off on 30 May 1928 into Dockyard control. She commissioned for trials on 30 April 1929. On 7 June 1929 she commissioned at Portsmouth under Captain E.C. Boyle VC as a seagoing gunnery firing ship, replacing the battlecruiser *Tiger*, which joined the Battlecruiser Squadron whilst the *Hood* was in refit. On 11 June 1931 she undertook firing tests off Bognor Regis, using her sister ship *Emperor of India* as a target. The *Emperor of India* was damaged and settled in shallow water, and was later salvaged and broken up. *Iron Duke* paid off in 10 November 1931 at Devonport to be demilitarised and for further service as a Gunnery and Boys' Training Ship. Her B and Y 13.5-inch turrets and her torpedo tubes were removed, together with her conning tower and belt armour. Her boiler power was reduced to 14,500-shaft horsepower, limiting her speed to 17.5 knots. She then had a range of 4,000 miles at 10 knots. Her standard displacement reduced to 21,250 tons. She commissioned on 6 September 1932 for trials and on 4 October 1932 at Portsmouth as a Gunnery firing ship. On 7 December 1935 she reduced to the equivalent of a reserve crew and on 4 January 1936 was placed at extended notice. She commissioned again on 21 May 1936 as a Gunnery Firing Ship and Boys' Training Ship. Her AA armament changed through the pre-war years. She was fitted with two single 4.7-inch AA guns in 1932. These were replaced by two single 4-inch in late 1935. These

HMS Iron Duke partially de-equipped as a training ship, but still an imposing sight. *(Ken Kelly Collection)*

were removed in 1936, but four single 3-inch guns were mounted instead.

She was present at the Silver Jubilee Review at Spithead on 16 July 1935, and also at the Coronation Review of the Fleet on 20 May 1937. From 1936 to the outbreak of war, she was used for trials of various guns. In May and June 1939 a prototype twin 5.25-inch turret, later to be fitted in the new battleships and light cruisers of the Dido class, was mounted in Y position for trials. She took part in the Review of the Reserve Fleet at Weymouth on 12 August 1939, just prior to the outbreak of war. She then sailed for Scapa Flow, arriving on 26 August 1939, to act as a depot ship and as part of the defences.

On 17 October 1939, whilst the main body of the fleet was at sea, the anchorage came under attack by twelve Ju.88 bombers and *Iron Duke* suffered a near miss off the port bow and another, slightly more distant, on the port quarter. One aircraft was shot down and one rating was killed during the attack. The bombs appeared to be 250-Kg. with delayed action fuses. C boiler room was flooded, together with Q and Y magazines. She finally developed a list of 20-25 degrees, and was beached at Ore Bay, and there was subsequent slow flooding which spread to all compartments abaft B boiler room. She was paid off on 26 October and re-commissioned the same day. She was moved to Longhope on 14 December and re-beached on 26 January 1940 in a position where she would be aground at all tides. She continued in commission as a base ship, with two quadruple 2-pounders and four multiple machine guns to enhance her AA battery of four 3-inch guns.

Ju.88s and He.111s attacked the Scapa Flow anchorage at dusk on 16 March 1940. The *Rodney*, *Renown* and *Norfolk* were present during the attack, and *Norfolk* was hit on the port side of the quarterdeck abaft Y turret by a bomb which exploded near Y shell room, making a hole in her side and starting a fire. Her after magazines had to be flooded. During that attack the *Iron Duke* had three near misses by delayed action-fused bombs, and suffered slight buckling of her hull plating by the bilge keel. She remained in commission and was finally paid off on 6 August 1945.

She was sold in 1946 to Smith and Houston, being handed over to Metal Industries on 2 March 1946. She arrived at Faslane in August 1946. Her hull was re-sold and taken to Port Glasgow on 30 November 1948 for breaking up. She had gained the Battle Honour 'Jutland 1916' for her name.

HMS WARSPITE

HMS Warspite as built with two funnels. *(Syd Goodman Collection)*

The *Warspite* was one of five Queen Elizabeth Class battleships. She was laid down on 31 October 1912 at Devonport Dockyard and was launched 26 November 1913. She was completed on 16 April 1915. On trials she achieved 77,510-shaft horsepower.

On 3 December 1915 she collided with her sister *Barham* and had to have a new stem fitted at Devonport. During the Battle of Jutland she came into action at 'Windy Corner' and was severely damaged. With her steering jammed with her helm hard over, she started circling as the German heavy ships closed to 12,000 yards. She came under intense fire, and luckily her steering defect suddenly cleared, possible shaken by the hits she sustained. Her armoured citadel was not breached, but all outside it, mess-decks, gun batteries etc, were a shambles. She returned to Rosyth for docking and repairs, which last till late July 1916. She had lost 14 killed and 17 wounded. In August 1916 she collided with her sister *Valiant* and was again docked at Rosyth.

Aircraft launching platforms were fitted on B and X turret in 1918. From 1919 she was in the Second Battle Squadron of the Grand Fleet until 1923, when she joined the First Battle Squadron. She was refitted from November1924 to February 1926. During this period her two funnels were trunked into one (to keep smoke clear of the bridge and fire control systems) and anti-torpedo bulges added. (increasing her beam to 104 ft from 90.5 ft), which reduced her speed to 23.5 knots. Her bridgework and control top were modernised, and she was fitted with additional AA guns. She was the first of her class to undergo this refit. She then commissioned for the Mediterranean Fleet. On 12 July 27 hit an uncharted rock in Aegean Sea and returned to the Portsmouth for repairs. She was again in the Mediterranean from 1929 until May 1930, when she returned to Home Waters to serve in the Second Battle Squadron.

She was refitted again from December 1933 to March 1937, but this time on a massive scale. She was re-engined and her 24 boilers were replaced by 6 new boilers. Additional horizontal armour was fitted. She could then develop 80,000-shaft horse-

HMS Warspite after her 1933-37 refit with new bridge and improved guns and machinery. *(Ken Kelly Collection)*

power giving her a speed of 24 knots. On trials she achieved 80,250- shaft horsepower with a speed of 23.8 knots. Her 15-inch guns were modified to increase their elevation by 10 degrees, increasing their range from 23,400 yards to 32,000 yards, and her secondary armament was reduced to eight 6-inch guns. She was also fitted with an AA battery of four twin 4-inch guns, four eight barreled pompoms and four quadruple machine guns. Eleven 20-mm guns were added in 1941, four more in 1942 and a further 16 in 1943. Four twin 20-mm guns were added in 1944 and by 1945 she carried 27 single and four twin 20-mm guns. Her whole bridgework was modified and her fighting top was removed. She had a hangar for aircraft fitted together with a cross deck catapult amidships, altering her appearance completely. Two sisters, *Queen Elizabeth* and *Valiant*, were to undergo similar refits but the outbreak of war prevented the other two being modernised.

She then joined the Mediterranean Fleet and was still there as Fleet Flagship when war was declared. In October, with the threat by German pocket battleships to convoys in the Atlantic, she was deployed to escort convoys in the North Atlantic. In November she was on duty escorting convoys to Halifax when the *Scharnhorst* and *Gneisenau* sank the *Rawalpindi*. She was then detached to cover the Denmark Strait.

The mining of the *Nelson* in December reduced the Home Fleet, and *Warspite* was detached to reinforce the Home Fleet, becoming Flagship on 6 December at Greenock. Later that month she sailed to cover the First Canadian troop Convoy as enemy movements had been noted in the central North Sea. However the Germans ships were on a minelaying sortie and no threat to the convoy arose. She then operated on Northern Patrols. It was decided to return her to the Mediterranean in March, but she was recalled whilst still on passage as the Norwegian campaign began.

She and the aircraft carrier *Furious* were ordered to join the Home Fleet on 9 April. Later that afternoon the fleet came under attack by bombers and the destroyer *Gurkha* was lost. The next morning the First Battle of Narvik took place when Captain Warburton-Lee took the Second Destroyer Flotilla into the Fjord to investigate whether there were any

enemy ships present. During the action that ensued, two large German destroyers were sunk and five others damaged with six merchant ships sunk for the loss of two British destroyers sunk and one damaged. *Warspite* and *Furious* joined the main fleet that day, bringing the fleet strength up to 3 battleships, one carrier, three cruisers and 18 destroyers. The Fleet then headed north to allow *Furious* to launch a torpedo-bomber strike against Trondheim.

On 13 April 1940 *Warspite* led nine destroyers into Narvik Fjord to complete the destruction of German naval forces remaining there, in an operation coordinated with an attack by aircraft from the carrier *Furious*. During the operation *Warspite*'s aircraft went ahead and sank the submarine U-64. All eight remaining German destroyers present were destroyed in the operation which involved *Warspite* engaging the enemy in the confines of the fjord - *Warspite* firing four salvoes at close range at the *Erich Koellner*. Two British destroyers were seriously damaged. Regrettably no British military forces were available to take advantage of this success, and the naval force was unable to provide a landing party large enough to cope with the 2,000 troops which had been landed by the German destroyers earlier.

On 24 April *Warspite* took part in a bombardment of Narvik, assisted by 3 cruisers (*Effingham*, *Aurora* and *Enterprise*) and the destroyer *Zulu*. That day she sailed from Narvik to return to the Mediterranean to be the Flagship of Admiral Sir Andrew Cunningham. Narvik was finally taken on 28 May, and the harbour was out of action until 8 January 1941.

Warspite hoisted the Commander-in-Chief's Flag on 11 May 1940. At that time the Mediterranean Fleet was being strengthened to counter the threat by the Italians. In June she took part in the first sortie of the Mediterranean Fleet against Italian shipping heading for Libya South of Crete. During the action off Calabria in July 1940, where both British and Italian Fleets were covering convoys, she hit the Italian battleship *Cesare* at a range of 13 miles. British cruisers also hit the Italian cruiser *Bolzano*. The action was hindered for the British by the comparative slowness of their battleships, and the unwillingness of the Italians to fight. During high level bombing by Italian aircraft, which proved accurate, fortunately only the cruiser *Gloucester* was hit, though other ship suffered splinter damage. During 22 raids 300 bombs were dropped on the Fleet. Later in July she covered convoys for the Aegean from Alexandria.

In 17 August she, *Malaya* and *Ramillies* with the *Kent* and 12 destroyers shelled Bardia and Fort Capuzzo. During their retirement, they came under air attack but suffered no hits. In late August to November she covered convoys and fleet movements in the Mediterranean. In November she was part of the covering force for the carrier *Illustrious* as she carried out the very successful attack on Taranto.

Later in November she again sailed from Alexandria to cover a convoy to Crete. In December she sailed again to cover attacks by aircraft from the *Illustrious* on Italian airfields on Rhodes and Stampalia. On night 18-19 she and *Valiant* shelled Valona. The battleships fired 96 rounds of 15-inch leaving the targets burning for hours.

In January 1941 she, with the *Malaya*, *Ramillies* and cruiser *Kent*, took part in a further bombardment of Bardia (captured by British troops 5 January) and Fort Capuzzo. On 10 January she was with the Fleet supporting convoys to Piraeus and Malta. These came under heavy attacks, during which the main fleet came under attack by German aircraft. These intense attacks by specialist anti-ship squadrons (Fliegerkorps X) concentrated on the carrier *Illustrious*, which was badly damaged, but managed to limp into Malta, where temporary repairs were carried out so that she could escape to Alexandria 13 days later. The carrier then underwent longer repairs in the USA. On 11th, during further air attacks, the cruiser *Southampton* was set on fire and had to be sunk.

On 27 March *Warspite* sailed with the *Barham* and *Valiant* and carrier *Formidable*, screened by nine destroyers to cover a convoy to Greece. A further force of 4 cruisers and 3 destroyers had been sent on ahead. Three enemy cruisers were sighted by reconnaissance aircraft, and later another enemy force, which included an enemy battleship, was sighted nearby. A third enemy force comprising

heavy cruisers and destroyers was also sighted in the area. Both British forces pursued the enemy, which headed west at high speed whilst air strikes from shore and carrier based aircraft were mounted, and these managed to slow the battleship (*Vittorio Veneto*) and stopped the heavy cruiser *Pola*. The Italians detached two heavy cruisers and four destroyers to stand by the *Pola*. The British light cruisers reported the position of the *Pola* and then proceeded onwards to seek the main force. The British battleships then closed the position of the *Pola* and she was detected by *Valiant*'s radar. The British battleships closed and also detected the other Italian ships standing by the *Pola*. The battleships opened fire at 3,000 yards range. One cruiser, *Fiume*, was wrecked by two broadsides from *Warspite* and sank 30 minutes later leaving 60 survivors. The second cruiser (*Zara*) was also engaged by *Warspite* and was finished off by torpedoes from the destroyer *Jervis*. *Warspite* also fired on an Italian destroyer and in the melee fired a salvo of 6-inch at the destroyer *Havock*. The British destroyers sank the *Pola* and two destroyers (*Giosue Carducci* and *Vittorio Alfieri*). The other two Italian destroyers escaped, though *Oriani* had been hit in her forward engine room by a 6-inch shell. Contact with the enemy battleship was not regained. This night action on 28 March became known as the Battle of Cape Matapan.

On 20-21 April she with *Valiant* and *Barham* and cruiser *Gloucester* bombarded Tripoli. The bombardment lasted 42 minutes during which time 530 tons of shells were fired. Whilst returning from this operation the *Valiant* was slightly damaged by a mine. In early May the Fleet again sailed to cover convoys from Alexandria to Malta. Later that month the Mediterranean Fleet was sailed to prevent German landings on Crete. The Fleet came under heavy air attacks, but countered all efforts by the enemy to land on the island by sea. On 22 May 1941 the *Warspite* was badly damaged by air attacks as she helped in the withdrawal of the lighter forces engaged to the north of the island. During the action she dodged over 400 bombs, but was hit by one 550-pound bomb on the starboard side of her forecastle which burst 12 feet in from her ship's side. Her starboard 6-inch and 4-inch batteries were wrecked and her speed reduced. Part of her upper deck (130 by 30 feet) was displaced by two feet and there was a hole 6 by 8 feet. One twin 4-inch gun was blown overboard, but the fires started were quickly brought under control. Smoke caused her No 3 boiler room to be evacuated. She had 19 killed and 72 wounded. She reached Alexandria at 0330 on 24 May, where she was classified as seaworthy in fine weather. Whilst there she was near missed by an 1100-pound bomb on 23-24 June. She proceeded to Bremerton, Seattle, via Port Said, Colombo and Sydney for permanent repairs.

She returned to operations, joining the British Eastern Fleet via Sydney in February 1942 and arrived at Trincomalee in March to become the Flagship of Admiral Somerville. The next month she was part of Somerville's fast division with two fleet carriers, 2 light cruisers and 6 destroyers. This force operated in the area of the Maldives seeking the opportunity for a night strike on the Japanese forces threatening Ceylon, knowing it could not afford a full engagement with the superior Japanese forces because of the need to retain a fleet in being. Contact was not established, and the Japanese force withdrew after sinking the carrier *Hermes* and cruisers *Cornwall* and *Dorsetshire*.

In August 1942 she with other units of the British Eastern Fleet transferred from Kilindini to Colombo. The force took part in decoy operations off the Andamans to divert attention from the US landings at Guadalcanal. In September she helped escort transports for the British occupation of Madagascar. In February 1943 she covered troop convoys taking 30,000 troops to Australia from Suez in five liners including *Queen Mary*.

In April 1943 she returned to the Mediterranean and became Flagship of Force H, part of the covering force for the landings in Sicily on 10 July (Op Husky). On 17 July she bombarded Catania with 57 15-inch shells. She also bombarded the coast between Reggio Calabria and Pessaro on 2 September preparatory to Operation Baytown, the British landings in Calabria.

She then took part in Operation Avalanche, the landings at Salerno on 9 September. The next day she, with *Valiant* and destroyers, escorted the Italian battlefleet from off Bone to Malta as part of the

HMS Warspite showing her enhanced AA armament in WWII. *(Ken Kelly Collection)*

Italian armistice conditions.

The fleet's bombardments at Salerno were vitally important to the success of the venture. *Valiant* and *Warspite* fired 62 rounds of 15-inch, 35 of which fell on the target, and another 8 within 100 yards. On 16 September she was attacked by ten to twelve FW.190 fighter-bombers of which one was shot down by her pompoms. As the attack developed three glider bombs were launched at her from 20,000-ft overhead. Avoiding action in the 7 to 10 seconds available was not possible in the congested waters off the beaches. One glider bomb hit amidships, going through No 4 boiler room and exploding in her double bottoms leaving a hole 20-ft by 7-14 ft and wrecking No 4 boiler room. The second near missed by No 5 boiler room and the third near missed on the starboard side aft causing little damage. Five of her six boiler rooms were flooded. Her one boiler room gave up after one hour, and flooding continued. She eventually had 5,000 tons of water onboard. All available salvage parties from US ships in company went to her assistance, including the salvage tugs *Hopi* and *Moreno*. The *Hopi* took her in tow for Malta. The cruiser *Delhi* provided radar and AA cover. The tow parted twice overnight and she passing through the Strait of Messina broadside on. She reached Malta at 0800 on 19 September. After temporary repairs she was taken to Gibraltar where large cofferdams were built on her bottom to permit her to continue to UK in March 1944. She then had two turrets out of action and No 4 boiler room inoperative. At Rosyth further repairs were started allowing a further turret to become operational, but all the damage could not be rectified before she was required to sail for the Normandy landings.

She was part of the bombardment force for D-Day at Sword Beach. During this action two torpedoes passed between her and the battleship *Ramillies*, and she was straddled by fire from the batteries ashore at Benerville. The *Warspite* carried out 20 shoots on 6 and 7 June, firing 314 rounds from her main armament, returning to Portsmouth to re-ammunition. On 10th she returned to the

beaches to support fire in the Utah area. Her accuracy and flexibility earned praise from the US Commander of the Army ashore. After one week she had to change her guns, and took passage to do this at Rosyth. On 13 July off Harwich she hit a mine, which damaged her hull portside aft. Her port outer shaft was seized for the rest of her career, and two other shafts were put out of true, limiting her speed to 15.5 knots.

She was repaired at Rosyth and returned to bombardment duties and on 25 August bombarded Brest, engaging batteries at 30,000 yards. Between 5 and 10 September she and the monitor *Erebus* were present to support operations for the 49 and 51 British divisions to take Le Havre, which surrendered on 12 June. *Erebus* was hit twice by shore batteries during this operation. *Warspite* was one of the ships singled out for special congratulations for her work by the Army. In all British battleships and monitors fired 3371 rounds of 16- and 15- inch and 1034 rounds of 6- inch in support of operations between D-Day and the fall of Havre.

On 1 November she and the monitors *Roberts* and *Erebus* took part in the Walcheren operation, which was to open the way for the Allies to use the port of Antwerp. They supported the troops with their 15-inch guns, which silenced several large German batteries. During her bombardment duties she had been mainly manned by officers and men of the passage crew who were returning to UK ready for leave from the Eastern Fleet. That they continued to serve with such good results reflected well on them and the spirit of the ship. By the end of her duties at Walcheren her guns were worn out, and this was effectively the end of her career. She started reducing to reserve in January 1945, and was placed in reserve category 'C' on 27 July.

She was sold on 12 July 1946 after 31 years service during which she had gained one battle honour in the First World War and 14 in World War II - the largest number of battle honours to any one ship in World War II. Whilst under tow to the breaker's yard on the Clyde she ran aground in Prussia Cove on 29 July. She was refloated and beached at Marazion, where breaking up took place in situ till 1956.

A sad view of *HMS Warspite* aground off Cornwall whilst being towed to a breaker's yard.
(T. Ferrers-Walker Collection)

HMS MALAYA

HMS Malaya which had been hard hit during the Battle of Jutland. *(Ken Kelly Collection)*

Malaya was, like *Warspite*, one of the five Queen Elizabeth laid down at the height of the Pre World War I arms race. *Malaya* was provided as a gift by the Federated Malay States at a cost of £2,945,709. She was the first ship of her name in the Royal Navy.

Malaya was laid down on 20 October 1913 by Armstrong Whitworth and Co. of Walker-on-Tyne at Elswick. She was launched on 18 March 1915 and commissioned on 27 January 1916. *Malaya* achieved 76,074-shaft horsepower on trials. This class was the first class of battleships to steam at this speed, which, for capital ships, had previously been achieved only by the lightly armoured battle-cruisers.

Malaya joined the Grand Fleet on 18 February and was with the Fifth Battle Squadron at the Battle of Jutland. During the early stages of the battle, *Malaya* was last in her line during a turn away from the enemy. She bore the brunt of the enemy fire for half an hour. She was hit below the waterline twice and started to list, and was then hit in the starboard 6-inch battery. The hit devastated the guns and their crews and started fires. The damage and injuries were made worse by a lack of screens between the 6-inch guns. In all she received seven hits, and had 63 killed and 33 wounded. Repairs were completed by the end of June 1916. She then she rejoined the Fifth Battle Squadron, remaining with the Grand Fleet until the end of the war. During 1917 Prince Albert, later King George VI, served onboard as a Lieutenant. In April 1918 she covered a raid by light forces on the Kattegat. She was present at the surrender of the German High Sea Fleet in the Firth of Forth on 21 November 1918.

In April 1919 she visited Cherbourg for the Peace Celebrations, and in January 1920 embarked the Allied Naval Armistice Commission to carry them on their inspection of German naval ports to ensure Treaty obligations were being fulfilled. In December 1920 she sailed from Portsmouth for India, embarking H.R.H. The Duke of Connaught from Marseilles to Madras. She then visited the Federated Malay States, calling at Port Swettenham, Singapore, Malacca, Port Dickson and Penang. She called at Bombay to carry H.R.H.

The Duke of Connaught back to Ville-France before arriving at Portsmouth in March 1921.

On return from the Far East she joined the 1st Battle Squadron of the Atlantic Fleet but in September 1922 was sent to the Mediterranean during troubles in Turkey. In November she embarked the Sultan of Turkey at Constantinople and took him to Malta. She then returned to Constantinople. She remained in the Mediterranean until March 1923 and rejoined that station 6 months later. In 1924 she underwent a minor refit during which time her 3-inch AA guns were replaced by 4-inch. In June to September two further single 4-inch HA guns were fitted at Portsmouth. She returned to the Mediterranean until 1927, when she returned to Portsmouth for a major refit, which lasted from September1927 to January 1929. During this period she was fitted with anti-torpedo bulges, increasing her beam to 104 ft. and reducing her speed to 23.5 knots. Her forward funnel was trunked into the after funnel to reduce fumes to the bridge and her gunnery fire control positions and her bridgework were modernised.

She then served in the Mediterranean from 1929 to 1930 and then the Atlantic and Home Fleets to 1934 prior to a second major refit. She was the Royal Guardship at Cowes in the summers of 1931, 1932 and 1934. Her second major refit was started on 1 October 1934 at Devonport Dockyard and lasted to 23 December 1936. During this refit she was fitted with extra armour. Her AA armament was enhanced with twin 4-inch AA guns in place of the singles; 8-barrelled 2-pounders were mounted to port and starboard of her funnel; and four multiple machine guns were fitted. AA directors, a twin hangar and catapult were also added, she being the first battleship to be fitted with hangars. Her forward torpedo tubes were removed, the after tubes having been removed in 1931. However, her 15-inch guns were not modernised, and the refit was not as comprehensive as that given to other ships of the class later, who had their machinery and AA capability upgraded together with improvements to their main armament increasing the range of their 15-inch guns. Her displacement had risen to 31,100 tons.

HMS Malaya after her 1934-36 refit, with single funnel. Note the anti-torpedo bulges along her sides. *(Syd Goodman Collection)*

On completion of the refit she sailed to rejoin the Mediterranean Fleet. On 7 February 1937 whilst heading south for Gibraltar, she encountered thick fog off Oporto and collided with the Dutch SS *Kertosono*. She returned to Portsmouth for repairs and her crew transferred to the battleship *Revenge*. The *Revenge*'s crew joined the *Malaya* and when repairs were completed on 24 May 1937 she sailed for the Mediterranean again. She was there in 1939 when the war broke out. She was then in the First Battle Squadron with the *Warspite* and *Barham*, and the aircraft carrier *Glorious*. In October she transferred through Suez with the *Glorious* to the Indian Ocean to form a hunting group against surface raiders. In December she was transferred to the Home Fleet to cover convoys across the Atlantic. She and her sister *Valiant* covered the third Canadian Troop Convoy from Halifax, arriving on the Clyde on 2 February 1940. The convoy comprised the liners *Aquitania*, *Empress of Britain*, *Chrobry*, *Monarch of Bermuda* and *Empress of Australia*. In March 1940 it was decided to transfer her to the Mediterranean to strengthen that fleet as the threat from Italy grew. She arrived at Alexandria on 3 May, with the battleship *Royal Sovereign*, and took part in covering convoys from Alexandria to Malta.

In July the British Fleet was covering two convoys from Malta to Alexandria, when they came under air attack. The *Malaya* suffered splinter damage to her forward AA director cabling but was able to complete temporary repairs in half an hour. The next day the Fleet encountered the Italian Fleet, which was also covering a convoy, to North Africa. The Italian force comprising two battleships, 12 cruisers and 20 destroyers which posed a great threat to the British convoys. The British ships closed to drive off the Italians, and the Italian battleship *Giulio Cesare* was hit at 26,000 yards, by the *Warspite*, whose guns had been modernised to increase their range. The *Malaya* was unable to close sufficiently to use her unmodernised guns. The British Fleet did not have the speed to follow the Italian ships, and withdrew to guard the convoys. They later came under heavy air attacks, fortunately without damage.

On 17 August 1940, with the *Warspite* and *Ramillies* and the cruiser *Kent* she bombarded Bardia and Fort Capuzzo (Operation MB2). She fired 62 rounds of 15-inch, 104 rounds of 6-inch at ranges from 6 to 8 miles. Although attacked by aircraft on their return to Alexandria the force was unscathed. From October to December 1940 she covered convoys, including some to the Dardanelles, whilst in November she was part of the covering force for the carrier *Illustrious*'s very successful air strike on the Italian Fleet at Taranto. In December *Malaya* headed west to join Force H. During her passage one of her escorts, the destroyer *Hyperion*, struck a mine and had to be sunk.

In January a series of convoy operations to Malta and Piraeus were mounted, and *Malaya*, then part of Force H, was in the covering forces operating in the Western Mediterranean. During this operation the Mediterranean Fleet came under heavy air attacks, during which the carrier *Illustrious* was severely damaged, and cruiser *Southampton* was set on fire and lost. On 31 January Force H sailed to carry out an air strike on the Tirso dam in Sardinia, but met strong defences. A bombardment of Genoa was cancelled due to bad weather. A second attempt at the bombardment was carried out on 9 February 1941, when *Malaya* and the battle-cruiser *Renown* and cruiser *Sheffield* bombarded the port for half an hour, starting large fires and hitting oil tanks, docks and shipping (Operation Result). The three ships fired 273 rounds of 15-inch, 782 of 6-inch and 400 of 4.5-inch. Four merchant ships and a training ship were sunk and 16 ships damaged. The Italian battleship *Diulio*, which was in dry dock, was not hit. *Ark Royal* was in company and her aircraft hit an oil refinery at Leghorn and laid mines at the entrances to the Italian base at La Spezia. The force returned safely, counter action having been delayed by a lack of communication between the Italian Naval and Air Commands.

Whilst escorting convoy SL 67 off Sierra Leone on 8 March 1941 *Malaya*'s aircraft sighted the German battle-cruisers *Scharnhorst* and *Gneisenau*. The *Malaya* also achieved a brief sighting, but the Germans decided not to attack a convoy so heavily defended, and, knowing they had been sighted, slipped away westwards using their superior speed towards the Halifax area. *Malaya* and other escorts

HMS Malaya in 1943. She was not given the same drastic modernisation as three of her sisters.
(Ken Kelly Collection)

set out to shadow the German ships but returned to the convoy when darkness fell. On 20 March 1941 *Malaya* was again escorting a convoy when she was torpedoed 250 miles WNW of Cape Verde Is. by *U106* ((Lt. Cdr. Oesten). She was hit at 2127 as she was zigzagging. Her armament was in the second degree of readiness, but her anti-submarine defences were at the first degree, so virtually all her vertical and horizontal watertight doors and hatches were closed. The torpedo which hit her was not seen until about two seconds before it hit the ship. Her main damage was to No.1 boiler room, which was put out of action. She suffered no casualties, there was no fire and her electrical supplies were undamaged. She took in 1,550 tons of water and ended up with a list of 1.5 degree to port after counterflooding. Several of her 6-inch guns were damaged. Her speed was reduced to 20 knots because of the loss of boilers. The convoy she was escorting (SL 68) was scattered and she proceeded to Trinidad, and then onto New York. She was repaired in the Brooklyn Naval Yard, the first British ship taken in hand in the U.S.A. under the Lease-Lend agreement. At this time her machine guns were removed and eleven single 20-mm guns fitted.

In July 1941 she escorted troops convoys, whilst being attached to the Second Battle Squadron of the Home Fleet. In September four more single 20-mm guns were added to her armament. In October she steamed to Gibraltar to join Force H, taking the Flag of Admiral Somerville from *Rodney*. On 10 November 1941 she sailed as Flagship of Force H to cover an operation (Perpetual) to fly aircraft to Malta. 37 Hurricanes and 7 Blenheim bombers were launched successfully, all but three of the Hurricanes landing at Malta. On the way back to Gibraltar the *Ark Royal* was torpedoed and subsequently sank. The next month *Malaya* was left as the only operational battleship in the Mediterranean, when *Queen Elizabeth* and *Valiant* were damaged at Alexandria, *Barham* having been

lost the previous month. *Warspite* was having action damage repaired in the U.S.A. The situation was worsened by the loss of the *Prince of Wales* and *Repulse* off Malaya on 10 December. The Home Fleet's only capital ships were the battleships *King George V* and *Rodney* and the battle-cruiser *Renown*.

In February 1942 an attempt to fly off aircraft from the carriers *Eagle* and *Argus* to Malta south of the Balearics had to be broken off because of trouble with the supplementary tanks of the aircraft. Another launch of aircraft to Malta was carried out in March 1942, again using the carriers *Eagle* and *Argus*. Seven Blenheims from Gibraltar and 15 Spitfires from the carriers reached Malta safely on 7th. These were the first Spitfires to join the defence of Malta. A further attempt to fly off aircraft to Malta at the end of March had to be cancelled, but a further attempt between 27-30 March was successful with 16 Spitfires reaching Malta.

In April *Malaya* was offered to the Eastern Fleet, but Admiral Somerville rejected her because of her limited endurance. That and the next month she escorted a troop convoy for the Middle East from Gibraltar to Freetown. At the start of April she sailed to cover the force heading to take Diego Garcia (Operation Ironclad), sailing from Freetown on 6 April. On 19th the force arrived at Capetown, and *Malaya* then returned northwards. In June 1942 she was part of the main escort for a convoy of 6 merchant ships to Malta (Operation Harpoon). The main escort included the aircraft carriers *Eagle* and *Argus* and cruisers *Kenya*, *Charybdis* and *Liverpool* and 8 destroyers, with a close escort of the AA cruiser *Cairo*, 9 destroyers, 4 minesweepers and 6 motor launches. The convoy came under attacks from enemy surface ships and also suffered heavy air attacks. The cruiser *Liverpool* was damaged by air attacks. Five fleet destroyers drove off an Italian force of two cruisers and five destroyers, but *Bedouin* and *Partridge* were hit and stopped. *Bedouin* was later lost to air attacks. The Polish destroyer *Kujawaik* was lost on mines at the approaches to Malta. Four of the merchant ships were lost and a fifth was mined but reached harbour.

HMS Malaya equipped with radar and extra AA guns, but reduced to a bombardment role at the end of 1943. *(Syd Goodman Collection)*

In July and August she was employed escorting troop convoys between Freetown and Capetown. In late August she returned to Gibraltar and at the end of September sailed for the UK for a refit at Rosyth. During this refit her catapult and aircraft handling gear were removed and two extra twin 4-inch guns added, together with two further eight-barreled 2-pounders and two single 20-mm. After the refit she joined the Home Fleet. In February and March 1943 she covered a convoy between the UK and Freetown. The convoy was shadowed but no attack developed. She then returned to Scapa Flow on 26 April. The *King George V* and *Howe* sailed south to the Mediterranean ready for the invasion of Sicily in July, leaving *Malaya* with the Home Fleet. On 8 July, the Home Fleet operated with US ships including the battleships *Alabama* and *South Dakota*, to carry out a demonstration off the Norwegian coast to divert the Germans attention from the assault forces gathering for Operation Husky. The Germans, however, did not detect the demonstration.

On 30 December 1943 she was placed in care and maintenance on the Clyde, releasing her crew for the manning of more modern ships. She took the Flag of Flag Officer Commanding the Reserve Fleet in 1944. On 22 June 1944 she re-commissioned for bombardment duties. By then her 6-inch guns had been removed, and she had an AA armament of six twin 4-inch, four eight barreled 2-pounders and forty-five single 20-mm guns. On 1 September 1944 she bombarded the Isle of Cezembre off St Malo. Her fourth salvo hit a large German battery and later two of her shells landed in the centre of the barracks at maximum range. Spotting was carried out by light aircraft. On 15 May 1945 she and the *Ramillies* became tenders to the training establishment HMS *Vernon* at Portsmouth, and were known as *Vernon II*.

In August 1946 approval was given for her to be reduced to reserve and scrapped. She was handed over to the British Iron and Steel Corporation on 6 April 1948, and arrived at Faslane 12 April 1948 to be broken up.

She had gained the following battle honours for her name:

Jutland 1916; Atlantic 1940-41; Calabria 1940; Mediterranean 1940-41; Malta Convoys 1941-42; and English Channel 1944

HMS REPULSE

HMS Repulse - a view that shows her side armour, and also her beautiful lines. *(T. Ferrers-Walker Collection)*

The battlecruisers *Repulse* and *Renown* were laid down on 25 January 1915 at Clydebank and Fairfield's respectively, their design having been approved in the remarkably short time of ten days. Their design followed the classical battlecruiser philosophy, a heavy armament of six 15-inch guns and a high speed of 32 knots, achieved by being sparing in the use of protective armour. They were originally ordered as battleships of the R class, but their hull design was cut in two and extended in length by 170 feet, to 794 feet. *Repulse* was originally to have been built by Palmers, but the work was transferred to John Brown's as her new designed length was too great for the former yard's slips. She was launched on 8 January 1916, and completed on 18 August of the same year, a record time for a ship of her size. Despite her speedy completion, events had occurred during the war at sea in that period, namely the loss of the battlecruisers at the Battle of Jutland, that made the Fleet look askance as she arrived at Scapa Flow. She arrived displaying two rows of scuttles along her sides, a sure sign of her lack of armour plate. Even her clean lines, with no torpedo net fittings on her sides, and no wood planking on her decks, could offset this lack of protection.

She joined the First Battlecruiser Squadron on 21 September 1916, and became the Squadron's flagship. During her sea trials in the Atlantic it was found that her hull was weak forward, and her deck bent and sagged inwards. Strengthening pillars were fitted to combat this. Another modification was the raising of her forefunnel by 6 feet to help clear the smoke from the bridge and fire control positions. However, despite this initial weakness of her hull, she proved a dry ship. Her hull above the waterline sloped outwards, and she had a good flare forward. She was also fast, her 42 boilers giving her steam for 31.5 knots on trials. She claimed high speeds during her service career.

On 1 October 1917 she made aviation history when Squadron Commander Rutland flew a Sopwith Pup off from her B gun turret. The flying off platform had been fitted on the turret to allow the turret to train into wind, thus avoiding the need for the whole ship to be turned for the flying-off operation. *Repulse* was the first capital ship so fitted.

On 15 November of that year she went into action in support of some British light cruisers that were operating off Heligoland. The cruisers were trying to surprise a German minesweeping operation, which was being supported by battleships and cruisers. The *Repulse* tried to lure the German heavy units into the North Sea, where there was a force of British battlecruisers, but the German refused to be drawn. However, during the action she achieved a hit on the *Konigsberg* with her 15-inch guns. She also took part in a raid on the Kattegat in mid April 1918, but had no opportunity to engage the enemy during that foray.

She took part in the surrender of the German High Seas Fleet on 21 November 1918, and was then sent to Portsmouth to refit. There she was fitted with a belt of 9-inch armour plate taken from the Chilean battleship *Almirante Cochrane*, which the Royal Navy had acquired whilst she was being built, and which was being converted into an aircraft carrier to be named *Eagle*. Although she, like her sister *Renown*, had been built with anti-torpedo bulges incorporated in her hull, further bulges were added, increasing her beam from 90 to 102.7 feet. In all, 4,500 tons were added to her original displacement of 26,500 tons. After this refit she could always be distinguished from her sister by the armour plate on her sides, *Renown* retaining the two rows of scuttles.

She rejoined the Atlantic Fleet's Battlecruiser Squadron in 1920, and in 1922 visited Rio de Janeiro with the new battlecruiser *Hood* for the Brazilian centennial celebrations. In November 1923 she and *Hood*, accompanied by five light cruisers, set out on a World cruise, visiting South Africa, Zanzibar, Ceylon, Malaya, Australia and New Zealand, returning via the United States and the Panama Canal, arriving at Portsmouth on 29 September 1924, after steaming over 30,000 ,miles.

HMS Repulse as modernised 1933-36 with aircraft catapult amidships, but with few AA defences.
(Syd Goodman Collection)

In 1925 she visited Lisbon for the 400th anniversary of the great navigator Vasco da Gama, and also took the Prince of Wales to South Africa and South America on a seven months' voyage. She reduced to a special two-fifths complement in January n1926, and spent the next few years with the Atlantic Fleet, with forays into the Mediterranean. In 1927 she lost two pilots in a flying accident in the Bay of Biscay.

In 1933 she started a large refit. An athwartships aircraft catapult was fitted together with a hangar capable of accommodating four seaplanes. Her general appearance was not much altered, and little was done to improve her anti-aircraft defences. The refit completed in March 1936, and she then joined the Mediterranean Fleet, but was at Spithead on 20 May 1937 for the Coronation Review of the Fleet. In 1937 she took part in the operations caused by the Spanish civil war, and on 23 August she, with the destroyer leader *Codrington*, procured the release of a British ship taken by the Republican cruiser *Miguel De Cervantes*.

In October 1938 she was again started a refit. On completion she carried a secondary and tertiary armament of twenty 4-inch guns and two eight barrelled two pounders. However, 12 of the 4-inch guns were in World War I triple mountings. It was only a short refit, and her engines and boilers were not modernised. Her sister ship was fortunately given a major modernisation bringing both her machinery and armament up date.

In April 1939 she sailed as escort to the liner *Empress Of Australia* which was carrying the King and Queen to Canada and the United States of America. Originally *Repulse* had been earmarked to carry the Royal Family, and had been refitted ready for this task, but, with the growing international tension, it was decided to retain her in Home Waters. Her role was limited to escorting the Royal Family on the first leg of their voyage.

The day before war was declared, all three battlecruisers were at Scapa Flow under the command of Rear Admiral W. V. Whitworth CB, DSO, with *Repulse* under the command of Captain E. V. Spooner DSO. By 7 September *Repulse*, with the destroyers *Electra* and *Escort*, was in the Iceland-Faroes Gap enforcing the blockade of Germany. She spent much of her time there and in the North Sea. In December, with the battleship *Resolution* and carrier *Furious*, she escorted the first Canadian troop convoy, which comprised five large liners carrying 7,400 soldiers of the First Canadian Division to Europe across the North Atlantic. Soon afterwards she escorted military convoys for North Africa and the Cape, providing protection against any German raider. This was a real threat, as the *Graf Spee* had shown all too well.

Not all this work was straightforward, for she was damaged at Halifax, Nova Scotia, when she hit the breakwater there on 3 November; and she had her after turret damaged by rough weather two weeks later whilst escorting a convoy with the *Furious*. There was no time for refits, nor any rest. By February 1940 she had already completed an exceptional 130 days at sea during the war.

The Norwegian campaign brought her no respite. On 5 April she was one of the ships sent to aid the destroyer *Glowworm* which had encountered German warships. She was then sent to join her sister *Renown* off the Lofotens on patrol. She helped search for, but did not find, the German battlecruisers *Scharnhorst* and *Gneisenau*, and had just returned to Scapa Flow on 15 April when she was detached to support the cruiser *Suffolk*, which had been severely damaged by bombing off Stavanger after she had carried out a bombardment there. *Repulse* continued to provide cover for the Norwegian campaign throughout, and in June helped cover the evacuation convoys. On 5 June she was sent northwards to investigate a report by RFA *Prunella* of two 'unknown' vessels. Whilst doing that she was diverted to Iceland, where landings had been reported. She was back at Scapa Flow again on 15th, only to have to dash eastwards in the hope of catching the *Scharnhorst*. The submarine *Clyde* had reported torpedoing the German battlecruiser. In fact the *Scharnhorst* had been damaged by the destroyer *Acasta* whilst trying to protect the carrier *Glorious*, and it was the *Gneisenau* that *Clyde* had hit. *Repulse* was bombed whilst heading for the reported position, but was not hit. Whilst on the way, a mine was washed aside by her bow wave and an emergency turn avoided any contact.

The next few months were spent operating from Scapa Flow, with a break on 1 October when she docked for 12 days. With no ships to spare, she was back at Scapa by 20th, and the next month covered the raid on German weather ships at Jan Mayen Island. A German scientific expedition was captured and a radio station destroyed. In November, when the *Jervis Bay* was sunk, she was deployed to cover the approaches to the Bay of Biscay. In December she covered minelaying operations east of Iceland, and also carried out an unsuccessful hunt for the *Scharnhorst* and *Gneisenau*. At the end of the month she, with the cruiser *Nigeria*, covered North Atlantic convoys, and in January 1941 was with the Home Fleet when it deployed south of Iceland to intercept the *Scharnhorst* and *Gneisenau* who had sailed for Kiel on 22 January

She docked again at Rosyth on 17 February 1941, but sailed a day later, this time for the warmer climes of Gibraltar and Freetown. At the start of May she escorted the Operation Tiger convoy as far as Gibraltar, but did not carry on into the Mediterranean because of her inadequate AA defences. Later that moth she was at Greenock ready to escort another convoy to the Cape. Instead she joined the Home Fleet in the search for the German battleship *Bismarck*, which had broken out and had sunk the *Hood*. She operated with the new battleship *King George V* during the search, but finally had to break off to head to Newfoundland for fuel. She was delayed there, in Conception Bay, by an intense gale,

Her Captain was now Captain W.G. (Bill) Tennant, CB, MVO (Dunkirk Joe). She remained in the North Atlantic for the next six weeks, operating from Halifax and Scapa Flow, until 19 July, when she arrived at Rosyth to dock and be fitted with 15 Oerlikon guns. On 10 August, after the short docking, she headed back to Scapa Flow, and then on to Greenock to escort convoy WS-11 (Winston Special), comprising troops and military equipment for Suez via the Cape. It was about this time it was decided to send her to the USA for a modification to her AA armament by fitting seven twin 4-inch mountings. The Commander-in-Chief had already insisted that she be given a proper refit before the end of the year. She reached Freetown on 13 September, and Durban on 3 October. After taking the convoy as far north as the Seychelles, she returned to Durban on 3 November. After a short stop she headed back into the Indian Ocean, escorting convoys off the East African coast and carrying out gunnery practice, joining the East Indies Squadron at Colombo on 22 November. She then went on to Trincomalee, which she left on 29 November in company with the battleship *Prince of Wales* and four destroyers (*Express, Electra, Encounter* and *Jupiter*). The *Encounter* and *Jupiter* had joined the force from the Mediterranean, and were bedevilled by mechanical problems, which led to their remaining in Singapore when the force sailed on 8 December.

The force reached Singapore on 2 December, *Repulse* anchoring out whilst *Prince of Wales* went into the base. It was at this time it was decided that *Repulse* should be refitted at Norfolk, Virginia. Already she had been operating under war conditions for over two years with just bare docking periods and had covered over 50,000 miles in that time. Her ship's company, many of whom had joined her in early 1939, had had little leave. Built for a complement of 1181, by mid 1940 she was crowded with 69 officers and 1240 men. On 5 December, she, with the destroyers *Tenedos* and *Vampire* sailed for Darwin to help persuade the Australians to provide a cruiser to assist in operations from Singapore. But the next day, when a Japanese convoy was sighted south of Saigon heading west, she was recalled and arrived back at noon on 7th. At 0400 on the 8th there was an air raid, and at 1735 she sailed with the *Prince of Wales*, escorted by the destroyers *Express, Electra, Vampire* an *Tenedos*. They headed up the east coast of Malaya searching for signs of Japanese landings. The Captain, addressing the ship's company, said : "We are off to look for trouble. I expect we shall find it. We may run up against submarines, or destroyers, or aircraft or surface ships."

On the 9th the force was sighted by a Japanese submarine (*I-65*) and later by an aircraft from the Japanese cruisers *Kinu* and *Kumano*. The *Tenedos* was detached to Singapore to refuel whilst the remainder of the force searched the coastline. That evening the force came within 15 miles of a squadron of four Japanese heavy cruisers escorted by four destroyers, but the Japanese squadron turned

HMS Repulse at sea in WWII with minimal AA armament. *(Syd Goodman Collection)*

north just as the British force turned south for Singapore.

On the morning of 10th the British force closed Kuantan to investigate reports of landings, unaware that they had been attacked by, and were being trailed by, a Japanese submarine (*I-58*). At 1015 the force was sighted by searching Japanese bombers, and attacks started at 1100. The *Repulse* received a bomb hit through her hangar, the bomb exploding on the armoured deck, killing one man and starting a minor fire. The *Prince of Wales* was crippled by a torpedo hit aft at 1144. The *Repulse* then took the brunt of the attacks, dodging torpedoes at high speed whilst also under high level bombing attacks. *Repulse* signalled requesting air cover at 1158, and 11 Brewster Buffalo aircraft arrived at 1315, but meanwhile air attacks had continued with unrelenting fury. The *Prince of Wales* was reduced to 8 knots with a heavy list, and *Repulse* closed to offer aid and support. The *Repulse*, after avoiding at least 16 torpedoes, was hit by a torpedo at 1225, and her speed was reduced to 25 knots. Then, in a further concerted attack, she was hit by three torpedoes to port and one to starboard. She started to list and slow down, and sank stern first at 1235. She had withstood the attacks of over 80 aircraft for 90 minutes, and finally sank in less than 5 minutes. Despite the speed of her loss, her ship's company reacted with courage and discipline and only 28 officers and 408 men (about 40 percent of her crew) were lost. The *Prince of Wales* abandoned ship at 1310 and sank at 1320, 8 miles from the *Repulse*. Eighty percent of the battleship's crew were rescued.

The *Prince of Wales* (modern, armoured and of 35,000 tons) was sunk by between five and seven torpedoes and one bomb, whilst *Repulse* (25 years old and of 32,000 tons) had succumbed after 5 torpedo hits and one bomb. It is interesting to compare the statistics when battlecruisers were subject to so much criticism. It is also interesting to consider what the effect would have been if the air cover had

been called for at 1015 when enemy aircraft were first sighted. Any aid to breaking up the enemy's attacks could have been invaluable. Perhaps the *Repulse* would have been under less pressure and been able to side step even more attacks. The Japanese aircraft had been returning to their bases when they sighted the British force, and so they did not have the fuel to spare to avoid even slow opponents. A sidelight is that the Japanese aircraft (which were naval manned) did not attack the destroyers which were rescuing survivors, and it has been reported, by a Japanese pilot that some aircraft returned to the area the next day to ensure that all the survivors had been rescued.

The survivors were picked up by the escorting destroyers and taken to Singapore. A few (some officers, officer candidates, specialist ratings and boys) were sent back to Britain, but most remained to help with the land fighting in Malaya. Some were lent to other ships that were operating from Singapore (*Mauritius, Exeter* and destroyers). Fifty sailors were sent to man the Penang ferry and others ran the trains from Kuala Lumpa to Singapore. 150 Royal Marines from both capital ships (both Devonport manned) formed 'The Plymouth Argylls' and helped defend Tengah airfield.

HMS RENOWN

HMS Renown making smoke probably causing the bridge to make an angry call to the engine room! Note the side scuttles denoting her lack of armour. *(T. Ferrers-Walker Collection)*

The *Renown*, like her sister ships *Repulse*, was originally to have been a battleship of the R class. At the design stage her hull was lengthened, extra machinery was added to improve her speed, and only three twin 15-inch guns were mounted. The reduction in gun armament was caused by availability, though eight big guns were considered better for a capital ship's broadsides. She emerged as a 26,500 ton battlecruiser.

She was laid down by Fairfield on 25 January 1915, was launched on 4 march 1916, and completed on 11 September 1916. Her arrival at Scapa Flow so soon after the Battle of Jutland, where the battlecruiser losses had been heavy, was greeted with dismay, as her rows of scuttles proclaimed her lack of side armour. However, additional plating had been incorporated over her magazines, and she and her sister were the first ships to have anti-torpedo bulges built into their hull structure. Extra deck protection was installed later after she had joined the fleet. On speed trials she achieved 32.68 knots. She served in the Grand Fleet for the remainder of the war, and was present at the surrender of the German High Seas Fleet in November 1918.

She was a handsome looking ship with a marked sheer forward and pronounced flare, and she carried a well positioned secondary armament of five triple 4-inch guns, with two single 4-inch guns on B gun deck. The triple mountings were awkward to operate, but were the forerunners of the very successful twin 4-inch mounting. Her 42 boilers gave her steam for 120,000 shaft horse power driving her four propellers to give a speed of 31.5 knots. On trials she reached 32.68 knots. She was also fitted with flying off platforms on B and Y turrets.

After the war she was employed on various

Empire Tours, carrying the Prince of Wales to Canada in 1919, to Australia and New Zealand in 1920, and to India and Japan in 1921-22. For these journeys the flying off platforms were removed from the turrets and an after triple 4-inch gun mounting was replaced by extra accommodation. In 1927 she took HRH the Duke of York to Australia. She also served with the Home and Mediterranean Fleets.

She was refitted in 1923-26 and 1936-39. She and her sister becoming known as 'Refit' and 'Repair'. During the earlier refit, carried out at Portsmouth, she was given extra protection against torpedo attacks. Armour from the Chilean battleship *Almirante Cochrane* (being completed as the British aircraft carrier *Eagle*) was added, and extra single 4-inch AA guns were mounted. In 1933 she was fitted with an athwartship catapult and a single seaplane. Her last major refit, just before the Second World War, was far more radical, giving her a complete new anti-aircraft armament of ten twin 4.5-inch guns and three 8 barrel two pounders. Her original triple 4-inch guns were removed. Her overall appearance was much altered, with new bridgework and funnels. Gone was her foremast with its control top, and in its place was a light tripod mast.

Later in the war six of the twin 4.5-inch turrets were removed and sixty-two 20-mm guns were added (eighteen twin and 26 single mountings). Her main armament of 15-inch guns had been modified to increase their elevation to 30 degrees. Additional protection was given to her magazines and machinery spaces. The weight compensation was achieved by fitting her with lighter machinery with high pressure small tube boilers. She retained her high speed, achieving 29.93 knots on her post refit trials.

In September 1939 she was serving with the Home Fleet, and was immediately employed patrolling between Iceland and the Faroes. Later that month she was part of the covering force for the return of the badly damaged submarine *Spearfish.* During that operation the fleet was bombed by German aircraft, but without damage. In October, she, the carrier *Ark Royal*, and the destroyers *Hardy, Hostile, Hasty* and *Hereward*, formed Force K, one of the many groups set up to search for German raiders in the South Atlantic. On 2 December this force intercepted the German liner *Watussi*, which scuttled herself, *Renown* sinking the wreck with practice 15-inch shells. When the German battleship *Graf Spee* was engaged off Montevideo, Force K was sent to the area at high speed. The force had to refuel at Rio de Janeiro on 17 December, and that day the *Graf Spee* scuttled herself.

The *Renown* remained in the South Atlantic until 4 March 1940, when she rejoined the Home Fleet on the Clyde. Three days later the Fleet left for Scapa Flow, and on 5 April the *Renown* sailed to support a minelaying force off the North Norwegian coast. One of her escorts, the destroyers *Glowworm*, was detached to search for a man lost overboard, and made contact with the German invasion force on 8 April. The next day *Renown* encountered the German battlecruisers *Scharnhorst* and *Gneisenau*, and in a running engagement, the *Renown* scored three hits on the *Gneisenau* with 15-inch shells, hitting her main fire control, her A turret and after AA guns. *Renown* was hit on the foremast and another shell hit her on the waterline but passed through and out the other side without exploding. On 20th the *Renown* left the Norwegian coast and docked at Rosyth, returning to cover the final evacuation of Norway in June.

In August 1940 she joined Force H, based on Gibraltar, replacing the battlecruiser *Hood* as the flagship. She covered the passage of reinforcements to the Eastern Mediterranean, and later sailed on a patrol to intercept three French cruisers which had passed through the Straits of Gibraltar to the west. The cruisers did reach Dakar, and were there when an Anglo-French expedition arrived and made an unsuccessful attempt to land on 23 September.

During the next year *Renown* with Force H took part in a variety of operations in the Mediterranean, covering the passage of reinforcements to Malta which included the flying off of fighter aircraft from aircraft carriers. During a convoy to the Eastern Mediterranean in November 1940, when troops were being taken to Egypt and four new corvettes passed to the Eastern Mediterranean, an Italian squadron, which included two battleships, intercepted the convoy. The action which followed off Cape Spartivento was inconclusive. The cruiser *Berwick* was hit and an Italian destroyer was damaged. The

Italian force broke off the engagement, and the main aim, which was the safe passage of the convoy, was achieved.

In December, *Renown* covered the passage of the battleship *Malaya*, five destroyers and two M.T. ships from Malta to Gibraltar, and shortly afterwards sailed to strengthen the escort of a troop convoy for the Middle East which had been attacked by the German cruiser *Admiral Hipper* enroute to Gibraltar.

In the first seven months of 1941 she took part in twelve operations in the Western Mediterranean, mainly covering reinforcement to Malta, but also, on 9 February, she, with the battleship *Malaya* and cruiser *Sheffield*, bombarded Genoa. Complete surprise was achieved and no casualties were incurred. Two hundred and seventy three rounds of 15-inch were fired, together with 6-inch and 4.5-inch shells. Four freighters and an old training ship were sunk. Damage was inflicted on other ships and the dock installations.

In May 1941, Force H was diverted to the North Atlantic to cover the possibility of the German battleship *Bismarck*, which had broken out into the Atlantic, heading south. In fact, Force H, which had been ordered to sea at 0500 on 24 May, and had cleared Gibraltar harbour an hour later, was well placed, as the *Bismarck* made for Brest. The *Ark Royal* was part of Force H and her aircraft carried out significant strikes, which slowed the German ship sufficiently for the Home Fleet to close and sink her.

Force H continued to cover reinforcements and supplies to Malta, including covering the convoy Operation Substance in July. In August 1941 *Renown* left Force H and refitted at Rosyth. Since the outbreak of war she had spent 381 days at sea, covering 135,347 miles. During this refit she was fitted with surface and air warning radar, and also radar for fire control of her main and AA armaments. Six single 20-mm AA guns were also added. She rejoined the Home Fleet at Scapa Flow on 22 November. In March 1942 she was part of the covering force for several Russian convoys, the German battleship *Tirpitz* being in a position to threaten them. The next month found her back in the Mediterranean escorting the American carrier *Wasp*, which was taking Spitfires to Malta. She left the Clyde on 15th and was back again by 26th, touching 32 knots on the way. A month later *Renown* carried out the same operation escorting the *Wasp* and the British carrier *Eagle*. She then returned to the Home Fleet, remaining there until October 1942.

She then rejoined Force H ready for the Allied landings in North Africa in November. She took part in these landings, and remained with Force H to January 1943, when she rejoined the Home Fleet on the Clyde, prior to a four month refit at Rosyth.

HMS Renown showing the radical nature of her pre-war refit, which upgraded her machinery as well as her guns. *(Portsmouth Royal Naval Museum)*

During this refit her Walrus aircraft were removed, her boats resited and 29 20-mm guns added. On 24 August 1943 she left Scapa Flow for Halifax Nova Scotia, where she embarked the Prime Minister, Mr. Churchill, the First Sea Lord and their staffs, who had been at the Quebec Conference. She was back on the Clyde on 19 September, after a 23.5 knot passage, much of which was through fog. In November she was again employed taking the Prime Minister to a conference, this time with the Allied leaders in the Middle East. She sailed from Plymouth on 12 November for Gibraltar, escorted by the destroyers *Rocket, Tumult* and *Ulster*, and carrying the Prime Minister, and the First Sea Lord. She then steamed on to Oran and Algiers with fresh escorts, returning to the UK on 2 December.

After a short docking during which she was fitted with 19 more 20-mm guns, she hoisted the flag of Vice Admiral Sir Arthur Power in command of the First Battle Squadron and Second in Command, Eastern Fleet. She sailed on 18 December 1943 from Rosyth to Scapa Flow. At the end of the month she sailed with the battleships *Queen Elizabeth* and *Valiant* to join the Eastern Fleet. They were joined by the carriers *Illustrious* and *Unicorn* on the Clyde. The force arrived at Colombo on 27 January 1944.

During 1944 she took part in various operations with the Eastern Fleet, including Diplomat in March, (an attempt to intercept possible Japanese raiders); Cockpit in April (a seaborne strike on Sabang), Transom in May (a strike on Sourabaya) and Pedal in June (a strike on Port Blair). During Operation Crimson in July (a strike on Sabang) the fleet carried out a bombardment as well as conducting the standard air strikes. In October she bombarded the Nicobar Islands. The next month the flag was shifted and the fleet divided. The modern ships formed the British Pacific Fleet, whilst the older ships, including the *Renown* and *Queen Elizabeth*, formed the Eastern Fleet. In December *Renown* went to Durban for a refit.

She returned to Trincomalee on 7 March 1945. At that time it was thought that the German fleet might stage a break out from their Eastern Baltic bases, which were becoming untenable. This sortie had been mooted at the end the First World War, though it was not put into effect. *Renown* was sailed from Colombo on 30 March, and arrived at Rosyth on 15 April. It was a distance of 7,642 miles which she covered in 306 hours, steaming at an average speed of almost 25 knots. The passage included the transit of the Suez Canal and a surface gunnery practice shoot carried out in the Mediterranean without slowing down. Three days after V-E Day – 8 May 1945, nine German naval delegates attended a meeting onboard the *Renown* at Rosyth, bringing details of enemy minefields, buoys and swept channels. She left Rosyth on 12 May for a refit at Portsmouth, and was then ordered to prepare for reserve. Her complement was reduced and six forward 4.5-inch gun mountings were removed. She was employed training Chinese naval personnel, who were to take over the cruiser *Aurora*. On 23 July she sailed for Devonport, where President Truman was received onboard her on 2 August by King George VI. The President was returning to the USA from Potsdam in the US cruiser *Augusta*.

From November 1945 to December 1946 she was employed as a part of the *Imperieuse* training establishment at Devonport. She was then placed in reserve. On 21 January 1948, it was announced that she was to be scrapped, and she paid off on 1 June 1948. She left Devonport under tow on 3 August 1948 and arrived at Faslane five days later to be broken up by Metal Industries. Her wardroom table was presented to HMS *Vernon*, the torpedo school at Portsmouth.

In a career spanning 32 years, the *Renown* had been at the forefront of the naval scene, both in peace and in war. In peacetime she had been an imposing and handsome looking warship to carry important people to all parts of the World. She carried a big punch for use against surface ships and shore targets, and had the ability to cope with heavy air attacks, demonstrated especially during her period in the Mediterranean in World War II. Her ability top steam at high speed for long distances proved invaluable on several occasions and allowed her to move from one theatre of operations to another quickly when the need arose. She showed how effective a battlecruiser could be in modern warfare if properly equipped, and when acting as part of a balance force. She had gained ten Battle Honours for her name.

HMS RODNEY

HMS Rodney showing the unusual arrangement of her main armament, all three turrets being forward of the bridge. *(Ken Kelly Collection)*

Towards the end of the Great War, plans had been made to construct five large 48,000-ton battlecruisers. With the coming of peace, and subsequent cuts in defence expenditure, in 1921 plans for these ships were cancelled. However, Britain's battleship force was aging, and it was decided to build two new ships, both of which were laid down on 28 December 1922. These two vessels (*Nelson* and *Rodney*) were to incorporate a new triple 16-inch gun turret originally designed for the battlecruisers. These ships also incorporated some of the material originally ordered for other battlecruisers which had been cancelled at the Armistice. These 16-inch guns fired shells of 2,461 pounds, three times that of the shells fired by the *Dreadnought*. The guns had an elevation of 40 degrees giving them a range of 35,000 yards, and permitting them to be used against aircraft. The cost of each salvo was £700. Each ship would carry three turrets. However, weight restrictions imposed by international treaties, limited the ships' displacement, and so a novel configuration of turrets, with three in line ahead of the bridge structure, with the middle turret superimposed, was adopted. There was, unusually, no main armament gun armament aft.

Their secondary armament was of a new type of 6-inch gun mounted in twin turrets, with three turrets on each side. These guns had a 60-degree elevation, again to allow their use in AA work, and were the first power worked 6-inch guns. Six single 4.7-inch high angle guns were added for anti-air-

HMS Rodney being manoeuvred in dock. Her massive 16-inch guns dominate the scene. *(Ken Kelly Collection)*

craft work, together with eight single 2-pounder pom-poms. The ships also carried two 24.5-inch submerged torpedo tubes, and were given a crane and catapult for spotting aircraft. The engine rooms were fitted forward of the boiler rooms to give the two propeller shafts a reasonably level inclination. The turbines developed 45,000-shaft horsepower and this gave a designed speed of 23 knots, a knot slower than the earlier Queen Elizabeth class battleships. However, *Rodney* achieved 23.8 knots on trials. The overall arrangement minimised the length of armoured citadel required to save weight. *Rodney*' s displacement was 33,900 tons.

Her overall length was 710 ft (over 60 ft more than the Queen Elizabeth class) and her beam was 106 ft 1 inch. The bridge structure was novel, being very tall, and with gunnery directors on top, obviating the need for fighting tops on the foremast. These structures were known as 'Queen Anne's Mansions'. The On 17 December 1925 *Rodney* was launched at Cammell Laird's, Birkenhead, by HRH Princess Mary. She was completed in 17 December 1927.

By July 1932 her single 2-pounder AA guns had been replaced by two eight barreled 2-pounders installed by the funnels, and two multiple machine guns were added by 1934. A further 8 barreled 2-pounder had been added by April 1939. By April 1942 she carried five eight barreled and one four barreled 2-pounders and 2 machine guns together with eighteen 20-mm guns. By August 1943 her 4.7-inch guns had been given shields, and the num-

HMS Rodney exercising her secondary armament of 6-inch guns. Note the aircraft catapult fittings on Q turret in the foreground. *(Syd Goodman Collection)*

ber of 20-mm Oerlikons had risen to 66, of which 10 were in twin mountings. The number of smaller guns was increased throughout the war to counter the air threat. At the end of the war her tertiary armament comprised six 4.7-inch, forty-four 2-pounders (five eight barreled and one four barreled), ten twin 20-mm and fifty-eight single 20-mm guns.

She served with the Atlantic Fleet/Home Fleet 1928-34. In June 1930 she took the British Parliamentary delegation to Iceland for the 1000th Anniversary celebrations of the Icelandic Parliament. She was at the Jubilee Review of the Fleet on 15 July 1935. In September 1937 she took part in RDF (Radar) trials during which she and other ships were detected at 3,000 yards by an aircraft fitted with RDF. In 1938 she was fitted with type 79Y radar, one of the first two ships to have operational radar, the other being the cruiser *Sheffield*.

At the outbreak of war she was with the Second Battle Squadron of the Home Fleet. Shortly after the outbreak of war, the Fleet sailed to search for enemy shipping. On 25 September she was part of the Home Fleet that sailed to cover the return of the damaged submarine *Spearfish*. The fleet came under air attack when 150 miles off the Norwegian coast, but suffered little damage, though the Germans claimed to have sunk the carrier *Ark Royal*. During these attacks she and *Sheffield* became the first ships to use RDF (Radar) operationally at sea.

On 8 October the Fleet sailed again when the German battlecruiser *Gneisenau*, a cruiser and 9 destroyers made a brief sortie off the Norwegian coast. This sweep proved abortive as the enemy ships withdrew through the Great Belt before the British force could arrive. Later that month the Fleet covered an iron ore convoy from Narvik. On 23 November, when the Armed Merchant Cruiser *Rawalpindi* was sunk by the battlecruisers *Scharnhorst* and *Gneisenau*, *Rodney* with *Nelson*, the cruiser *Devonshire* and 7 destroyers sailed from the Clyde, and headed north to carry out searched for the German ships, but could not find them.

That December she developed steering defects and had to be docked in Liverpool from 9th to 29th. She rejoined the Fleet on New Year's Eve. The next day, she took over Flagship duties from her sister, *Nelson*, who had been damaged by a magnetic mine and had to go to Portsmouth for repairs.

She sailed with the Home Fleet on 8 April 1940 (still as Flagship) when German forces were sighted at sea. It was believed that the Germans were breaking out into the Atlantic, but in fact it was the opening moves in the German invasion of Norway. The Germans invaded Norwegian ports on 9 April. One part of the Fleet was detached to carry out an attack on Bergen. That raid was subsequently cancelled, and whilst the detached force was rejoining the main body, both sections came under air attack. During the bombing which lasted for three hours the destroyer *Gurkha* fell astern of the detached group and was sunk. *Rodney* was hit by a 1,000-lb. bomb which failed to explode and broke up on her deck. She had 15 casualties. During these attacks the Fleet used 40 percent of its AA ammunition and four Ju.88s were shot down. The Fleet turned away from the Norwegian coast. *Rodney* returned to Scapa Flow on 15 April.

On 9 June the *Rodney*, the battlecruiser *Renown* and 6 destroyers left Scapa Flow to cover the returning troop convoys from Norway. When it was realized that German heavy ships were in the area threatening British shipping, the carrier *Ark Royal* was ordered to join the battleships, and searches were made without success. During this period German heavy ships sank the carrier *Glorious* and her escorting destroyers. On 12-14 June the *Rodney* was with the carrier *Ark Royal* whose aircraft carried out an attack on the German battlecruiser *Scharnhorst* at Trondheim. One bomb hit the German ship, but did not explode, and eight aircraft were shot down.

The Commander-in-Chief's Flag was transferred back to *Nelson* on 24 July, and the next month *Rodney* underwent repairs at Rosyth. In September she, the *Hood*, *Nelson*, cruisers and destroyers were transferred from Scapa Flow to Rosyth in order to be in a position to cover any possible sortie by the German Fleet into the Channel.

In early November the heavy cruiser *Scheer* attacked convoy HX 84 which was heading from Halifax, Nova Scotia to Britain. The Armed

HMS Rodney in wartime camouflage with main armament trained to port. *(Syd Goodman Collection)*

Merchant Cruiser *Jervis Bay* scattered the convoy and delayed the German ship by engaging her, though she herself was sunk. The delay meant that *Scheer* was only able to sink five ships and damage three others out of the 37 strong convoy. As a result of *Jervis Bay*'s enemy sighting report, *Rodney* and *Nelson* were sailed to cover the Iceland Faeroes passage against surface raiders. Later *Rodney* was diverted to escort convoys from Halifax to protect them from the threat of surface raiders, though *Scheer* had, in fact, headed for the South Atlantic. Normal convoy traffic did not resume until 17 November. Whilst covering convoys in the Atlantic in December, she encountered heavy weather and was damaged. Repairs were carried out at Rosyth.

In January 1941 she with *Nelson* and *Repulse*, eight cruisers and 11 destroyers sailed into the Atlantic in a search for the German battlecruisers *Scharnhorst* and *Gneisenau*, which had passed north between the Shetlands and Norway on 23 January. The cruiser *Naiad* sighted the German ships briefly, but the Germans had detected the British cruiser and turned away at high speed. Thus a chance for the Home Fleet to engage the German battlecruisers was lost.

In March she was covering convoy HX 114 from raiders and briefly sighted the German battlecruiser *Gneisenau* on 16 March. The German ship, which had been rescuing survivors from a ship she had just sunk, used her speed to escape. *Rodney* returned to the area of the sighting and rescued 27 men, survivors from the motor vessel *Chilean Reefer*, which had been sunk by the *Gneisenau*. In the previous two days the *Gneisenau* had sunk seven ships and captured three of a dispersed convoy, whilst *Scharnhorst* had sunk six. Sweeps were carried out to prevent the Germans returning to Germany, but the battlecruisers headed for the French coast instead, reaching Brest on 22 March.

On 24 May the battleship *Bismarck* and cruiser *Prinz Eugen* were caught trying to break out into the Atlantic on an operation against the convoys. In the ensuring engagement, the battlecruiser *Hood* was sunk. Nearby convoys were diverted. *Rodney*, which was enroute to the USA with 4 destroyers escorting the troopship *Britannic*, was ordered to take the destroyers *Somali*, *Tartar* and *Mashona*, and join the Home Fleet, leaving one destroyer to escort the *Britannic*. She joined the Home Fleet on 26 May and was with the main force, which included the battleship *King George V*, that closed the German ship on 27 May. The *Bismarck*'s opening salvoes fell close to her, but the accuracy soon fell off. *Rodney* opened fire a minute before the *King George V*, at 8 miles range. Her third salvo achieved the first hit on the German battleship. Within 15 minutes the *Bismarck* was heavily hit, and after ninety minutes was a burning shambles. *Rodney* fired 380 rounds of 16-inch, and 716 rounds of 6-inch, and also launched 12 torpedoes, of which one was claimed to have hit the German ship. The British battleships, being low on fuel, headed back for port whilst the cruisers *Norfolk* and *Dorsetshire* finished off the German battleship with gunfire and torpedoes. The *Bismarck* sank at 1036, less than two hours after she had been sighted. Just 110 survivors were rescued by *Dorsetshire* and the destroyer *Maori*, and another five later by *U-74* and the weather ship *Sachsenwald*. Whilst returning to harbour the British ships were attacked by aircraft, one of which was hit by the *Rodney*. In another attack the destroyer *Mashona* was sunk.

Rodney then proceeded to the USA for a refit at Boston, which lasted from 13 June to 12 August 1941. In late August she sailed from Bermuda to search for German raiders in the Atlantic, joining a US Task Group, which included the carrier *Wasp*.

In September 1941 she joined Force H and on 24 September sailed as part of the close escort of a convoy to Malta (Operation Halberd). The escort comprised three battleships, a carrier, five cruisers and eight destroyers, and the convoy comprised nine merchant ships. On 27th the convoy came under air attack during which the battleship *Nelson* was torpedoed. The Italian Fleet with two battleships sailed to intercept the convoy but was kept at bay by the heavy escort. One transport was hit and later had to be sunk, but the main body of the convoy arrived safely.

On 16 October, wearing the flag of Vice-Admiral Somerville, she left Gibraltar with the carrier *Ark Royal*, which flew a squadron of torpedo bombers to Malta. This operation was successful, but on the next, when *Rodney* was not involved, the *Ark Royal* was torpedoed and lost. In November she returned to the colder waters off Iceland to cover convoys against attacks by raiders.

In February 1942 she started a refit at Liverpool

HMS Rodney at Malta in WWII with protective nets alongside. *(Maritime Photo Library)*

which completed on 5 May. In May 1942 there had been plans for her and *Nelson* to sail for the East Indies, but these were cancelled. The next month she escorted a convoy to Freetown, returning to Scapa Flow in July. That month she was diverted from convoy duty in the South Atlantic to form part of the cover for the August convoy to Malta (Operation Pedestal). The convoy comprised 14 merchant ships escorted by 3 separate groups of warships, totaling 2 battleships, 3 carriers, 7 cruisers, 25 destroyers and 8 submarines. There were also diversionary operations. During sustained attacks, nine of the merchant ships were lost, together with an aircraft carrier (*Eagle*), two cruisers (*Cairo* and *Manchester*) and a destroyer (*Foresight*). Another carrier, two cruisers were badly damaged. During the operation *Rodney* opened fire with her 16 inch against attacking aircraft at 9 miles range. She also suffered a near miss, which reduced her speed to 18.5-knots. The five ships that arrived, including the tanker *Ohio*, helped Malta survive the siege. The submarines torpedoed two Italian cruisers and one Italian submarine was sunk. This was the largest single naval operation of the war at sea at the time.

After a docking in Rosyth, she escorted a convoy to North Africa in preparation for the landings there (Operation Torch). During that operation, in November, she was part of Force H with the battleships *Duke of York* and *Nelson*, battlecruiser *Renown*, carriers *Victorious*, *Formidable* and *Furious*, 3 cruisers and 17 destroyers. They operated off Oran to cover the transports carrying troops, equipment and stores against surface attacks. As French coastal guns opened fire on the assault forces, *Rodney* engaged them with her 16-inch guns. Her special target was Fort Santon, which was bombarded for three days before it surrendered. She remained with Force H covering follow up operations in North Africa. The force came under attack by human torpedoes at Mers-el-Kebir on 23 March, but the attackers were repelled without achieving any success.

In May 1943 she returned to Plymouth for a docking, rejoining Force H in June. Force H was part of the covering force for the landings in Sicily (Operation Husky) on 10 July, during which 115,000 British troops, and 66,000 American troops were put ashore. For the first two days the force cruised off the landing beaches and was not called upon to bombard, and then she sailed to Malta for her first visit to the island since December 1940. She returned to the landing area and on 31 August she and the *Nelson* together with the cruiser *Orion* escorted by destroyers sailed into the Straits of Messina to bombard Calabria, as part of the preparation for Operation Baytown, the British landings in that area.

In September 1943 she was in Force H as Flagship of Rear-Admiral Rivett-Carnac, as part of the covering force for the landings at Salerno (Operation Avalanche). Force H came under attack from enemy torpedo aircraft and *Warspite* and *Formidable* were narrowly missed. The Force's AA fire destroyed at least three, and possibly six, of the attacking aircraft. With the surrender of the Italian Fleet, Force H was no longer required.

Rodney returned to the Clyde in November 1943 for repairs, and the next month rejoined the Fleet at Scapa Flow. She docked in Rosyth again in February and March prior to the Normandy landings, for which *Rodney* was part of the reserve bombardment force for the Eastern Naval Task Force. She was engaged in gunfire support, and helped the army Third Division to hold off an enemy counterattack. The Germans were surprised to come under 16-inch shellfire 17 miles inland from the Gold Area, the shells arriving with devastating effect. On 26 June she operated with other ships supporting attacks by British units in the Caen area. On 7 July 1944 she shelled the Houlgate area and on 8th the Caen area, which surrendered the next day. During the operation she was attacked by human torpedoes, bombs and shells but was undamaged.

On 12 August she bombarded the artillery ashore at Alderney to deter action against passing ships. 3 of the 4 guns targeted were damaged. She then sailed Scapa Flow via Portland, arriving on 14 September. Two days later she was at sea again, heading north to provide cover for convoys to and from Russia lest the German battleship *Tirpitz* should make a sortie. On 30 November she again became flagship of the Home Fleet, based on Scapa Flow. She remained there until April 1945. She was

then relieved by the battlecruiser *Renown*, which had returned from the East Indies to strengthen the Home Fleet lest the German heavy ships made a final attempt to break out into the Atlantic.

When the war had ended *Rodney* was placed in reserve at Rosyth, having steamed 156,000 miles on war service and without a proper refit since 1942. She was broken up at Inverkeithing arriving there on 26 March 1948. She had gained eleven battle honours for her name.

HMS NELSON

HMS Nelson fitting out. She would soon be spick and span as a flagship. *(Ken Kelly Collection)*

The battleship *Nelson* and her sister ship *Rodney*, were built between the wars to a design heavily influenced by current armament treaties, and utilizing material available from cancelled ships. She was laid down at Armstrong's at Newcastle-on-Tyne on 28 December 1922, was launched on 3 September 1925 and completed in June 1927. She had a standard displacement of 33,950 tons and was 710 feet long (660ft between perpendiculars) and had a beam of 106 feet, just small enough to let her pass through the 110 feet wide locks of the Panama Canal, which she did in 1931.

Her tall bridge structure (called 'Queen Anne's Mansions after the Admiralty building in London) carried the directors for her 16-inch, 6-inch and 4.7 inch guns. Her nine 16-inch guns were mounted in three turrets sited forward of the bridge. Her secondary armament of six twin 6-inch guns were mounted to port and starboard of her superstructure together with four single 4.7-inch AA guns, and she also carried a pair of 4.7-inch AA guns on her quarterdeck. She had a single amphibian aircraft handled by a crane on her port side, whilst *Rodney* carried two aircraft with a catapult on her third (C or Q) turret. Although these ships lacked the elegant lines of earlier capital ships, their layout made optimum use of armour . They earned the title 'The Cherry Tree' ships, having been 'cut down by Washington'.

The main engines, which were forward of her boilers as part of the weight saving design, could develop 45,000 shaft horse power, driving her via twin shafts at a maximum of 23 knots. She achieved 23.55 knots on trials. Other weight saving measures was the use of aluminium kit lockers, pine instead of teak for deck planking and plywood for non-load bearing bulkheads. She carried 1314 officers and men when a private ship, which was rarely, for she was commissioned as the flagship of the Atlantic Fleet on 15

August 1927, relieving the *Revenge*, and wore the flag of the next seven Commanders-in-Chief of the Atlantic/Home Fleet.

The triple 16-inch guns had been intended for the battlecruisers ordered in 1921 but subsequently cancelled. Each shell weighed 2461 pounds (a 14-inch shell weighed 1590 pounds). The guns could elevate to 40 degrees and had a range of 35,000 yards. The 6-inch guns had a 60 degree elevation and an AA capability and were the first power-worked 6-inch guns in service. Their prototype had been tried in the cruiser *Enterprise*. By 1939 her AA armament was six 4.7-inch guns and two 8 barrelled two pounder pom poms and eight single 2 pounders with 12 machine guns.

When war broke out in 1939, *Nelson* was the flagship of the Commander-in-Chief Home Fleet, Admiral Sir Charles Forbes, and was based at Scapa Flow. At that time the Home Fleet searched the Norwegian Sea for returning German merchant ships. Three weeks after the start of the war, she came under air attack whilst covering the return of the damaged submarine *Spearfish* from Norway. She escaped unharmed. In October she carried out searches for the German battlecruiser *Gneisenau* and an accompanying cruiser and destroyers, but without success. She also searched for the *Scharnhorst* and *Gneisenau* after they had sunk the armed merchant cruiser *Rawalpindi* on 23 November.

On 4 December she entered Loch Ewe, which had become the Fleet's base instead of the lightly defended Scapa Flow. Whilst doing so, she ran over a magnetic mine laid by *U-312* five weeks before. She was badly damaged, and, after temporary repairs and awaiting the clearance of other mines that had been laid in the area, she steamed to Portsmouth for permanent repairs. Whilst there some of her crew were detached to take part in the Norwegian campaign, some landing at Aadalsnes on 17 April. Because of the fall of France, and the danger of invasion, it was decided that work on her should be completed on the Clyde. Whilst being escorted there in June, the minesweepers accompanying her exploded two mines which lay in her track. In that June she carried out trials of a gunnery radar, but landed the set on completion of trials. It was not policy at that time for flagships to carry radar as it was thought it might interfere with communications. However, some wags allege that radar would have vied with the admiral's flag for

HMS Nelson showing her tall bridge structure with gunnery directors soaring above.
(Portsmouth Royal Naval Museum)

the top of the mast! *Rodney*, not a flagship, was the first British battleship fitted with radar.

In September 1940 she took part in a sortie to attack shipping off the Norwegian coast. During this two ships were detected and one was sunk and the other damaged by aircraft from the carrier *Furious*. Two months later she sailed again to search for the German battleship *Admiral Scheer* in the Iceland Faroes passage after the sinking of the armed merchant cruiser *Jervis Bay*, but without success. A similar unsuccessful search for the battlecruisers *Scharnhorst* and *Gneisenau* was carried out by the *Nelson*, *Rodney*, *Repulse*, eight cruisers and eleven destroyers in January 1941. The Germans were sighted by the cruiser *Naiad* on 28th, but the German's radar had already detected the British force and they were able to use their superior speed to avoid being followed, and narrowly escaped running into the Home Fleet ships. The next month she again sailed in search of a suspected enemy warship but without any contact being made. In March she was part of the covering force for Operation Claymore, when the Lofoten Islands were raided. The operation went well, wit the destruction of German shipping and shore installations, the capture of German prisoners and the bringing back of Norwegian volunteers. Furthermore, the destroyer *Somali* boarded the patrol vessel *Krebs* and captured valuable codes.

Later that month she carried out patrols with the cruiser *Nigeria*, covering convoys, minelaying operations in the Faroes-Iceland area and searching for surface raiders. This included a search for the *Scharnhorst* and *Gneisenau*, which were expected to return to German after a sortie against the Atlantic convoys. However, they made for Brest instead. Towards the end of the month she again sailed from Scapa Flow and acted as ocean escort to convoy WS 7 which was taking troops to the Middle East. She arrived at Capetown on 16 April and then proceeded to Durban to carry out docking and essential repairs. She left Durban on 10 May for Freetown escorting the carrier *Eagle*. On that passage the raider *Atlantis* (Ship 16) passed the two ships at 7,000 yards at night, but was not herself detected.

Later that month she headed for Gibraltar to join convoy SL 75, and on the way intercepted the German patrol ship *Gonzenheim* (4,000 tons), which had been sighted by an aircraft from the *Victorious*. The cruiser *Neptune* was ordered to board the German ship, but the German scuttled herself before this could be carried out. *Neptune* torpedoed the burning wreck. *Nelson* returned to Scapa Flow on 8 June.

The next month she joined Force H, operating from Gibraltar. She then carried out exercises before taking part in Operation Substance, the passage of a convoy comprising a troop transport and six merchant ships to Malta. The escort comprised *Nelson*, *Renown* and *Ark Royal* together with four cruisers and seventeen destroyers together with a fast minelayer. The convoy was attacked by submarines and aircraft. The troop transport ran aground and had to return to Gibraltar, the cruiser *Manchester* was damaged and the destroyer *Fearless* hit and had to be sunk. *Nelson* returned to Gibraltar on 27 July, but three days later sailed again for Operation Style, the transport to Malta of personnel and stores from the troopship that had run aground during Operation Substance. During this and the covering operations and aircraft strike and bombardments were carried out, and the cruiser *Hermione* rammed and sank the Italian submarine *Tembien*. *Nelson* relieved the *Renown* as flagship of Vice Admiral Sir James Somerville.

Her next operation was to escort the *Ark Royal* during an attack on Sardinia, and on 10 September, she covered an operation ferrying aircraft to Malta. Later that month she took part in Operation Halberd, another convoy to Malta. It was a convoy of nine 15 knot merchant ships, escorted by *Rodney* and *Prince of Wales*, four cruisers and twelve destroyers. The *Nelson* and *Ark Royal* together with a cruiser and six more destroyers provided a covering force. On 27th air attacks developed and *Nelson* was torpedoed by an aircraft south of Sardinia. Her speed was reduced to 15 knots. By 1900 that day the convoy had reached the Narrows, and the heavy escort stood off whilst the cruisers and destroyers went on with the merchant ships. One of the merchantmen was hit by Italian torpedo aircraft. It had to be sunk after the troops onboard had been transferred to other ships. Temporary repairs to *Nelson* were carried out at Gibraltar, and then she sailed to Rosyth for full repairs and a refit. She reached Rosyth on 23 November, carrying some survivors from the *Ark Royal*, which had been lost on 14 November. Repairs were completed on 30 April 1942, when she returned to the Home Fleet. Shortly afterwards she escorted a convoy to Freetown, returning to Scapa Flow on 26 July.

At the start of the next month she took part in another convoy to Malta, Operation Pedestal. The convoy comprised fourteen merchant ships and was provided with a strong escort comprising three battleships, three carriers, six cruisers, an anti-aircraft cruiser and 24 destroyers. The convoy came under heavy attacks. The carrier *Eagle* was sunk by *U-73* on 11 August, and the carrier *Indomitable* was heavily damaged in air attacks on 12 August. One merchant ship was damaged on 12th and had to be sunk later. The destroyer *Foresight* was also disabled and had to be sunk. About 30 enemy aircraft and two submarines had been destroyed by the time the covering force retired at 1900 on 12th. Shortly afterwards the cruisers *Cairo* and *Nigeria* were torpedoed by the Italian submarine *Axum*, the former having to be abandoned and the latter having to return to Gibraltar. Two merchant ships were sunk and another damaged. The cruiser *Kenya* was torpedoed but was able to stay with the convoy. Early next morning the cruiser *Manchester* was torpedoed by an E-boat and subsequently lost. Four more merchant ships were lost during E-boat attacks. A further merchant ship succumbed to air attacks later in the day and a straggling merchant ship was sunk on the evening of 13th. Only five ships of the convoy reached Malta. These included the tanker *Ohio*, which was much damaged and only arrived after an epic struggle by her crew and survivors from other ships, and with assistance by the escorts.

On completion of that operation, *Nelson*, the carrier *Furious*, and other ships, sailed from Gibraltar on 20 August. *Nelson* underwent repairs at Rosyth, which took until 16 October. Once repaired she sailed for Gibraltar to rejoin Force H under the command Admiral Syfret. She arrived a few days after the initial landings in North Africa.

She spent the first half of 1943 with Force H operating from Gibraltar, and during Operation Husky, the landings in Sicily, she was the flagship of Vice

HMS Nelson showing the secondary armament of 6-inch guns in turrets, an innovation at the time.
(T. Ferrers-Walker Collection)

HMS Nelson firing her nine 16-inch guns. *(Steve Bush Collection)*

Admiral Sir Algernon Willis and was operating in the Ionian Sea to prevent any interference by the Italian fleet. On 31 August she, and her sister ship *Rodney*, together with the cruiser *Orion* and nine destroyers entered the Messina Strait and carried out a bombardment of two coastal defence batteries north east of Reggio. (Operation Hammer). This was in preparation for the British landings in Calabria (Operation Baytown).

She and the *Rodney* were also in the covering force for Operation Avalanche, the landings at Salerno. On 29 September the *Nelson* was in Malta, and the Italian Armistice was signed onboard by General Eisenhower and Marshal Badoglio. In November, *Nelson* returned to the United Kingdom for a refit and repairs. These were completed in the middle of May 1944, and she was allocated as a reserve bombardment ship for the Western Task Force for Operation Neptune, the landings at Normandy. She arrived off Gold Beach just after noon on 11 June, remaining there until 18th, carrying out twenty bombardments. She was damaged by a mine at 1930 on her last day there. She was one of the ships selected for special mention by the Army for her support. This included firing a 16-inch shell at Caen every minute throughout the night 12/13 June to demoralise the German defenders. Two days later she sailed for the United Sates of America for a refit at Philadelphia. This lasted until 14 January 1945. She then returned to Portsmouth via New York for more refit work and trials before sailing for the East Indies on 29 April via Malta and the Suez Canal. She reached Colombo in July 1945. Her AA armament then comprised six 4.7-inch guns, sixteen 40-mm, forty-eight two pounders and sixty-one 20-mm guns. She became the flagship of the Third Battle Squadron on 12 July, relieving the *Queen Elizabeth*.

She took part in a series of bombardments and air strikes off Puket, the Malay Peninsula, during July. During these she recovered 94 personnel from the minesweeper *Vestal* which was sunk by a Japanese aircraft in a suicide attack, the first on any unit of the East Indies Fleet. The carrier *Ameer* was also damaged in this attack. On 17 August she operated in support of minesweepers in the Nicobar area in preparation for the occupation of Penang. She sailed from Rangoon to arrive at Penang on 28 August, with the cruiser *Ceylon* and escort carriers *Hunter* and *Attacker* together with three destroyers. Senior Japanese officers came onboard to sign undertakings that there would be no attacks on the Fleet. They also brought documents concerning mine barrages in the area. The formal surrender of Penang was signed on board on 2 September by Vice Admiral Uzumi on the same table as the Italian Armistice had been signed.

She sailed five days later to take part in the occupation of Western Malaya. She, and the French battleship *Richelieu*, was part of the covering force for Operation Zipper, when 100,000 troops were landed in three days. *Nelson* was present at Singapore on 12 September when the official surrender ceremony of all Japanese forces in South East Asia was carried out, the surrender being signed by Lt. General Itagaki and Vice Admiral Fukudome. *Nelson* then returned to Trincomalee and sailed from Colombo on 11 October for Kilindini, Suez, Malta and Gibraltar. She reached Portsmouth on 17 November 1945. She then became a training ship, relieving the battleship *Valiant*. She arrived at Portland on 29 December and carried out a cruise to Gibraltar and Lisbon in the spring 1946. However, she operated mainly from Portland. On 22 September 1947, she was replaced in the Training squadron by the carrier *Victorious*, and was then used in bombing trials.

She arrived at Inverkeithing on 15 March 1949 to be broken up by Wards. She had earned six Battle Honours for her name, which is now continued in use by the Barracks at Portsmouth. Despite the treaty limitations which had led to her unusual appearance, she had survived mine and torpedo damage and air attacks, and had given over twenty years of valuable service.

HMS DUKE OF YORK

HMS Duke of York showing the balanced profile of this class. *(MoD/Crown Copyright)*

The *Duke of York* was the third of the King George V Class battleships to be laid down. She was built by John Brown on the Clyde, was laid down on 5 May 1937 and war had begun by the time she was launched on 28 February 1940 by H.M. The Queen who had been the Duchess of York. She was completed on 4 November 1941.

Originally to be called *Anson* her name was changed in December 1938. She was of 35,000 tons standard displacement, a measure limited by international treaty. She had a full load displacement (in 1945) of 44,790 tons. Her armament comprised ten 14-inch guns, mounted in two quadruple turrets, one forward and one aft, with a superimposed twin turret forward. Her secondary armament comprised eight twin 5.25-inch guns, together with 48 2-pounders and 14 20-mm guns. By 1945 her tertiary armament comprised eight octuple and six quadruple 2-pounders, two quadruple 40mm and 55 20-mm (39 single and 8 twin) guns. The 14-inch guns had a range greater than the 15-inch previously mounted in battleships, each round weighing 1,590 lbs with a maximum range of 36,000 yards. Her turrets weighed 1500 tons (quadruple 14-inch), 900 tons (twin 14-inch) and 80 tons (5.25-inch twin). She had over 14,000 tons of armour. Her length was 745 ft and beam 103 ft. Her engines were designed to develop 110,000 shaft horse power giving a designed speed of 27 knots, though these ships did develop 125,000 shaft horse power giving 28.5 knots, with over 29 knots being logged.

On completion, she became flagship of Vice-Admiral A.T.B. Curteis, Second in Command Home Fleet, vice *Renown*. The next month she carried Winston Churchill to the USA, disembarking him and his party at Annapolis on 22 December. She then went on to Hampton Roads where Churchill and his party re-embarked and was taken to Bermuda, from where the Prime Minister flew home. The *Duke of York* then worked up in the area for 12 days before heading back to Scapa Flow for a further month's work up.

On 28 February she sailed for Iceland, and on 3 March she sailed from Hvalfjord with the battle-cruiser *Renown* to search for the German battleship *Tirpitz* which was reported south of Bear Island. On 22 March she sailed with her sister ship *King George V* to cover Russian Convoys PQ.13 and QP.9, during which the cruiser *Trinidad* was disabled in action with German destroyers, one of which Z.26 was sunk. The next month she covered convoys PQ 14 and QP 10. Later in April, whilst covering PQ.15 the *King George V* rammed and sank the destroyer *Punjabi*. Because the battleship was damaged when the destroyer's depth charges exploded, the *Duke of York* had to relieve her temporarily as Fleet Flagship. She then also covered convoys PQ.16 and QP.12 in May.

Many of the Home Fleet ships were despatched to provide extra cover for the convoy to Malta in June 1942. During this lull, King George VI visited the ships remaining at Scapa Flow, including the USS *Washington*. He stayed onboard the *Duke of York* whilst there. The late June convoy to and from Russia, PQ.17 and QP.13, were also covered by a force, which included the *Duke of York*. The German battleship *Tirpitz* was believed to threaten the Russia bound convoy, which was scattered, but the *Tirpitz* remained at anchor at Altenfjord. The convoy then came under attack from submarines and aircraft, and 24 out of the 36 ships in the convoy were lost.

In September she was part of the distant covering force for convoy PQ.18 to Russia,. This force comprised *Anson*, *Duke of York*, *Jamaica* and five destroyers. The convoy was also given a special fighting destroyer escort comprising the cruiser *Scylla* and 16 destroyers as well as the usual close escort and cruiser covering force. There was also a carrier force, Spitzbergen fuelling force, submarine patrols, and 2 cruisers and a destroyer taking reinforcements and stores to Spitzbergen, together with a specially strengthened close escort to cope with aircraft and submarine attacks. The convoy came

HMS Duke of York - note the unusual quadruple 14-inch gun mounting aft. Forward she had another quadruple mounting with a superimposed twin 14-inch turret. *(MoD/Crown Copyright)*

under intense attacks and three ships were lost to U-boats and ten to air attacks, but 27 reached Archangel.

In October 1942 she became Flagship of Vice-Admiral E. Neville Syfret, commanding Force H, for the North African Landings (Operation Torch). Force H then comprised the battleships *Duke of York*, *Nelson* and *Rodney*, battlecruiser *Renown* and the carriers *Victorious*, *Formidable* and *Furious* and the cruisers *Argonaut*, *Bermuda* and *Sirius* together with 17 destroyers. They covered operations in the Mediterranean for the landings. Once the operation had been completed successfully, the Flag was transferred to the *Nelson* on 15 November and *Duke of York* returned to Scapa Flow before proceeding to Rosyth for a refit whish lasted until March 1943.

On 8 May 1943 she became the Flagship of Admiral Sir Bruce Fraser (Commander-in-Chief Home Fleet), who was relieving Admiral Sir John Tovey. In July she, with the battleships *Anson* and *Malaya*, the carrier *Furious*, two cruiser squadrons and three destroyer flotillas together with a US Task Force (comprising the battleships *Alabama* and *South Dakota*, the cruisers *Augusta* and *Tuscaloosa* and five destroyers) carried out an operation off the coast of Norway as a diversion for the landings in Sicily. The German air reconnaissance did not detect the forces, and so the diversion failed. Another demonstration was carried out later in the month, which was more successful. During it five German reconnaissance aircraft were shot down by Martlet fighters.

In October she carried out a raid on German Shipping off Bodo (Operation Leader). The US Carrier *Ranger* flew off aircraft to attack two German convoys and shipping in the roads. Four steamers were sunk, six damaged together with a ferry for the loss of five aircraft.

Russian convoys resumed with JW 54A in November 1943, and the first few passed through unmolested. In December 1943, it was anticipated that the Germans would attack a Russian convoy. They only had the battlecruiser *Scharnhorst* available in northern Norway. The battleship *Tirpitz* had been put out of action by midget submarines the previous September, and furthermore the smaller battleship *Lutzow* had sailed for the Baltic in the September. A strong force of the *Duke of York*, cruiser *Jamaica* and four destroyers was sailed to cover the convoy (JW 55B) with a further force of three cruisers, *Norfolk*, *Belfast* and *Sheffield* operating closer to the convoy. The convoy comprised 19 merchant ships with a close escort of ten destroyers, two corvettes and a minesweeper, sailing from Loch Ewe on 20 December.

Scharnhorst sailed with five destroyers on the evening of 25 December, using convoy positions given by U-boats and aircraft. The weather was bad with a force 7 blowing from the south. The German destroyers reported that the weather would reduce their gunnery ability and speed. The next morning the destroyers were ordered to sweep ahead of the battlecruiser, but then the battlecruiser altered course without informing the destroyers. Meanwhile British stations had monitored the German signals and informed Admiral Fraser that the Germans were at sea. He turned the convoy to the north to allow his forces to get into a position between them and the approaching German forces. At 0840, on 26 December, whilst the cruisers were still 50 miles east of the convoy, *Belfast* detected a radar contact at 17.5 miles between the cruisers and the convoy. It was thought to be the convoy, but was probably a German destroyer. At 0915 the cruisers formed a line of bearing, and at 0921 the *Scharnhorst* was sighted from the *Belfast*. *Belfast* opened fire three minutes later with starshell, and the *Norfolk* followed with her 8-inch. *Scharnhorst* altered away from the direction of the convoy and increased speed to 30 knots. *Norfolk* achieved several hits, putting *Scharnhorst*'s radar out of action.

Scharnhorst retired at speed, but, as anticipated, circled round to close the convoy again. Meanwhile the German destroyers were ordered to undertake various sweeps to find the convoy. These orders involved a turn, which led them away from the convoy's track and hence they missed making contact by 8 minutes. They took no further part in the action.

The three British cruisers again intercepted the *Scharnhorst* at noon, just one hour after the late dawn. The cruisers were only 9 miles ahead of the convoy, and had been joined by 4 destroyers from the convoy, and these were sent on ahead as the

HMS Duke of York looking weatherbeaten - she spent much of her time in northern waters and sank *Scharnhorst* in a gale. *(T. Ferrers-Walker Collection)*

cruisers turned to engage the enemy once more. The British opened fire and the *Scharnhorst* replied and turned away at speed, and a further chase developed, though the German had a 6-knot advantage in the prevailing weather conditions. *Norfolk* was hit in X turret and had to flood the magazine, and *Sheffield* was straddled. The cruisers managed to close to 7 miles, but this was outside visibility range, and the German ship steadily drew away. The cruisers continued to shadow the German, reporting her position to the *Duke of York*, which was escorted by the cruiser *Jamaica*. The British battleship was closing fast.

At 1617 the *Duke of York* established contact by radar, with the *Scharnhorst* at 45,500 yards. By 1632 the *Duke of York* gunnery radar had acquired the German at just over 15 miles, and the destroyers with the battleship were ordered to prepare for a torpedo attack. At 1640 the *Belfast* was ordered to open fire with starshell, illuminating the German ship which was surprised by the arrival of 14-inch shells from the *Duke of York*. *Duke of York* achieved hits with her first and third salvoes, starting a fire amidships and putting her forward turret out of action. *Jamaica* opened fire shortly afterwards. However, the German ship turned to the north and then the east, turning occasional to fire a broadside at *Jamaica*. One 11–inch shell fired at the *Duke of York* passed through her mainmast damaging her radar. The cruiser force continued to engage her whilst the destroyers closed to attack with torpedoes. However, the German ship was drawing clear ahead, and just as the range became too great for the *Duke of York*'s guns, a further 14-inch shell caused damage between wind and water, bursting in her Number 1 boiler room. Her speed fell to 20

knots. A further hit damaged her starboard 5.9-inch gun, killing all the men in the magazine.

The destroyers were then able to close and fire their torpedoes. Although the *Scharnhorst* started to increase speed, it was too late. One torpedo hit her boiler room, and her propeller shaft was damaged, slowing her again. The *Duke of York* was able to close and open fire again once the destroyers were clear. Within five minutes fires were breaking out in the battlecruiser, with only the occasional shot being fired from her main armament. Her speed reduced even more, and her ammunition started to explode. The *Duke of York* withdrew and allowed the cruisers and destroyers to engage with gunfire and to close to fire torpedoes. At least eight torpedo hits were achieved, and the battlecruiser was surrounded by smoke and mist, through which could be seen a dull red glow. *Jamaica* closed and fired torpedoes, and two explosions were heard. At 1945 the battlecruiser sank slowly, and more underwater explosions were heard. The destroyers *Scorpion* and *Matchless* closed to rescue survivors from the Arctic waters, but found pitifully few, only 36 out of the 1973 officers and men onboard. At least 13 14-inch shells, 12 8-inch or 6-inch shells and eleven torpedoes had hit the *Scharnhorst*. The *Duke of York* had fired 443 rounds of 14-inch from her main armament in 52 salvoes, of which 31 were straddles and 16 more fell within 200 yards of the battle-cruiser.

With the removal of this threat to the northern convoys, the Navy was able to use escort carriers to augment the escort to the convoys against submarine and aircraft attacks. Furthermore heavy ships could be released from their protection duties and be transferred to the Eastern Fleet, and the bases at Scapa Flow and the Clyde could concentrate on the preparations for the D-Day Landings.

On 30 March 1944 she sailed again as part of the covering force for a Russian convoy (JW.58 and RA.58). Part of the covering force detached to make an air strike on the carrier *Tirpitz* (Operation Tungsten) at Altafjord. The strike achieved 14 hits on the German battleship and put her out of action for 3 months.

In July she covered a further strike on the *Tirpitz*, lying in Kaafjord, by aircraft from three carriers. The incoming raids were detected early enough for

The battleship *USS Missouri* passing *HMS Duke of York* in November 1948 as the latter departed New York. *(Ken Kelly Collection)*

the Germans to screen the battleship with smoke and the AA defences were fully alerted, making the attack unsuccessful. One reason that the Germans were able to react in time was the slowness of the Barracuda aircraft.

In mid August she again provided distant cover for Russian convoy (JW 59/RA 59A), whilst also covering carrier strikes against the *Tirpitz*, still lying in Kaafjord. The first attack on the battleship *Tirpitz* on 20 August was prevented by weather, whilst during the second, the German defences and smoke screen again protected the battleship. However, the smoke did not cover the battleship ompletely and bombs were dropped and the attackers claimed one 500-lb. bomb hit, though the Germans claimed that there were no hits. The escort carrier group involved in the operation was attacked by U-boats, and the carrier *Nabob* torpedoed and damaged, and the destroyer escort *Bickerton* was also hit and had to be abandoned.

That September the *Duke of York* underwent a long refit in Liverpool, which completed in March 1945, when she worked up. In April she sailed for the British Pacific Fleet with her sister *Anson* and other ships, arriving at Sydney in July. She was at Manus on 15 August 1945 as Flagship of Admiral Sir Bruce Fraser (Commander-in-Chief British Pacific Fleet) when the Japanese surrendered.

She entered Sagami Bay on 28 August for the preparations for the overall Japanese surrender on 2 September onboard the US battleship *Missouri* by the Foreign Minister Shigemitsu and the Chief of the Army General Staff, General Umezu.

She remained with the British Pacific Fleet until June 1946 and then returned to the UK, arriving at Plymouth on 11 July 1946. In December 1946 she became the flagship of Admiral Syfret again, this time he was Commander-in-Chief Home Fleet. She was relieved as Flagship by the carrier *Implacable* in April 1949, when she paid off into reserve at Portsmouth, becoming flagship of the reserve fleet vice *Ausonia*. She was relieved as Flagship by the cruiser *Dido* in August 1951, and that November was laid up in the Gareloch.

She arrived to be broken up at Faslane on 18 February 1958. She had gained three battle honours for her name, Arctic 1942-43, North Africa 1942, and North Cape 1943.

HMS INDOMITABLE

HMS Indomitable distinguished by her large gunnery director on her island. She carried two twin 4.5-inch guns on each corner of the flight deck. *(Syd Goodman Collection)*

The fleet carrier *Indomitable* was built by Vickers Armstrong, Barrow-in-Furness, who also supplied her machinery. She was authorised in the 1937 building programme, and was laid down on 10 November 1937. She was launched on 26 March 1940, commissioned on 26 August 1941and was completed on 10 October 1941. She was named by Mrs. Winston Churchill. She differed from her earlier sisters (*Illustrious*, *Formidable* and *Victorious*) in having an extra half hangar and thinner plating to the hangar sides. She had a standard displacement of 23,500 tons, later rising to 29,730 tons. She was 754 feet long and had a beam of 95.75 feet. Her engines drove three shafts and developed 110,000-shaft-horse-power giving her a speed of 30.5 knots. Her endurance was 9,000 miles at 18 knots. She was armed with sixteen 4.5-inch guns, mounted in pair of twin turrets at each corner of her flight deck, and carried 65 aircraft. She also carried 48 two- pounder guns, and later carried 12 40-mm, 34 Oerlikons and 43 two-pounder guns. Two further ships of the class were built later (*Implacable* and *Indefatigable*), but they were completed to a modified, larger design and had two hangars and had bigger engines with four shafts giving them a speed of 32.5 knots.

Immediately on completion she was sent at once to the West Indies for a short 'work-up'. Unfortunately she grounded on a coral reef off Kingston, Jamaica, on 3 November 1941 during this period, which entailed docking at Norfolk, Virginia. On 14 January 1942 she, escorted by three Australian destroyers (*Napier*, *Nestor* and *Nizam*), sailed from Port Sudan. She flew off 48 Hurricane fighters to Batavia on 27 and 28 January from a position south of Java to reinforce the air defences of Java. Most of the aircraft went straight on to Singapore. She reached Trincomalee on 2 February. On 25 February *Indomitable* called at Port Sudan again to collect more fighters to ferry them to the Far East.

At the end of March she joined the Eastern Fleet under Admiral Sir James Somerville. This Fleet operated south of Ceylon, and also included her half sister *Formidable* and the smaller, older carrier *Hermes*. The three carriers had between them only 57 strike aircraft and three dozen fighters. It should also be noted that there were insufficient shore-based long-range reconnaissance aircraft and virtually no shore-based air striking forces. The two larger Fleet carriers were put into the fast division (Group A) of the Fleet. The Group searched in vain for the Japanese forces, which had just entered the Indian Ocean, in the hope of carrying out a night attack on them. At one point they were within 200 miles of the main Japanese striking force in the Indian Ocean, which consisted of five fleet carriers, four battleships, three cruisers and eight destroyers. Admiral Somerville was hampered by lack of reconnaissance aircraft, and recognised that, with the state of the Navy world wide – fighting in every ocean and with far too few ships available in every Fleet - he could not hazard his weak fleet against such odds in a daylight action. On 9 April Group A proceeded to the safer region of Bombay, whilst the slower group of the Fleet retired to Kilindini on the East African coast. Despite losses, including the carrier *Hermes* and heavy cruisers *Dorsetshire* and *Cornwall*, the 'Fleet-in-being' had been maintained and the Japanese fleet withdrew eastwards.

Indomitable, with her half sister *Illustrious*, provided cover for the landings at Diego Suarez, Madagascar (Operation Ironclad) on 5 May. *Indomitable* and two destroyers joined the assault forces from the Eastern Fleet on 3 May, and for this operation she was flagship of Rear Admiral D.W. Boyd. Her aircraft struck at positions ashore, concentrating on the airport, and also forced the gunboat *D'Entrecasteaux*, which had been supporting the defenders, to be beached. The submarine *Monge* made an unsuccessful attack on *Indomitable* on 8 May, but was afterwards sunk by the destroyers *Active* and *Panther*.

In August 1942 she took part in covering an important convoy to Malta from the West (Operation Pedestal), the last convoy to reach the island before its relief in November 1942. Fourteen merchant ships set out with an extremely heavy escort, which included the carriers *Indomitable*, *Victorious* and *Eagle*. Between them the three carriers could put up 72 fighters. The opportunity was also taken to send the carrier *Furious* with 38 more Spitfires to be flown to Malta to boost the defences there. The convoy came under severe attacks from U-boats, aircraft and motor torpedo boats. The carrier *Eagle* was torpedoed on 11th by *U-73*. She sank in 8 minutes but destroyers rescued 900 of her crew. Air attacks took place that evening, and the next day they intensified. *Victorious* was hit, but the bomb broke up on her armoured deck. The Italian submarine *Cobalto* was detected and sunk by the destroyer *Ithuriel*, and that evening the destroyer *Foresight* was hit and disabled and had to be sunk. *Indomitable* suffered three heavy bomb hits, putting her flight deck out of action, and she suffered three or four near misses. She had a 30-ft hole below the waterline. She was stopped, but was able to steam at reduced speed within three hours. Her aircraft had to land on *Victorious*, then the only effective carrier remaining. That evening the Italian submarine *Axum* torpedoed the cruisers *Cairo* and *Nigeria*. The former had to be sunk and the latter had to turn back for Gibraltar. An hour later the cruiser *Kenya* was damaged by a torpedo from the Italian submarine *Alagi* but was able to continue with the convoy. Early the next morning the cruiser *Manchester* was disabled by enemy motor torpedo boats, and was later scuttled. Meanwhile the merchant ships were under continuous attack, and finally just five reached Malta. *Indomitable* was under repair at Liverpool until February 1943.

Early in 1943 she resumed service, this time with the Home Fleet. In June 1943, however, she, with other units of the Home Fleet, was lent to the Mediterranean Fleet to cover the landings in Sicily on 10 July (Operation Husky). For the landings she was part of the covering force operating in the Ionian Sea. On 16 July she was damaged by a torpedo dropped by an Italian aircraft when 90 miles east by north of Malta. She was hit on her port side and the port boiler room was extensively damaged, but she was able to proceed the 90 miles to Malta under her own power. Repairs were executed in the United Sates at Norfolk, Virginia, and it was not until April 1944 that she was able to sail for the United Kingdom. In May 1944 she took part in a Home Fleet operation off Norway.

In June 1944, she was allocated to the Eastern Fleet and sailed from the Clyde. She arrived at Trincomalee on 5 July with her half sister *Victorious*. At that time she carried 29 Hellcats and 15 Avengers.

In August 1944, she took part in Operation Boomerang, providing air rescue cover for a US bombing attack on North-West Sumatra. This was followed on 24th by air strikes by aircraft from *Indomitable* and *Victorious* on Padang, South-West Sumatra (Operation Banquet) without significant results.

On 18 September 1944 aircraft from *Indomitable* and *Victorious* carried out strikes on Sigli, Northern Sumatra again without significant results. Her aircraft also carried out photo-reconnaissance over the Nicobars (Operation Light). Between 17th and 19th October she took part in Operation Miller, a diversion for the imminent US landings at Leyte. The carriers' aircraft struck at targets on the Nicobar Islands, and bombardments were also carried out. Of 12 enemy aircraft that attacked the fleet, seven were shot down by the fighter cover.

On 20 November, she, with *Illustrious*, flew off aircraft to strike against Pangkalan Brandan, North-West Sumatra (Operation Outflank), but weather caused the aircraft to be diverted to the oil installa-

HMS Indomitable with aircraft ranged on deck and with her forward lift lowered. *(Syd Goodman Collection)*

HMS Indomitable -note the light AA guns fitted under the flight deck to protect her stern.
(Syd Goodman Collection)

tions at Belawan Deli and the airfields near Sabang. The force suffered no losses.

Later in November 1944 *Indomitable* was allocated to the newly formed British Pacific Fleet under Vice Admiral Rawlings. On 17and 20 December 1944 *Indomitable* took part in Operation Robson, carrier strikes on the oil, harbour and railway installations at Belawan-Deli in Northern Sumatra. These strikes proved more successful, causing a great deal of damage.

On 4 January she, with *Victorious* and *Indefatigable*, took part in the successful raid on the oil refineries of Pankalan Brandan, Sumatra (Operation Lentil). 28 attacking aircraft were in the strikes, escorted by 32 fighters. Three aircraft were lost and 15 Japanese aircraft destroyed.

On 16 January 1945 the British Pacific Fleet sailed from Trincomalee for the Pacific. It had been decided to carry out strikes on Sumatra en route (Operation Meridian). On 20/21 and 22/23 January the weather was unsuitable for flying, but on 24th strikes were launched from *Indomitable*, *Illustrious*, *Victorious* and *Indefatigable* to make successful attacks on the oil refinery at Pladjoe, north of Palembang. These were the two largest refineries in South East Asia, and provided three quarters of Japan's requirements for aviation fuel. Despite the strong defences, the output of the Pladjoe refinery was halved by the attacks. 14 enemy aircraft were shot down and 38 destroyed on the ground. The British lost 7 aircraft to enemy action and 25 due to crashed landings. This was followed by strikes on 29 January against the oil refineries at Soengi-Gerong near Palembang, 30 Japanese aircraft were shot down and 38 destroyed on the ground. The British force lost 16 aircraft. A Japanese attack on the force by 12 bombers resulted in all the enemy aircraft being shot down by fighters or the fleet's AA fire. The Fleet arrived at Fremantle on 4 February.

The Fleet, including *Indomitable*, *Victorious*, *Illustrious* and *Indefatigable*, sailed from the base at Ulithi Atoll, Caroline Islands, on 23 March and replenished on 25th. On 26 and 27 March air strikes were carried out on the Sakishima-Gunto group of islands of the southern Ryukyus to neutralise the airfields. The Fleet then replenished before renewing attacks on 31 March. Strikes were conducted each day to 2 April, and then the Fleet retired to replenish. The destroyer *Ulster* was hit by Kamikaze aircraft of the 1st Air Fleet and had to be taken in tow by the cruiser *Gambia* and was taken to Leyte. On 13th *Indomitable* was dive bombed by four aircraft but was not hit. She also carried out night strikes, her aircraft making use of moonlight.

After their last strikes on 20 April the Fleet returned to Leyte, sailing for operations again in early May. The carrier force then comprised *Indomitable*, *Victorious*, *Formidable* and *Indefatigable*. After replenishing on 3 and 4 May a carrier strike was carried out against the Sakishima-Gunto group, whilst the battleships, cruisers and destroyers bombarded the islands and airfields. On 4 May 1945 *Formidable* was attacked by Japanese aircraft. A few minutes later *Indomitable* was approached by a Zeke diving at 60 degrees. *Indomitable* was under full helm at the time. Despite heavy AA fire, the Zeke flattened her dive at the last minute and landed on *Indomitable*'s armoured flight deck (forward lift), bounced over the side and the bomb it carried appeared to explode under water, missing the ship by ten yards. No personnel were injured nor were any aircraft damaged in the attack, the only casualty being the ship's radar. About 10 minutes later another attack developed but the Kamikaze aircraft was shot down by gunfire from *Indomitable* and the destroyer *Quality*. Ten minutes later a further attacker was shot down. In all, during those attacks, 14 enemy aircraft were destroyed, 11 by fighters and 3 by gunfire. Repairs were carried out and strikes resumed on 5 May. At 0524 on the morning of 20 May the destroyer *Quilliam* was severely damaged by a collision with the *Indomitable* in thick fog. *Indomitable*'s bow and forepeak were slightly damaged. The destroyer, whose bow was wrecked, was towed to the replenishment area by the destroyer *Norman*, escorted by the cruiser *Black Prince*. She was then towed the 700 miles to Leyte by the tug *Weazel*. The Fleet continued operations and replenishments through until 25 May, and then returned to Leyte. It had spent 62 days at sea with only eight days break at Leyte for storing. Air strikes had been flown on 23 days.

HMS Indomitable smartly painted in peace time. *(MoD/Crown Copyright)*

Indomitable arrived at Sydney, New South Wales, on 7 June, and was there waiting to become flagship of 11th Aircraft Carrier squadron comprising new unarmoured light fleet carriers *Colossus*, *Venerable* and *Vengeance*, when the Japanese surrendered. She left on VJ-Day (15 August) as part of the force (TG 111.2) to occupy Hong Kong, flying the flag of Rear Admiral C.H.J. Harcourt, commanding the 11th Aircraft Carrier Squadron. The force, which included the *Indomitable* and the light fleet carrier *Venerable*, sailed from Subic Bay on 27 August. On 29 August the force started entering Hong Kong, but there were attacks by Japanese explosive boats. Aircraft from *Indomitable* and *Venerable* attacked the anchorage at Lamma Bay and destroyed the enemy craft. Hong Kong was occupied on 30 August.

Indomitable returned to Portsmouth on 30 November 1945, and was then employed on trooping duties calling at Malta, Port Said, Aden, Singapore, Colombo, Aden and arriving at Portsmouth on 13 March 1946. Between 1948 and 1950 she underwent an extensive refit and modernisation at Portsmouth, her bow and stern being rebuilt on lines of light fleet carriers, and her bridge remodelled. On completion she joined the Home Fleet, in which she became the flagship of the Commander-in-Chief, Admiral Sir Philip Vian, early in 1951. She was the first of HM Ships to be fitted with a helicopter. In May 1952 the flag of the Commander-in-Chief was transferred to the battleship *Vanguard*, and *Indomitable* became the flagship of the Flag Officer, Heavy Squadron, Home Fleet. Later that year she was replaced by the new fleet carrier *Eagle*.

She sailed for the Mediterranean with the Home Fleet on the Spring Cruise early in 1953. While off Malta on 3 February 1953 leaking petrol in the ship's hangar exploded when aircraft were being refuelled on the flight deck during an exercise. Three ratings were killed, six died later, and three officers and 27 ratings were injured. Ten awards for gallantry and three posthumous commendations were announced in the London Gazette of 27 July.

Indomitable was present at the Coronation Review of the Fleet at Spithead on 15 June 1953. She was towed from Portsmouth to the Clyde to be placed in reserve on 5 October 1953, where she remained until approval to scrap her was given on 21 September 1955, when she was handed over to the shipbreakers for breaking up at Faslane, arriving there on 30 September, 1955.

She had gained six Battle Honours, Malta Convoys 1942, Diego Suarez 1942, Sicily 1943, East Indies 1944-45, Palembang 1945 and Okinawa 1945. This brought the total for the name to eight.

County Class Cruisers

These cruisers were the first post World War I design for the Royal Navy, and were built to the strict international treaty limits then agreed by Great Britain. Limited by international treaties, the design of these heavy cruisers was a compromise. The limit of 10,000 tons displacement meant that armour and speed had to be restricted. However, these ships were well armed, with four twin 8-inch guns, four single 4 -inch and four 2-pounders, and also two quadruple torpedo tube mountings. Three groups of this class were built, the first being launched in 1927-28, comprising five ships for the Royal Navy (*Kent, Cornwall, Cumberland, Berwick* and *Suffolk*), and two for the Royal Australian Navy (*Australia* and *Canberra*). A second group of four cruisers for the Royal Navy (*London, Devonshire, Shropshire* and *Sussex*) was launched in 1927-28, and two further vessels (*Dorsetshire* and *Norfolk*) followed in 1928-29. Another pair of heavy cruisers (*York* and *Exeter*) of a modified design, smaller and armed with only three twin 8-inch turrets, were also launched in 1928-29. Although much criticised for their appearance and lack of armament, these ships proved themselves during the Second World War. With their good endurance and seakeeping qualities they were much in demand for protection of the trade routes.

Cornwall and *Dorsetshire* were lost to Japanese air attacks off Colombo in April 1942. *Canberra* was lost in August 1942 at the Battle of Savo Island, and was replaced in the Royal Australian Navy by the transfer of *Shropshire. York* was lost in Suda Bay in May 1941, and the *Exeter* was sunk in the Java Sea in March 1942.

HMS CUMBERLAND

HMS Cumberland as built, showing her substantial freeboard. *(Syd Goodman Collection)*

The *Cumberland* was a County Class cruiser of the first (*Kent*) group. *Cumberland* was laid down on 18 October 1924 by Messrs. Vickers-Armstrong Ltd., Barrow, launched on 16 March 1926 and completed on 23 January 1928, and was the first of the County class. She commissioned for trials on 22 November 1927, and commissioned fully on 15 December 1927. These ships had three funnels, which, after initial trials, were raised in height by 15 ft. to reduce the effect of funnel fumes on the bridge and gunnery controls. Their engines developed 80,000-shaft horsepower driving them at 31.5 knots, though on trials all ships exceeded this speed, *Cumberland* achieving 32.6 knots. They had a range of 13,300 miles at 12 knots and 2,300 miles at full speed.

Cumberland was 629ft 11ins long, and had a beam of 68 ft 5 inches over torpedo bulges. The next group of the County class was narrower, being completed without the bulges. These ships were designed by Sir Eustace H. Tennyson d'Eyncourt of Australia, and because of their high sides were known as "Whited Sepulchres" or "Tin-clads". However, despite the treaty limitations which had cut their protection and speed, and despite initial problems with the then new 8-inch guns, they proved popular in service. Their main armament provided a broadside of eight guns fired shells totaling 2,048 lbs. The guns had an elevation of 70degrees, and a range of 29,200 yards. At first they also experienced difficulty in launching torpedoes from the height of their upper deck. On completion these ships were found to be 250 tons under the treaty limit, and so aircraft, catapult and cranes could be fitted and their ammunition stowage increased. Despite teething problems, they proved good seaboats.

Cumberland was allocated to the China Station on completion, arriving at Hong Kong on 12 March 1928. In October 1929 she carried the Secretary of State for War and Parliamentary and Financial Secretaries of the Admiralty and their private secretaries from Gibraltar to Chatham. After a refit when a catapult and crane for one aircraft were added and a high angle director was fitted in place of the rangefinder on the after superstructure, she re-commissioned and returned to the Far East, arriving at Hong Kong in April 1930. She again returned to Chatham to re-commission for the Far East in December 1932. She returned to Chatham in January 1935, paying off into Dockyard hands on 12 March 1935 for a major refit which lasted until 31 July 1936. During that refit she was fitted with an aircraft hangar and catapult abaft her funnels, and given a pair of twin 4-inch AA guns in place of her after single mountings. A narrow belt of 3-5 inch armour was added at her waterline over the machinery spaces. To compensate for the extra top-weight, her hull was cut down abaft Y turret. Her torpedo tubes were removed. Her sister *Suffolk* was given also modernised with the same cut down stern.

In 1936 she returned to the China Station, and in August 1937 she and *Suffolk* stood off the Putu Islands to assist in the defence of the Shanghai International Settlement. On 14th Chinese aircraft attacked Japanese shipping in the vicinity. The USS *Augusta* was damaged by bomb splinters and two bombs near missed the *Cumberland*. The next day her sailors and Marines took over the defence line between Soochow Creek and the French concession. At the end of the month she was about a mile from the US Dollar Liner *President Hoover* when it was mistaken for a Japanese transport and was dive-bombed. *Cumberland* closed her to give assistance to two serious casualties. In October she visited Shanghai to protect British property, remaining there until November. In 1938 she carried the Commander-in-Chief on an inspection of his command, the first visit being to Singapore for the opening of the new base there on 14 February.

In September 1938 she took up her war station at Wei-Hai-Wei when the Munich crisis occurred, but later that month she sailed from Hong Kong, arriving at Sheerness in November 1938 to undergo a refit at Chatham. Her anti-aircraft armament was enhanced, with her forward single 4-inch AA guns being replaced by twin mountings, and two quadruple 2-pounders were fitted port and starboard forward of her forefunnel. Two quadruple machine guns were also fitted on her hangar roof. Her original four single 2-pounder guns were removed. Her

HMS Cumberland when refitted with aircraft hangar and one pair of 4-inch AA guns port and starboard.
(Portsmouth Royal Naval Museum)

armament then comprised four twin 8-inch, four twin 4-inch, four quadruple 2-pounders, two multiple machine guns and four 3-pounder guns and two Walrus aircraft.

She re-commissioned in March 1939 for the Second Cruiser Squadron of the Home Fleet, and at the outbreak of war was in the South Atlantic protecting the trade routes as part of the 8th Cruiser Squadron. The German pocket battleship *Admiral Graf Spee*'s reconnaissance aircraft sighted her on 11 September in mid Atlantic. The battleship, which was with the oiler *Altmark*, was able to slip away unnoticed. That month she and the cruiser *Neptune* and destroyers *Hunter* and *Hyperion* searched for German shipping south of Ascension Island. In October she was allocated to Force G with *Exeter*, later joined by *Ajax* and *Achilles*, to search off the South East Coast of South America for the surface raider known to be at large in the South Atlantic. On 5 October she was passed a message by a merchant ship that had picked up a distress message from the *SS Newton Beach*, which had been attacked by the *Admiral Graf Spee*. The cruiser, which was keeping radio silence, assumed that the Commander-in-Chief at Freetown had already received the message, which he had unfortunately not. Had this message been passed on immediately there was a possibility that *Admiral Graf Spee* and her supply ship would have been caught within days. On 5 December she and the *Ajax* located the blockade-runner *Ussukuma* (7834 tons) which scuttled herself.

Admiral Graf Spee was brought to heel by the cruisers *Exeter*, *Ajax* and *Achilles* on 13 December off the River Plate, whilst the *Cumberland* was at Port Stanley boiler cleaning. *Cumberland* was sailed at once, working up to top speed to relieve the damaged *Exeter*. She arrived at 2200 on 14th, just 34 hours after Commodore Harwood had broadcast the enemy's position. She arrived to find that the German ship had taken shelter in Montevideo harbour, outside which the *Ajax* and *Achilles* were patrolling. The *Admiral Graf Spee* emerged from harbour and scuttled herself on 17 December.

She entered Montevideo after *Admiral Graf Spee* had been scuttled, and then returned to the Falklands prior to a docking in Simonstown. She remained with the South American until March, and then joining the 6th Cruiser Squadron in the South Atlantic to July 1941. In May she and her half sister *Shropshire* escorted the New Zealand and Australian troop convoy US.3 from Capetown to Freetown, arriving on 7 June. She remained with the convoy to the Clyde. The convoy escort was strengthened north of Freetown and she and the convoy arrived on the Clyde in June 1940.

That month she sailed again from the Clyde to escort the first of the famous series of WS convoys (Winston Specials) carrying troops from the UK to the Middle East. She arrived at Colombo on 29 July in company with her sister ship *Kent*. These WS convoys were to take hundreds of thousands of men and large quantities of equipment to the Middle East and India. In July she became part of the South Atlantic command, protecting trade routes. That month she was sent from Simonstown, and was joined by her half sister *Dorsetshire* from Freetown, to search for a disguised raider, but it was like looking for a needle in a haystack, with too few ships being available to establish an adequate search.

On 31 August she and the cruiser *Cornwall* were detached to join the ill-fated expedition to Dakar (Operation Menace), which had been instigated after the fall of France. The expedition carried British and Free French Forces. A patrol was established off Dakar on 14th. The force arrived too late to prevent French Vichy cruisers entering harbour. On 16 September *Cumberland* intercepted and sank the French merchant ship *Poitiers* (4185 tons) which had been sailing for the Ivory Coast with ammunition. On 19th three French cruisers were sighted at sea, and *Cumberland* and her Australian sister ship *Australia* shadowed them The French *Gloire* broke down and after being intercepted agreed to go to Casablanca, but the other two (*Georges Leygues* and *Montcalm*) were followed, and, despite a parley by the *Cumberland*, re-entered the port of Dakar.

The main assault force arrived off Dakar on 23rd, and efforts at diplomacy failed. French naval forces sailed from the harbour and attempts were made to drive them back. Shore batteries opened fire and a large calibre shell hit *Cumberland* when she was

engaging Fort Manuel. The shell hit her port side and wrecked her main switchboard and damaged steam pipes. She was temporarily immobilized and had to flood her 4-inch magazines as a precaution. She was forced to withdraw. Two destroyers, *Foresight* and *Inglefield*, were also damaged. On the third day of the bombardment the battleship *Resolution* was torpedoed by the French submarine *Beveziers*. It was decided that little more was to be gained by further bombardment, and that the assault force was liable to receive further damage. The expedition therefore withdrew. The *Resolution* was out of action for year, and the cruiser *Fiji* had been torpedoed on the outward voyage and had to return to the UK for repairs.

In November 1940 she with the cruiser *Newcastle* was sent to reinforce the South Atlantic Division in a search for enemy surface ships. The pocket battleship *Admiral Scheer* and raider *Thor* were known to be at large, and thus a force capable of dealing with a pocket battleship was concentrated in areas off Rio de Janeiro or the River Plate. The next month she joined the cruiser *Enterprise* in a search for the raiders off South America, and they were joined later by the *Newcastle* in the Rio-Montevideo area. She carried out patrols off South America to June 1941.

On 28 June she arrived at Sheerness for a refit which lasted to October 1941. Tripod masts replaced her original pole masts, and four single 20-mm guns were added. Extra radar was also mounted and shelter provided for the 4-inch guns' crews. She then joined the First Cruiser Squadron of the Home Fleet.

In November 1941 she suffered gale damage off Iceland, and in December was refitted for Arctic service. In January 1942 she carried Stafford Cripps from Russia to the UK, escorted by the destroyer *Tartar*. In March-April 1942 she was underwent repairs at Chatham when four more 20-mm guns were added and her machine guns removed.

She was part of the distant covering force, which included the battleships *Duke of York* and USS *Washington* and aircraft carrier *Victorious*, for Russian Convoy PQ.17 in July 1942. The convoy was ordered to scatter on 4 July because of a threat from attack by German heavy surface ships. Although the threat did not materialise, the ships of the convoy were heavily attacked by submarines and aircraft. Twenty-four ships (including 1 rescue ship) totaling 142,695 tons were lost. In all 3,350 vehicles, 430 tanks, 210 aircraft and 99,316 tons of other equipment went down with the sunken ships.

In September 1942, when the next Russian convoy PQ.18 was sailed, she and the cruiser *Sheffield* and a destroyer carried reinforcements and stores to Spitzbergen. *Cumberland* landed stores at Barentsburg on 17th, whilst *Sheffield* landed her stores the next evening. The operation was conducted in clear weather, but the enemy did not detect them. That month she also provided distant cover for PQ 18 and the return convoy QP 14. PQ 18 lost 13 ships out of 40, 3 to U-boat attack and 10 to torpedo bombers. QP 14 lost 3 of its 15 ships to U-boats, whilst of its escort the destroyer *Somali* and minesweeper *Leda* were lost together with the tanker RFA *Gray Ranger*.

On 31 October she and her half sister *Norfolk* with 5 destroyers sailed from Scapa Flow for the Azores to provide cover for the North African landings. On completion of that duty she returned to the Arctic and in December she was part of the distant cover force for Convoy JW 51B. *Cumberland*, with the battleship *Anson* and three destroyers escorted the convoy to 15 degrees East. Two days later, when the convoy had reached 30 degrees East, it came under attack by the German heavy cruiser *Admiral Hipper*, the pocket battleship *Lutzow*, and destroyers. However, the destroyers of the escort, aided by the close support force comprising the cruisers *Jamaica* and *Sheffield*, drove off the enemy for the loss of the destroyer *Achates* and minesweeper *Bramble*, whilst the German destroyer *Friedrich Eckoldt* was sunk by the *Sheffield*. All fourteen ships of the convoy arrived safely.

In February 1943 she with the cruisers and *Sheffield* were the covering force for Convoy JW 53 to Russia. After severe weather the *Sheffield* was forced to return to harbour with considerable damage. Submarines and aircraft attacked the convoy, but the threat from enemy surface vessels did not materialise. 22 out of 28 ships arrived, the other 6 were forced to return to Iceland by bad weather. On 17 April 1943 she grounded off Hvalfjord entrance.

HMS Cumberland with tripod masts and cut down stern. *(Author's Collection)*

The next month she, with cruiser *Bermuda* and the destroyers *Eclipse* and *Athabaskan*, left Greenock to relieve Spitzbergen again. The force had to shelter from bad weather in Akureyi but arrived at Spitzbergen on 10th June, returning to Scapa Flow on 14th.

From August to November1943 she underwent a refit on the Tyne. Her hangar and catapult removed and extra radar fitted. On completion she was armed with four twin 8-inch, four twin 4-inch, two quadruple 2-pounders, five twin and four single 20-mm guns. After work up at Scapa Flow she sailed for the Eastern Fleet, passing through Alexandria in February 1944. On 21 March she sailed from Trincomalee with the Eastern Fleet on Operation Diplomat, when the US Naval forces comprising the carrier *Saratoga* and destroyers joined the British Eastern Fleet. The combined force returned to Trincomalee on 2 April, the same day as four escort carriers arrived. Shortly afterwards the French battleship *Richelieu* joined the combined force, which included Dutch, as well as Australian and New Zealand vessels.

In July 1944 she was with the Eastern Fleet when it carried out a bombardment at Sabang. (Operation Crimson). Capital ships, cruisers and destroyers of the force shelled the area whilst aircraft struck at the local airfields. Many shells, including 134 eight-inch shells, were fired at the shore targets. This was the first shore bombardment of Japanese positions by the Eastern Fleet.

In September 1944 she took part in Operation Light, where aircraft from the carriers *Victorious* and *Indomitable*, covered by the battleship *Howe*, cruisers and destroyers carried out attacks on Sigli in North East Sumatra. The aircraft also undertook photo-reconnaissance of the Nicobar Islands.

In October she was part of the force that took part in Operation Millet, a diversion for the then imminent landings on Leyte by the US Forces. The force sailed from Trincomalee on 15th and on 17th and 19th the carrier aircraft attacked the Nicobar Islands. On 17th the group which included *Cumberland* shelled the islands. The Japanese sent out a strike of 12 torpedo aircraft against the force. Seven of the attacking aircraft were shot down by the carrier aircraft for the loss of three of their own number, The diversion failed as by then the American forces had already struck at the Philippines.

In November, when the British Pacific Fleet was formed, *Cumberland* remained as part of the British East Indies Fleet. She refitted at Simonstown from January to March 1945, when she was fitted with two extra single 20-mm guns. In April 1945 she accompanied the battleships *Queen Elizabeth* and *Richelieu* for a bombardment of Sabang on 11 April (Operation Sunfish), covering a reconnaissance of Port Swettenham and Port Dickson by aircraft from the carriers *Emperor* and *Khedive*.

In late April and early May the covering force for the landings near Rangoon shelled Car Nicobar and Port Blair, whilst accompanying carriers carried out strikes in the area. The force returned to Trincomalee on 9 May, A few days later a Japanese surface force comprising the cruiser *Haguro* and destroyer *Kamikaze* were detected leaving Singapore to evacuate Japanese troops from the Nicobars and Andamans. The Eastern Fleet sailed from Trincomalee to intercept the Japanese ships. On 14 May *Cumberland* with the 21st Carrier Squadron (comprising the cruiser *Royalist*, four escort carriers and 8 destroyers, and 26th destroyer Flotilla (*Saumarez*, *Verulam*, *Vigilant*, *Venus* and *Virago*) was detached to an area west of the Six Degrees Channel. Air reconnaissance from the carrier *Shah* sighted the Japanese force on 15 May north east of Sabang, but the Japanese ships were seen to be heading back to Singapore. The 26th Destroyer Flotilla closed the Japanese force during the night 15-16 May in the Malacca Straits south west of Penang. The destroyers carried out a night pincer attack and sank the *Haguro* with torpedoes. The *Kamikaze* escaped with slight damage and the *Saumarez* was received three heavy hits.

On 2 September *Cumberland* and her half sister *London* landed Royal Marines at Sabang. She was present at Singapore on 12 September when the official surrender of all Japanese forces in South East Asia took place. On 15 September she arrived off Jakarta with one frigate and four Australian minesweepers to make contact with Allied

HMS Cumberland as a trials ship with twin 6-inch forward and twin 3-inch aft. *(Syd Goodman Collection)*

HMS Cumberland with a 4.5-inch gun to port of her bridge and a miscellaneous array of radar and radio antennae for trials. *(Syd Goodman Collection)*

Prisoners of War and to withdraw the Japanese forces to limited areas pending their final withdrawal. Japanese naval and military officers embarked to supply charts of minefields and provide information about the Prisoners of War. The next day another frigate, two minesweepers and 4 landing craft and the Dutch cruiser *Tromp* arrived. Merchantmen with food for the population arrived soon after, but conditions ashore proved difficult, as there was considerable civil unrest and virtually a civil war. A British battalion was not landed until 29 September.

In October 1945 she left Trincomalee for Plymouth, where, after repairs, she undertook trooping duties between England and Colombo, returning to Chatham in January 1946. She then carried out a trooping voyage to Sydney, returning to the UK in April. After a further passage to Colombo, she returned to Devonport and was put in care and maintenance. In June 1949 she started conversion at Devonport to a trials ship. Work was completed in April 1951. Her fore and aft superstructures had been enlarged, lattice masts fitted fore and aft and most of her armament removed. She emerged initially with a twin 4-inch and a twin 40-mm gun on her port side and a single 4.5-inch gun on her starboard side.

During the next few years she was used as the platform for a variety of gunnery trials. She also carried out trials of pre-wetting equipment, roll stabilisers, seaboats, torpedo tubes and also new messdeck equipment, such as plastic covered tables. Trials took place in the Mediterranean in 1951 and 1954,and on 16 August 1954 she was at Cannes for the 50th Anniversary of the Entente Cordiale. In September 1954 she carried 42 Commando back to Devonport. In 1955 she visited the Mediterranean to try the new twin 3-inch gun, which was fitted in X position. That year she carried trials of a new seaboat. She returned to the UK in September 1955. In May 1956 she sailed for the Mediterranean again for more trials with the 3-inch gun and the new automatic twin 6-inch gun, mounted in B position. A MRS 3 director was mounted on her bridge to control the guns. The 6-inch and 3-inch were the prototypes for the automatic guns to be fitted in the new Tiger Class cruisers. In October 1956 she carried out trooping duties between UK and Malta prior to the Suez operation. After refitting in Devonport in 1957, she sailed for the Mediterranean in June 1958 for more trials on the new 6-inch and 3-inch guns, firing 645 rounds of 6-inch and 6400 rounds of 3-inch in one month. She also carried out trials of new propellers, with glass windows installed in her bottom to permit observation. She was also employed on transporting troops between Gibraltar and Benghazi. In October 1958 she visited Barrow for two days, 31 years after she had been built there. She sailed for her final gunnery trials, which took place the next month off Gibraltar.

She arrived at Devonport for the last time on 11 December 1958, and paid off on 14 January 1959, having steamed 685,166 miles since her completion. She underwent de-equipping until May, when she went into extended reserve at Devonport. She was taken in tow on 30 October 1959 bound for Newport where she arrived on 3 November for breaking up. The first of the Counties, she was also the last.

She gained the following battle honours for her name:

Arctic 1942-43; North Africa 1942; Sabang 1944 (25 July); East Indies 1944-45, Burma 1945 and Malaya 1945.

This brought the ship's total Battle Honours to twelve.

HMS LONDON

HMS London in the piping days of peace in the Mediterranean. *(Ken Kelly Collection)*

The cruiser *London* was built at Portsmouth Dockyard. She was laid down 23 February 1926, launched on 14 September 1927 by the Lady Mayoress of London and completed on 31 January 1929. Of the second group of the County Class heavy cruisers, she was armed with four twin 8-inch guns, four single 4-inch (later increased to 8 singles), four single 2-pounders and two quadruple torpedo tubes. She displaced 9,850 tons, and her engines, built by Fairfield, developed 80,000-shaft horsepower giving her a speed of 32.25 knots. On trials she reached 32.91 knots. 630 ft long, with a beam of 66 ft., these ships were 2.5 ft narrower than the first group as they had no bulges.

She served in the 1st Cruiser Squadron Mediterranean from 1929-39, returning to Spithead for the Jubilee Review in July 1935 as Flagship of the Squadron. During her time in the Mediterranean she took part in 'Non intervention' patrols and the rescue of refugees from Republican Spain. *London* paid off on 15 March 1939 and then started a major refit at Chatham, emerging in 1941 with a new bridge structure on the lines of the Colony Class cruisers. During the refit she was given thicker armour and her AA armament was improved. She then was armed with four twin 8-inch, four twin 4-inch, two eight barreled 2-pounders and eight machine guns, together with two quadruple torpedo tubes. She also carried 3 aircraft. She recommissioned on 7 February 1941. Over 1200 tons had been added to her displacement, increasing it to 11,015 tons.

She then served on the Home and South Atlantic Stations. On 26 May she was escorting the SS *Arundel Castle* with evacuees from Gibraltar when she and her sister *Dorsetshire* were diverted to search for the German battleship *Bismarck* in the North Atlantic. The *Dorsetshire* was to deliver the final torpedo attacks on the German ship on 27 May. On 4 June she and the destroyer *Brilliant* intercepted the surface raider tanker *Esso Hamburg*, (9849 tons) on the Freetown-Natal route. The tanker scuttled itself. Again with the *Brilliant* she intercepted the U-boat tanker *Egerland* (9798 tons),

which also scuttled herself. On 21 June 1941 she intercepted the German supply vessels *Babitonga* (4422 tons) which had been supporting the raider *Atlantis*. This vessel, which was disguised as the Dutch *Japara*, also scuttled itself.

She carried the British and American supply missions led by lord Beaverbrook and Averell Harriman from Scapa Flow to Archangel for their meetings in Moscow, and brought them home again in late September (22-27). In late September/early October 1941 she was part of the escort of convoy QP1, the first homebound convoy from Russia comprising ships that had carried Hurricanes to Archangel. She underwent a refit on the Tyne from 30 October to late January 1942 during which eight single Oerlikons were fitted and her multiple machine guns removed.

In April 1942 she was with the *Nigeria* as cover for convoy PQ 15 to Russia. The convoy came under air attack, but the cruisers provided a strong defence and the attack became scattered and ill coordinated. *London* then withdrew from the convoy as it approached the submarine danger area. 22 out of the 25 ships in the convoy arrived safely. The three vessels lost were sunk by torpedo bombers that attacked later during the passage.

In July 1942 she was part of the cruiser escort for convoy PQ 17, which came under threat from German surface forces. The convoy was ordered to scatter and the cruisers and fleet destroyers headed west at high speed to meet challenge the German force believed to comprise the battleships *Tirpitz*, *Lutzow* and *Admiral Scheer*, heavy cruiser *Admiral Hipper* and destroyers. However, the German ships had returned to harbour and the expected action never materialised. The scattered ships of the convoy came under heavy air and submarine attack and suffered heavy losses.

In September the next convoy to Russia, PQ 18, was given a strong escort supplemented by a Fighting destroyer escort. *London* was again in the covering cruiser force. The *Tirpitz* sailed for exercises, and her movements caused anxiety, but no threat to the convoy developed. The convoy came under heavy air attack, and ten ships were lost whilst 40 aircraft were shot down. Three ships were lost to U-boats, but 27 of the original 40 ships arrived safely.

In November she helped cover a special convoy carrying the large number of allied merchant ships

HMS London with her spotting aircraft amidships. *(T. Ferrers-Walker Collection)*

HMS London after her long refit. Her funnel arrangement resembles the Colony class, but her slab sides reveal her true identity. *(Syd Goodman Collection)*

which had been waiting many months in Russia. 28 ships sailed from Archangel on 17 November, and underwent the passage in near total darkness, escorted by an AA ship and ten smaller vessels, reinforced by five destroyers in the Barents Sea. *London* and *Suffolk* with destroyers covered the convoy west of Bear Island.

In December 1942 to May 1943 she refitted on the Tyne where extra strengthening was fitted to her hull to cope with the extra loading brought about during her major refit. Her aircraft and catapult were removed at this time and extra radar and more Oerlikons added. She then returned to the Home Fleet and operated mainly in Northern waters until October 1943, when she sailed to Alexandria to bring the Defence Staff back to the UK after the Tehran Conference.

In December she entered Rosyth Dockyard for a refit which lasted to February 1944. She joined the Eastern Fleet on 13 March 1944. Her tertiary armament then comprised two eight barreled two pounders, and four twin and eight single 20-mm guns. On 21 March to 2 April took part in Op Diplomat, when the British Eastern Fleet was joined by American ships of US TG 58.5 (which included the carrier *Saratoga*). She took part in the carrier raid on Sabang on 19 April 1944 in company with the battleships *Queen Elizabeth*, *Valiant* and French *Richelieu*, battlecruiser *Renown* and carriers *Illustrious* and USS *Saratoga*. The raid was successful and achieved complete surprise. Oil tanks and installations were damaged and destroyed, and 24 enemy aircraft were destroyed on the ground with the loss of one aircraft, whose pilot was rescued by the submarine *Tactician*. In May she escorted the replenishment group for the carrier raid on Soerabaya (Operation Transom), again involving aircraft from the *Illustrious* and USS *Saratoga*. On 17 October 1944 she was with the Eastern Fleet when they bombarded the Nicobar islands and air strikes were carried out This was a diversionary operation for the imminent US landings on Leyte.

In November 1944, when the Eastern Fleet was

divided into two sections to form the British Pacific Fleet, *London* remained with the East Indies Fleet. In April 1945 she took part in Op Sunfish, where part of the Eastern Fleet including the battleship *Queen Elizabeth*, and French *Richelieu* shelled Sabang on 11 April. The escort carriers *Khedive* and *Emperor* provided air cover and their aircraft also attacked Port Blair and Emmahaven on 11 April. On 16th there were more air strikes against Emmahaven and Padang.

She then underwent a refit at Simonstown until July 1945. Her tertiary armament then comprised two eight barreled two pounders, four single 40-mm, eight twin 20-mm and four single 20-mm guns. On 28 August she anchored off Sabang, where a Japanese delegation brought documents onboard showing positions of mine barrages and giving assurances of peaceful intentions. On 31 August Vice-Admiral Hirose surrendered on behalf of the forces in Sumatra onboard. On 2 September 1945 she and the cruiser *Cumberland* put their marine detachments ashore at Sabang.

She was in the 5th Cruiser Squadron East Indies to January 1946. She then returned to the UK and then carried out two round trips, the first to Sydney and then Singapore carrying troops to Britain. The second trip completed in June 1946, when she went in to refit at Chatham after a short spell as flagship of the Reserve Fleet On completion of the refit she rejoined the British Pacific Fleet in September 1947 as part of the 5th Cruiser Squadron. On 21 April 1949 she was badly damaged on the Yangstse whilst trying to rescue the frigate *Amethyst*. She suffered 23 hits and lost 13 dead and 15 wounded. Her 4-inch guns could only operate in local control and A and B turrets were put out of action. She had many holes in her hull and fires were started. After withdrawing from the action she proceeded to Shanghai to act as the local Naval headquarters until mid May. She left the Far East Station on 10 June 1949, six weeks prior to the *Amethyst*'s break out, and arrived at Sheerness on 6 September. She was honoured by a civic reception by the Mayor and Aldermen of London and then paid off.

After a short period when she was laid up at Falmouth, she was towed to Barrow to be broken up, arriving there on 25 January 1950

She had gained the battle honours Atlantic 1941, Arctic 1941-3 and East Indies 1944-45 for her name, bringing the total for that name to seventeen. A further Honour, Kuwait 1991, has been earned by the later frigate of the name.

HMS SUSSEX

HMS Sussex, this second group of the County class had no external anti-torpedo bulges. *(Ken Kelly Collection)*

The *Sussex* was, like *London*, in the second batch of the between wars County class heavy cruisers. Built by Hawthorn Leslie, she was laid down on 1 February 1927, launched on 22 February 1928 and completed 19 March 1929.

She had a displacement of 9,830 tons, and was 633-ft long with a 66-ft beam. This class had no torpedo bulges, unlike the first group of County class. Her main armament comprised four twin 8-inch guns; with a secondary armament of four single 4-inch guns (later increased to 8), four single two-pounders and machine guns. Her 8-inch guns had an elevation of 70 degrees and a range of 29,200 yards. She also had two quadruple torpedo tubes. Originally she did not carry aircraft, though designed to carry one. One was installed in the early 1930s. During 1942 her AA armament was completely refitted, and in 1943 the number of 20-mm guns carried was raised to 22. In 1945 her X turret was removed, together with her catapult and torpedo tubes. Four more eight barreled pom-poms were fitted (bringing the total to six mountings), and her 20-mm gun armament brought up to a total of 14, four twin and six singles. The single 20-mm were removed in 1947 at Devonport.

Her engines developed 80,000-shaft horsepower (81,763 on trials) giving her a speed of 32.25 knots. She had a range of 12,800 miles at 10 knots, and 3,000 miles at 30.7 knots.

From 1929-1934 she was with the 1st Cruiser

HMS Sussex as modernised, with no hangar and retaining her high quarterdeck. *(Syd Goodman Collection)*

Squadron, Mediterranean Fleet. In July 1934 she exchanged duties with the Australian cruiser *Australia* for 2 years. During that period she returned to the Mediterranean in August 1935 to reinforce the Mediterranean Fleet during the Abyssinian crisis. She returned to the Royal Navy in December 1935 at Alexandria. After a refit in Chatham she recommissioned in June 1937 for the 1st Cruiser Squadron, Mediterranean Fleet. During the refit four extra single 4-inch guns were added together with two quadruple two-pounders and extra 0.5-inch machine guns. The four single two-pounder guns were removed. In October 1937 she embarked members of the Higher Arab Committee at Haifa for deportation to the Seychelles.

On the outbreak of war she was at Alexandria and was with her sisters *Devonshire* and *Shropshire* in the First Cruiser Squadron of the Mediterranean Fleet. In October, as Italy had not yet entered the war, she was transferred to the South Atlantic Station and formed Hunting group H with her sister *Shropshire* searching for the pocket battleship *Admiral Graf Spee* in the South Atlantic around the Cape of Good Hope. Force H was reinforced by Force K (comprising the aircraft carrier *Ark Royal*, battlecruiser *Renown* and cruiser *Neptune*). On 2 December she intercepted the German blockade-runner *Watussi* (9,552 tons) off South Africa. The German ship scuttled herself when the *Renown* opened fire. The *Sussex* took the German ship's passengers and crew to Simonstown. After the Battle of River Plate, she stood watch in the South Atlantic lest the German pocket battleship made a break for Germany. After the German ship had scuttled herself, *Sussex* was transferred to the East Indies Station.

In February she escorted the first Australian and New Zealand troop convoy for Europe. At the end of that month she was recalled from the East Indies to join the Home Fleet, returning through the

Mediterranean. She joined the 1st Cruiser Squadron of the Home Fleet in late May 1940, having given leave to her ship's company and refitted in Liverpool. She was then employed on patrols and other minor operations with the Home Fleet.

In June she was with *Repulse* and *Newcastle* escorting troopships from Harstad, Norway, to the UK. She was also detached with other ships of the Home Fleet to search for non-existent ships falsely reported to be breaking out through the Iceland-Faeroes gap. On 16 July she sailed with other units of the Home Fleet to intercept German ships thought to be making a sortie in the North Sea. The German ships returned to harbour, but the British force, whilst returning to Scapa Flow, met a thick fog. In the poor visibility the cruiser *Glasgow* collided with and sank the destroyer *Imogen*.

On the night 17/18 September 1940 she was bombed whilst in dock at Greenock. A 500-Kg bomb passed through her first whaler, the Wardroom Pantry and into her after engine room and started a serious fire, which was fed by fuel from an oil tank. Because the fire threatened the *Sussex*'s magazines, the surrounding area had to be evacuated for 12 hours until the fire could be brought under control. Her magazine had to be flooded and she capsized and was severely damaged. Immediate repairs took till October, when she was refloated and towed to Stephen's dry dock at Linthouse and rebuilt. Full repairs took until August 1942. By the time she was ready for sea again, her AA armament had been replaced. The single 4-inch guns had been replaced by four twin mountings. Two eight-barreled pom-poms were fitted together with ten 20-mm AA guns, including some on B and X turrets. Radar was fitted on the mastheads of new strengthened, tripod masts and also abaft B turret. The radar abaft B turret was found to have a blind arc and was later sited higher amidships to improve its coverage. Extra close range gunnery directors, fitted with radar, were mounted on the after superstructure.

She rejoined the 1st Cruiser Squadron of the Home Fleet, but four months later was transferred to the Eastern Fleet. Prior to departure she refitted on the Tyne. She sailed for Aden in February 1943 via the Cape. Whilst on passage, she took part in anti-blockade runner patrols. An American Liberator sighted the German supply tanker ship *Hohen Friedberg* (7892 tons) enroute to France in the Central Atlantic with a cargo of Vegetable oil. The tanker was reported and shadowed by the aircraft. *Sussex*, which was 190 miles away on patrol, intercepted the report and closed. On the evening of 26 February she arrived in the position and sank the tanker, an ex-Norwegian prize. The tanker was being escorted by three U-boats (*U-258*, *U-264* and *U-437*). One, *U-264*, fired a salvo of 4 torpedoes at the cruiser, but *Sussex* was able to avoid all of them. However, because of threat posed by these submarines, *Sussex* was unable to stop to rescue any survivors from the tanker.

In early March she escorted a convoy from Freetown to Durban. This was a WS convoy, carrying troops to the Middle East. From Durban she escorted another convoy to the Middle East. From July to September 1943 she was the Flagship of Admiral Somerville. In September 1943 she returned to Durban for a refit and repairs to her turbine. She was there until December. In January 1944 she arrived at Trincomalee in company with the battleships *Queen Elizabeth* and *Valiant*, battlecruiser *Renown*, aircraft carriers *Illustrious* and *Unicorn*, the Dutch cruiser *Tromp* and 12 destroyers, to reinforce the Eastern Fleet. In Mid March she took part in Operation Sleuth with the carrier *Illustrious*, cruiser *Gambia* and destroyers *Rotherham* and *Tjerk Hiddes* (Dutch) against suspected blockade-runners in the area south west of the Cocos Islands.

She returned to Chatham in June 1944 for docking. During the docking she had her X turret, catapult and torpedo tubes removed, and her radar and AA armament were enhanced. The refit lasted until March 1945. She then worked up with the Home Fleet before sailing from Scapa Flow on 25 April for the Mediterranean. On arrival at Gibraltar she was diverted to Bermuda, sailing on 1 May and returning to Gibraltar on 4 May. She then spent a period in the Eastern Mediterranean prior to rejoining the Eastern Fleet in July.

Between 24 and 26 July she was part of the force, including the battleship *Nelson*, that covered the minesweeping operations around Phuket Island off the west coast of the Kra Isthmus. On 26 July the force came under Kamikaze attacks, the first such on the East Indies Fleet. The carrier AMEER was damaged and the minesweeper VESTAL sunk. During these attacks the *Sussex* shot down two enemy aircraft and sustained slight damage when one enemy aircraft that had been shot down crashed 50 yards from her. Luckily the aircraft's bomb did not explode but wreckage stove in an 8-ft length of her side plating. The damage was above her waterline and did not affect her fighting efficiency.

On 31 August 1945 she sailed from Trincomalee flying the flag of Rear-Admiral C S Holland, commanding the occupation force for Singapore. On 4 September she arrived at Singapore with the 7th Minesweeping Flotilla, a destroyer, and a convoy which included the Headquarters ship *Kedah*, with the 5th Indian Division, XV Corps HQ and the British 3rd Commando Brigade onboard. The troops were landed and there were no untoward incidents ashore. Lt. General Itagaki and Vice-Admiral Fukudome surrendered on board on behalf of the Japanese forces in Singapore and Johore area. Finally on 12 September Admiral Mountbatten as the Supreme Commander, Allied Powers South-East Asia, accepted the surrender of General Itagaki in the Singapore Municipal Buildings. *Sussex* was amongst the Allied warships present at Singapore for that ceremony.

In November the Indian 5th Division were taken to Sourabaya in Indonesia in a convoy under the command of the HQ ship *Bulolo*, with the *Sussex* together with the destroyers *Caesar*, *Carron* and *Cavalier* providing a covering force. From December to February 1946 she was engaged in operations off Java. On 3 December she shelled areas east and south-east of Samarang where hostile Indonesian forces were reported.

She sailed for the UK on 6 March 1946, and arrived at Chatham later that month. She was then employed on trooping runs to and from the Far East. She paid off at Devonport on 18 September 1946, and underwent a refit during which all her single Oerlikons were removed. The refit lasted until April 1947, when she left Devonport to work up at Malta. She then joined the 5th Cruiser Squadron of the British Pacific Fleet. In December 1948 she was relieved as Flagship of the Squadron by the *Belfast*. In February 1949 she paid off at Portsmouth and was then de-equipped at Portsmouth and placed in reserve. She arrived at Dalmuir for breaking up on 23 February 1950, her hull being towed to Troon in July 1950. Breaking up was complete by January 1955.

She had gained the battle honours Norway 1940 and Burma 1945 for her name, bringing the total to four.

HMS EXETER

HMS Exeter showing her distinct appearance with upright masts and two funnels.
(Portsmouth Royal Naval Museum)

The cruiser *Exeter* was built at Devonport Dockyard, being laid down on 1 August 1928, launched on 18 July 1929 and was completed on 23 July 1931. She was one of two heavy cruisers completed to a lighter design than the standard County class vessels of the late twenties. She was armed with three twin 8-inch guns and displaced 8,390 tons. She was 575 feet long overall, with a beam of 57 feet. Her engines developed 80,000 shaft horse power giving her a speed of 32.25 knots. A half sister to the *York*, she benefitted by being the second ship of the class, being given a modern, square bridge and upright masts and funnels. Her after funnel was four feet wide than *York*'s, giving her a sturdier appearance. Minor modifications were carried out in the pre-war days, the side plating at main deck level being extended aft, her catapults were improved, and quadruple machine guns were fitted on either side abreast the catapult. She was also fitted with a bullet proof cover over her bridge.

She spent her first few years with the Atlantic Fleet, but in 1933 joined the America and West Indies Station as the Commodore's ship. Apart from a temporary absence for a short period from September 1935, when she, with other units from around the World, joined the Mediterranean Fleet at Alexandria during the Abyssinian Crisis, she spent six years on that station. Her last peacetime commission had been the usual round of work and play, visiting ports in South America and the United States of America as well as the Falkland Islands and the West Indies. She, with the *Ajax*, had aided the civil power at Trinidad during riots in June 1937, and, again with *Ajax*, helped earthquake victims at Talcahuano in January 1939. She returned to Devonport to pay off on 17 August 1939.

Her respite was short, for her crew were recalled on 23rd, and she sailed on the evening of 25th under the command of Captain S.F. Bell for the Cape Verde Islands, escorting the troopship *Dunera* on the way. She carried the flag of Commodore H. Harwood in command of the South American Squadron. She met the other ship of the Squadron, the cruiser *Ajax*, on 9 September and then guarded the River Plate area, while *Ajax* headed for the Falklands. They were joined by the cruiser *Cumberland* and the destroyers *Havock*

and *Hotspur*, whilst the oiler *Olwen*, later relieved by the *Olynthus*, supported them. The oiler was vital, as, even with her 10,000 mile endurance, the *Exeter* needed to refuel, and many ports were, by then, neutral and could only be used by her as a belligerent on a restricted basis.

In October 1939, when the German raiding operations were plain, the cruisers, re-inforced by the New Zealand manned cruiser *Achilles*, concentrated off the River Plate. The Commodore transferred his flag to the *Ajax* later in the month, while *Exeter* went to Port Stanley for maintenance. On 12 December, *Exeter* rejoined *Ajax* and *Achilles* 250 miles east of the River Plate, and at 0610 the next morning, the German pocket battleship *Admiral Graf Spee* was sighted.

The German ship opened fire with her 11-inch guns seven minutes later, concentrating her fire on the *Exeter*. The British force split into two divisions, *Exeter* taking one flank, whilst the *Ajax* and *Achilles* heading onto the other. Within five minutes *Exeter* had been hit twice, once by the starboard torpedo tubes, and then on the forecastle. Shortly afterwards B turret received a direct hit, wrecking both guns, and a second hit on the after part of the turret showered the bridge structure with shrapnel, killing many there. The Captain went aft to continue to control the ship, using boat's compass and passing messages to the after steering compartment via a chain of sailors. In the first 15 minutes of the action the *Exeter* had been hit by at least five 11-inch shells, and had been peppered with shrapnel from near misses. She continued to engage the enemy, firing her starboard torpedoes in local control. A further 11-inch shell put A turret out of action, and another exploded in the Chief Petty Officers' flat.

In view of her damage, the Captain considered ramming the enemy as a last resort. Y turret, the last in action, was firing with difficulty, one rammer was jamming and had to be moved with a hand-spike. Power supplies had failed for a time, but were restored, and local control was exercised by an officer sitting on the turret with binoculars. *Ajax* and *Achilles* closed the *Admiral Graf Spee* to draw her fire, and *Exeter* finally turned away at 0730, and headed the 1,200 miles to the Falklands at 18 knots. Five officers and fifty-six ratings had been killed, and many more were wounded, and the ship was badly damaged. *Ajax* and *Achilles* continued to hound the *Admiral Graf Spee*, who finally sought shelter in Montevideo and then scuttled herself on 17 December.

Exeter reached the Falkland Islands safely, and it was decided to repair her at Devonport. After temporary repairs, she was escorted from the Falklands by the cruisers *Shropshire* and *Dorsetshire*, relieved by the battlecruiser *Renown* and aircraft carrier *Ark Royal*, and later by nine Western Approaches destroyers. She reached Devonport on 15 February 1940 to a hero's welcome, being met by many VIPs, including the First Lord.

Her refit included the replacement of her single 4-inch AA guns by twin mountings; a new catapult and tripod masts. Her new captain, Captain Beckett, died on commissioning day, and he as relieved by Captain O.L. Gordon. The *Exeter* left Devonport on 24 March 1941, her repairs not quite completed, but the air raids on Plymouth were too intense to risk her remaining longer. She joined the First Cruiser Squadron at Scapa Flow to work up. She then conducted a patrol in the Denmark Strait. On 22 May she sailed from the Clyde as part of the escort of an important troop convoy (WS 8B), but by 25 th she was the only escort remaining with the convoy. The other ships, which included Captain Vian's destroyers, had been withdrawn to assist in the hunt for the German battleship *Bismarck*. In fact, at one time, the convoy crossed less than 100 miles ahead of the *Bismarck*, and at that point *Exeter* was the nearest British warship to her. She escorted the convoy to Freetown, and then on to the Cape and to Aden. She returned to Durban and spent the next few months on convoy escort duty between Aden and Durban.

In September she docked at Colombo, and then operated in the Indian Ocean until 7 December, when she was ordered to join the battleship *Prince of Wales* and battlecruiser *Repulse*. She was hurrying through the Malacca Strait when heard of the loss of these two ships. She was diverted to Singapore and then escorted convoys of troops and stores from India to Singapore. In February she joined the Allied American, British, Dutch and Australian ships in escort duties off Java.

She was at Tanjong Priok when she was detailed to join the multi-national (ABDA) force at Sourabaya. She sailed at 1400 on 25 February, in company with the Australian cruiser *Perth* and the British destroyers

HMS Exeter returning to Devonport for repairs after the Battle of the River Plate. *(Syd Goodman Collection)*

Electra, Encounter and *Jupiter*, leaving harbour while the port was under air attack, with the oil tanks on fire. The small force reached Sourabaya at mid-day on 26th, and, after negotiating the minefield in the approaches, went alongside at 1600. They sailed again within two hours, joined by Dutch and American ships, and searched for the Japanese invasion forces.

The Allied force was just returning to harbour to fuel at 1400 on 27th, and the leading destroyer had entered the swept channel through the minefield, when a report of the enemy units was received. The force immediately turned back to sea and headed towards the enemy, who came into sight a few hours later. The Japanese force comprised five Sendai class cruisers (with seven 5.5-inch guns each) and fourteen destroyers in two groups. They were soon joined by two Myoko Class cruisers (each with ten 8-inch guns). The Allied force comprised five cruisers and nine destroyers. The Japanese opened the engagement, firing at 28,000 yards, whilst the *Exeter* and USS *Houston*, the only two allied cruisers with 8-inch guns, replied at 27,000 yards. The Japanese had the benefit of aircraft spotting for their gunfire. The *Exeter* was second in the line, and was hit at 1700 by an 8-inch shell which went through the starboard after 4-inch gun mounting into the after boiler room. She lost speed and fell out of line. The following ships lost station in the confusion.

The *Encounter* and *Jupiter* at once made smoke to protect her, whilst the *Electra* closed three Japanese destroyers that were only 6,000 yards away. The *Electra* was overwhelmed and lost. The *Exeter*'s speed fell to 5 knots, but she soon recovered and was able to make 15 knots. However, she was in no condition to rejoin the cruiser line, so made her way back to Sourabaya escorted by the Dutch destroyer *Witte de With*. They arrived at 2300 and anchored. At 0700 the next morning she went alongside where she undertook emergency repairs. The crew also transferred 8-inch shells between magazines to balance the round remaining for each turret. Meanwhile, the two Dutch cruisers in the Allied force (*Java* and *De Ruyter*) were lost overnight together with the British destroyer *Jupiter*. The Australian *Perth* and the USS *Houston* were also lost the next morning in a fierce action in the Sunda

Strait against a superior Japanese surface force.

Three American destroyers at Sourabaya set out for Australia using the Bali Channel, leaving one of their number (USS *Pope*) to escort the *Exeter*. Another escort was to be the *Encounter*, who had returned to Sourabaya at midnight with 116 survivors from the Dutch destroyer *Kortenaer*, which had been sunk in the previous day's battle. The *Exeter* drew too much water to negotiate the Bali Channel, so she sailed at duck on 28th on a route to the north, and then turned west for Sunda Strait. Because of the damage to her boilers, her maximum speed was 23 knots.

At 0730 on 1 March, enemy ships were sighted, but seemed to have been evaded successfully until their reappearance at 0930. They turned out to be four cruisers, *Nati, Haguro, Myoko* and *Assigara* (each with ten 8-inch guns), escorted by three destroyers, *Kawakaze* (Wind on the River), *Yamakaze* (Wind on the Hill) and *Inadzuma* (Lightning) (each armed with 5-inch guns). They opened fire at once and *Exeter* weaved through a smoke screen made by her two escorts, and she also used the shelter of rain squalls. Her engineers, working under incredibly difficult conditions, managed to continue repairs to the boilers and gave steam for 26 knots, but this was still 7 knots less than the enemy ships. At 1120 she received a direct hit in her forward, undamaged boiler room. Not only did she lose speed, but she also lost all power to her turrets, and fires had sprung up throughout the ship. The *Encounter* closed to assist, but was told to escape. At about 1135 the order was given to abandon ship and she rolled over to port. Japanese destroyers closed and finished her off with torpedoes, firing 18 of which at least 4 hit.

Fifty-four officers and men were lost in this battle, a very similar number to that she lost in the River Plate action. It is also interesting to note that in her last actions her machinery was badly hit and guns were relatively unscathed, whereas the reverse was true in the River Plate action. 714 of her crew were taken into captivity, together with the survivors from the *Encounter* and *Pope*, which had succumbed to gunfire and air attacks during the day.

Just over three years later the *Haguro* was sunk by the 26th Destroyer Flotilla South West of Penang in a classic torpedo action, perhaps in part avenging the loss of the *Exeter*.

Exeter had earned three Battle Honours for her name: 'River Plate 1939'; 'Malaya 1942'; and 'Sunda Strait 1942', previous ships of the name gaining three, and a recent destroyer earning two more.

HMS Exeter after repairs with new masts and AA guns. *(Syd Goodman Collection)*

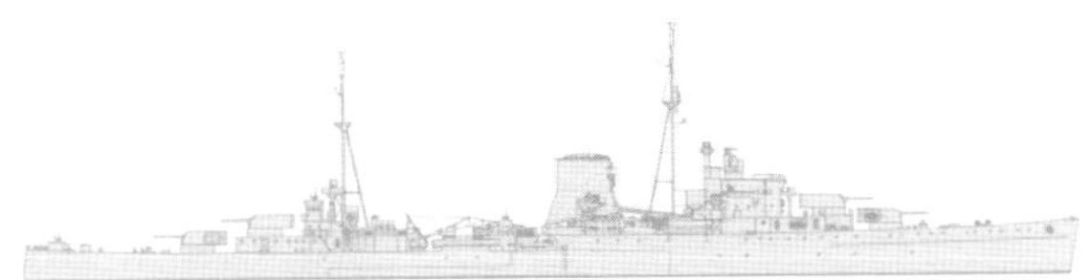

Leander Class Cruisers

After the building of heavy cruisers in the late 1920s, there was a lull before the next cruiser building programme started. It was then decided to build light cruisers armed with twin 6-inch guns. The Leander class was the first of these. They were a complete change from the previous heavy cruisers of the County class. Their main armament comprised four twin 6-inch turrets, and their appearance was dominated by their single, broad funnel amidships. Five of the class were built:- *Leander, Orion, Neptune, Achilles* and *Ajax*. A further three were built to a slightly modified design with two funnels (*Amphion, Phaeton* and *Apollo*, which transferred to the Royal Australian Navy as *Perth, Sydney* and *Hobart*). They all had a good war record, but paid a high price, *Sydney* being lost with all hands in November 1941off Western Australia; and *Neptune* being mined in the Mediterranean in the next month with but one survivor. *Perth* was sunk in the Sunda Strait action in February 1942 losing many men, both during her sinking and later in prisoner of war camps. *Orion* was hard hit during the evacuation of Crete, but survived to continue onward to gain the second highest total of Battle Honours of any ship in the Second World War.

HMS/HMNZS LEANDER

HMNZS Leander in wartime camouflage. *(MoD/Crown Copyright)*

The *Leander* was laid down on 8 September 1930 at Devonport Dockyard. Her displacement was 7,270 tons. She was armed with four twin 6-inch guns, which had a 60-degree elevation. This type of gun had already been fitted in the battleships RODNEY and NELSON. She was launched on 24 September 1931 and was completed on 24 March 1933. Despite the unusual single, large funnel, her overall profile was balanced, with two turrets forward and two aft, together with a modern, clean looking bridge. Her method of construction had been unusual in that she was the trial ship for welding techniques. Her engines, provided by Vickers-Armstrong Ltd. Developed 72,000-shaft horse power and her four propellers could drive her along at 32.5 knots. Originally wet amidships, extra plating was added along the waist area to counter this problem.

Leander served with the Light Cruiser Squadron of the Home Fleet for her first four years, and in March 1937 was transferred to the New Zealand Division. On 20 May of that year she represented New Zealand at the Coronation Review at Spithead. On completion of the Review she sailed for Auckland.

When war broke out in 1939, she and her sister ship *Achilles*, who was also in the New Zealand Division, covered the South Pacific trade routes. By January 1940 she was in the Indian Ocean checking for German whalers, and was also busy escorting convoys carrying Australian and New Zealand troops to Suez. *Leander* joined the East Indies

HMNZS Leander showing her large single funnel and with two twin 6-inch turrets fore and aft.
(Ken Kelly Collection)

Station in May 1940 after escorting troop convoy US-3 from Fremantle, and the next month she relieved the cruisers *Liverpool* as the Senior Naval Officer's ship in the Red Sea.

In October 1940, she was escorting convoy BN-7 off Massawa when it was bombed, but without damage. The same night the convoy was attacked by four Italian destroyers and in the ensuring action another escort, the destroyer *Kimberley*, drove one of the Italian ships, the *Francesco Nullo*, ashore. However, the *Kimberley* was hit by shore batteries and had to be towed clear by the *Leander*. The next month *Leander* bombarded Mogadishu and her Walrus aircraft bombed a fish factory as part of the campaign against Italian Somaliland.

After a refit in Bombay in December 1940, she was employed escorting troop convoys in the Indian Ocean. Shortly after leaving convoy US-9 off Bombay in February 1941, she sighted the Italian auxiliary cruiser *Ramb I* off the Maldive Islands. After a short engagement the raider exploded, but the *Leander* was able to rescue 103 of her crew. On 4 March she was with the Australian cruiser *Australia* off the Seychelles when they intercepted the German raider supply ship *Coburg* from Massawa together with the Norwegian tanker *Ketty Brovig*, which had been captured by the battleship *Admiral Scheer*. Both vessels scuttled themselves. Nineteen days later she intercepted a Vichy French steamship, the *Charles L.D.*, bound for Reunion, and sent her to Mauritius under guard.

In April she was an escort to convoy BM-7, which was carrying an Indian Brigade and an Artillery Group for Basra, where the troops landed unopposed after a German inspired revolt in Iraq. At the time, *Leander* was flying the flag of Vice Admiral Leatham, the Commander-in-Chief, East Indies. The next month *Leander* sailed for the Mediterranean, arriving at Alexandria on 4 June, where her catapult and Walrus aircraft were replaced by two multiple pom-poms. The Syrian campaign started on 8th, and on 16th the *Leander* was in a night action against two French destroyers off Beirut. The French flotilla leader *Guepard* was hit

but managed to escape using her superior speed. In July *Leander* helped reinforce Cyprus, and at the end of the month left Alexandria to return to New Zealand.

The New Zealand Navy Board was thanked by the Admiralty for the generous way they had placed *Leander* at the disposal of other commands, and they expressed their admiration of her excellent work on the East Indies and Mediterranean Stations.

In December 1941she escorted reinforcements from New Zealand to Fiji and joined the ANZAC Force when it was established in January 1942. The Force formed in Suva on 12 February 1942 under Rear Admiral Grace of the Royal Australian Navy, and joined Task Force 11 under Vice Admiral H.F. Leary, US Navy. The Force covered the eastern and north-eastern approaches to Australia and New Zealand, protecting shipping, supporting the island defences and harrying the Japanese forces ashore and afloat.

On 13 July 1943, four Japanese destroyers carrying 1,200 troops, covered by a cruiser and four other destroyers, entered the Kula Gulf. An Allied Task Force, which included the *Leander*, was deployed to stop the enemy movement. The Japanese sighted the Allied Force first and the cruiser *Jintsu* fired her torpedoes before being sunk. The *Leander*, then under the command of Captain S.W. Roskill, was hit and severely damaged. Two other cruisers, the US Ships *Honolulu* and *St. Louis*, and a destroyer of the Allied Force were also hit, the destroyer (the USS *Gwin*) sinking. The *Leander* had a hole 9 metres by 6 metres in 'A' boiler room. Three men had been killed, 24 were missing and eight more were injured. She arrived at Auckland on 29 July and initial repairs were carried out there. She went on to the US Navy Yard at Boston, Mass., where further repairs were carried out together with modifications. These included the removal of her X turret and the installation of a quadruple 2-pounder pom-pom in its place. Whilst there she ceased to be a part of the New Zealand Division.

HMS Leander modernised with AA guns on B turret and with twin 4-inch AA guns amidships.
(T. Ferrers-Walker Collection)

At the end of August 1945 she sailed from Boston for Rosyth via Montreal. She carried out trials in September 1945 and joined the First Cruiser squadron in the Mediterranean in August 1946. She was present at the Corfu incident on 22 October 1946, when the destroyers *Saumarez* and *Volage* were damaged by mines. She left Malta for the last time on 15 December 1947 and was laid up in the River Fal. She was sold on 15 December 1949 and arrived at Blyth on 15 January 1950 for breaking up.

HMS/HMNZS ACHILLES

HMNZS Achilles with tripod masts and radar added during the war. *(Syd Goodman Collection)*

The *Achilles* was the second of the Leander class cruisers to be built. She was laid down at Cammell Laird's on 11 June 1931, and launched on 1 September 1932. Of 7,030 tons standard displacement, and with four twin 6-inch guns, she had the same distinctive, single funnel profile as her sisters.

When she completed on 6 October 1933, she was allocated to the Second Cruiser squadron of the Home Fleet, with Captain Colin Cantlie, DSC, Royal Navy, in command. She carried out a work up cruise to Gibraltar in November 1933, proceeding from Portland to Gibraltar at an average speed of 28.5 knots. The following spring she was with the Home Fleet on its cruise to the West Indies, visiting Montserrat, St. Lucia, Barbados, St. Kitts, the Azores, Gibraltar and Arosa Bay, meeting heavy weather whilst crossing the Atlantic. During the summer cruise she exercised with three of her sister ships as well as visiting Milford Haven, Scapa Flow, Portland, Plymouth and passing through the Kiel Canal to Gavie (in Sweden) and Kiel. On completion of this summer cruise she docked at Chatham before taking part in the autumn cruise to Portland, Rosyth, Invergordon and the Humber.

The spring cruise 1935 followed the same pattern, visiting the West Indies. However, for the summer cruise she embarked the Duke of Gloucester for the Northern Ireland Silver Jubilee Celebrations, calling at Belfast and Arran as well as Scapa Flow before going to Spithead for the Silver Jubilee Review of the Fleet by King George V. On completion she docked at Chatham. The next Home Fleet autumn cruise was cancelled because of the Abyssinian crisis. Instead, she joined her sisters *Orion* and *Neptune* and took passage from Portland to Gibraltar, exercised in the Mediterranean and showed the Flag in the Atlantic. Visiting the Azores, Las Palmas and Funschal. On 13 November she returned to Chatham to reduce to special complement, and reverted to 14 days' notice for sea.

On 24 March 1936 she re-commissioned under Captain I.G. Glennie, with a ship's company of 60 percent New Zealanders and 40 percent 'Imperials', to join the New Zealand Division in place of the older cruiser *Dunedin*. Hence the outbreak of war in

September 1939 found her working the South Pacific trade routes with her sister *Leander* (also part of the New Zealand Division).

In October she joined Force G, one of the groups hunting for the German pocket battleship *Admiral Graf Spee*. She passed through the Straits of Magellan from the Pacific to join up with the cruisers *Exeter* and *Cumberland*. She replaced the *Exeter*, who proceeded to Port Stanley on 27 October. She then joined the *Ajax*, a sister ship, wearing the flag of Commodore Harwood, and covered the River Plate area. By the start of December the *Achilles* was off Rio de Janeiro and the *Ajax* was rejoining her from Port Stanley, where the *Exeter* and *Cumberland* were. The *Ajax* and *Achilles* met on 10th, and two days later they were joined by the *Exeter*. The next morning, the three cruisers encountered the *Admiral Graf Spee*. Immediately the *Ajax* and *Achilles* formed one division, attacking from the east, whilst the *Exeter* attacked from the south. One 11-inch shell burst just short of *Achilles*, its flying splinters killing three men in the gunnery control position, wounding and half stunning the Gunnery Officer, Lt. Washbourne, and several others. The splinters also wounded the Captain (W. Edward Parry) and Chief Yeoman of Signals Martinson on the bridge. Though none of the fire control instruments was seriously damaged, the position was temporarily out of action, and the secondary control had to take over for several minutes during the action. Despite the damage to all three British ships, the *Admiral Graf Spee* turned away. She was hounded by the *Ajax* and *Achilles* until she sought shelter in Montevideo, whilst the badly damaged *Exeter* returned to the Falklands to tend her wounds. The *Achilles* fired the parting shots before the pocket battleship slid into territorial waters. The two cruisers, joined on 16th by the *Cumberland*, stood on guard outside the harbour, but the battleship did not re-emerge, scuttling herself instead on 17 December. The British cruisers steamed past the wreck at 8pm on that day. Admiral Harwood's report (he had been promoted immediately after the action) of the action included the following comment: ' New Zealand has

HMNZS Achilles entering Malta in August 1946 with X turret replaced by AA guns. She was on her way back to the UK to be returned to the RN. *(Syd Goodman Collection)*

every reason to be proud of her seamen during their baptism of fire'.

After a triumphal return to Auckland on 22 February 1940, *Achilles* was tasked with escort duties in the Indian Ocean. In May 1940 she spent 26 days at sea and covered 9,575 miles, bringing her total distance steamed in the war to that time up to 125,125 miles. In November, she was part of a force which carried out an unsuccessful search for the raiders *Orion* and *Komet*. The raiders had just sunk the British liner *Rangitane*, which had recently sailed from Auckland.

In December 1941, she, with the Australian cruisers *Canberra* and *Perth*, met the USS *Pensecola* and eight transports from San Francisco heading for Brisbane via the Philippines. She then escorted convoy ZK-5, which comprised three large transports (including the *Aquitania*) carrying 4,250 troops and 10,000 tons of supplies from Sydney to Port Moresby.

On 12 February 1942, an ANZAC force was formed comprising the Australian cruiser *Australia*, the American cruiser *Chicago*, the New Zealand cruisers *Leander* and *Achilles* and two US destroyers. This force joined U.S. Task Force 11, and then U.S. Task Force 17, off the New Hebrides on 6 March. On 16-18 March the *Achilles* and Leander escorted the auxiliary cruiser *Westralia*, bringing a battalion of the U.S. American Division from Noumea to Efate in the New Hebrides. In April 1942, Captain C.A.L. Mansergh took over command from Capatin H.M. Barnes, and in July her operational control was transferred to the Commander South West Pacific. As she departed from the US Pacific Fleet, Admiral Nimitz signalled his appreciation " for the splendid manner in which every task assigned while you were under my direct command has been carried through to a successful conclusion. Well done".

On 4 and 5 January 1943, the *Achilles* was part of Task Force 67 covering operations in South-West Solomons. She carried out a night diversionary bombardment of an airfield and installations at Muna, New Georgia, with three American cruisers and three destroyers. While withdrawing on 5th the force was attacked by aircraft and *Achilles* was hit on X turret by a dive-bomber. Temporary repairs were carried out, though the turret remained out of action. In February she sailed from New Zealand to the United Kingdom via the Panama Canal for repairs. It was a measure of the difficulties caused by the loss of Singapore and other overseas bases that she had to travel half way round the World for such a refit.

She arrived at Portsmouth in March 1943 and started her refit, where X turret was removed. Extra AA guns and tripod masts were fitted. Her crew recommissioned the Colony class cruiser *Gambia* on 22 September 1943, while the crew of the *Leander*, repairing in the USA after being damaged in the action in Kula Gulf in July 1943, were shipped to the U.K. to re-commission the *Achilles* in March 1944, under Captain F.J.Butler. She left the United Kingdom in August for Colombo, where she became part of the Eastern Fleet.

In November, she became part of the British Pacific Fleet under Admiral Sir Bruce Fraser when it was formed from the modern ships of the British Eastern Fleet. This Fleet was to cooperate with the U.S. Fleet in carrying the war closer to Japan. She left Colombo on 9 December for Australia. In January 1945, she helped escort the liner *Rimutaka*, which was carrying H.R.H. the Duke of Gloucester to Sydney on the last leg of his journey to take up his appointment as Governor General of Australia.

In May 1945 she joined Task Force 57, which had been carrying out attacks on the Sakishima-Gunto group of islands in the Pacific. In June she took part in Operation Inmate, where the British carriers *Implacable* and *Ruler*, under Admiral Brind, carried out attacks on Truk. The carriers, escorted by four cruisers (including the *Achilles*) and five destroyers left Manus on 12 June and on the night 14/15 *Achilles*, with the cruiser *Uganda* and destroyer Tenacious, shelled the island of Dublon. 113 air attacks were launched by the carriers, and 103 Combat Air Patrol sorties were flown before the force returned to Manus on 17 June.

The next month the *Achilles* and the other New Zealand cruiser *Gambia* were part of British Task Force 37, joining U.S. forces in attacks on the Tokyo and Yokohama area. On 2-3 August the force had to move north clear of typhoons, which precluded air attacks on Japan for several days. Attacks

HMS Achilles in June 1948 having been renamed *Delhi* and transferred to the Royal Indian Navy.
(Syd Goodman Collection)

were resumed against North Honshu and Hokkaido on 9 August, and further attacks took place against North Honshu on 10th. Most of the British ships had to return to Manus on 12 August.

After the war, the *Achilles* sailed for New Zealand, arriving at Auckland on 30 August. She left New Zealand in July 1946 to return to the United Kingdom. She was handed over to the Royal Navy on her arrival at Sheerness on 10 September. She was then put into reserve. On 5 July 1948, after a long refit, she re-commissioned at Chatham for the Royal Indian Navy, being renamed *Delhi*. In August and September she passed through the Mediterranean and Suez Canal, arriving at Bombay on 15 September 1948. There she hoisted the flag of Rear Admiral J.T.S.Hall, Flag Officer Commanding Indian Naval Squadron, and she was received by the Prime Minister, Jawahalar Nehru. During 1949 she visited ports in the Indian Ocean. On 26 January 1950 she became the Indian Naval Ship *Delhi*, having her first Indian Captain, A.K.Chattergee, in June 1950. She returned to Britain in 1953 to attend the June Coronation Review at Spithead. She finally paid off on 23 December 1977, thirty years after commissioning as the Indian Navy's first flagship. She was discarded in May 1978. She had gained three Battle Honours for her name: 'River Plate 1939', Guadalcanal 1942-43', and 'Okinawa 1945', bringing the total for the name to six.

HMS ORION

HMS Orion gained thirteen Battle Honours for her name in World War II. *(Syd Goodman Collection)*

The fourth of the Leander class cruisers to be laid down was the *Orion*, on 26 September 1931, at Devonport Dockyard. She was launched on 24 November 1932 and completed on 18 January 1934. Of 7,215 tons standard displacement she was 554.5 ft long with a beam of 55.66 ft. She was armed with four twin 6-inch turrets, four single 4-inch (in 1936-37 these were replaced and repositioned) and three quadruple machine guns. She carried two quadruple torpedo tubes and was designed to carry two aircraft but only carried one. Her engines, provided by Vickers-Armstrongs, developed 72,000-shaft horsepower giving her a speed of 32.5 knots. Her endurance was 10,200 miles at 12 knots, and 2,200 at 30.75 knots.

She was in the 2nd Cruiser Squadron Home Fleet 1934-37, and was Flagship of the Squadron for the Jubilee Review of the Fleet on 16 July 1935. She then joined the 8th Cruiser Squadron (with *Berwick*, *York* and HMAS *Perth*) on the America and West Indies Station, relieving the *Dragon*. In October 1939 she reported the German tanker *Emmy Friedrich* in the Yucatan Channel. The tanker was later scuttled when intercepted by the cruiser *Caradoc*. In December she was directed to the German freighter *Arauca* off Miami by US Naval Aircraft, but as the German ship was in US (neutral) waters she was unable to capture her. During the first 120 days of the war she spent 102 days at sea on patrol and escort duties.

In February she returned to Britain carrying the ashes of the Late Lord Tweedsmuir, Governor General of Canada, and escorting the troopship SS *Duchess of Bedford*. She gave leave and was degaussed before returning to the America and West Indies Station in March. In April she was transferred to help strengthen the Mediterranean Fleet as the Italian threat developed. She became the Flagship of Rear Admiral (Destroyers), Mediterranean Fleet.

In early June she took part in the first sortie by the Mediterranean Fleet against the Italian shipping heading for Libya. The Italians sent out two forces to counter the British ships, but made no contact. On 21 June 1940 she was Flagship of Admiral Tovey for a bombardment of Bardia with *Neptune* and HMAS *Sydney*, the French *Lorraine* and 4 destroyers. This was the last joint Anglo-French operation in the Mediterranean. Only slight damage was caused by the bombardment.

A week later (28 June) she was with HMAS *Sydney* and the cruisers *Gloucester*, *Liverpool* and *Neptune* covering convoys to Malta, when three Italian destroyers were located taking supplies to Tobruk. The cruisers attacked the destroyers and *Sydney* sank the *Espero*, which was covering the escape of the other two destroyers.

On 9 July 1940 she was off Calabria, when the Mediterranean Fleet encountered the Italian Fleet. An Italian battleship was hit and damaged, together with the cruiser *Bolzano*. The cruiser *Gloucester* was slightly damaged by air attacks. However, the action proved inconclusive.

On 23 July she and 2 destroyers carried out a diversion off Castellorizo for an Aegean convoy operation. On night 3-4 September 1940 she, *Sydney* and the destroyers *Ilex* and *Decoy* bombarded the Dodecanese Islands. The *Ilex* later sank the Italian *MAS 537* when she and *MAS 536* attempted to attack the force. On 2 October 1940 she and *Sydney* bombarded the Maltezana area of Stampalia. Both before and after this she was

HMS Orion departing Malta in October 1945. *(Portsmouth Royal Naval Museum)*

engaged in covering convoys to Malta. On 15 October she towed the damaged cruiser *Liverpool* to Alexandria after the *Liverpool* had been hit by aerial torpedo. Later that month she and *Sydney* with the destroyers *Jervis* and *Juno* conducted a contraband control sortie into the Aegean as far North as the Dardanelles.

She was with the main battlefleet for the 11 November air strike on Taranto, and then carried out a raid on the Straits of Otranto. On night 11-12 November 1940 she with *Ajax* and *Sydney* sank one ship and set two on fire out of 4 ships of an escorted convoy heading for Brindisi. The escort, the auxiliary cruiser *Ramb III* and old torpedo boat *Fabrizi* escaped with some damage.

Later that month she took troops to Piraeus and covered Operation Collar, a raid on Rhodes by aircraft from the *Illustrious*. In December she made another sortie into Strait of Otranto with other cruisers and destroyers. In January took part in Operation Excess, a convoy to Malta and Piraeus.

On 28 March 1941 she was flagship of Vice-Admiral Light Forces (Vice-Admiral H D Pridham-Wippell) and operating off Gavdo Island protecting British convoys to Greece. It was known that enemy surface forces were in the area, and the convoys were turned away and the Mediterranean Fleet sailed to the area. *Orion*'s force sighted three enemy cruisers and soon afterwards also sighted another force, which included a battleship. Later a third force including heavy cruisers was also sighted in the area. The *Orion*'s force, followed by the main Mediterranean Fleet, chased the Italian ships. Air strikes were launched which damaged the Italian battleship, causing it to slow down, and stopped the cruiser *Pola*. Two other cruisers were left astern by the Italians to support the *Pola*. During the night *Orion*'s force detected the stopped cruiser and reported her position to the main fleet, whilst continuing their chase of the Italian battleship. TheBritish battleships closed and sank the two enemy cruisers standing by the *Pola*, whilst the destroyers in company sank the *Pola* and two Italian destroyers. Unfortunately the Italian battleship was able to carry out repairs which allowed her to increase speed and, with the remainder of the Italian force, she made good her escape. The action became known as the Battle of Cape Matapan.

On 12 April she with *Ajax* and *Perth* covered six destroyers on a sortie along the North African coast in support of the Army in its withdrawal. She then covered convoys to and from Malta, and later that month she took part in evacuation of British troops from Greece (Operation Demon). She was still Admiral Pridham-Wippell's flagship, who was in command of the forces involved. The evacuation started on 23 April, and lasted till the 29th. In all 50,732 troops were recovered, 80 percent of those landed earlier in Operation Lustre. Early in May she covered convoys to Malta and to Alexandria.

Later that month the Mediterranean Fleet deployed to prevent any seaborne landings on the Island of Crete. They came under heavy air attacks but achieved their aim. On the night 21st *Orion* was in a force comprising *Dido*, *Orion*, *Ajax* and four destroyers that encountered an enemy convoy north of Crete, and for 2.5 hours they engaged the enemy inflicting heavy losses. On 28th she (with *Ajax*, *Dido* and 6 destroyers) sailed to evacuate Heraklion. The force was attacked on the way in and two ships were damaged. That night the troops were embarked, and early in the morning they sailed for Alexandria, with the entire garrison of 4,000 embarked. The force was delayed when the destroyer *Imperial*'s steering gear jammed, and *Hotspur* closed her to take off her troops and crew and to sink her. This delay left the force close to the island at daybreak, and heavy air attacks developed. The destroyer *Hereward* was hit, damaged and lost, and *Dido* and *Orion* damaged in the bombing.

At 0710 *Orion* was near missed by a 500-Kg bomb that grazed her upper deck and exploded in the water off her starboard quarter, causing oil leaks into her after 6-inch magazine. At 0730 her Captain (Captain G R B Back) was wounded and he died 2 hours later. Commander T C T Wynne took over command. At 0915 she came under attack by dive-bombers and was hit by a 500-Kg bomb, which went through her forward turret and exploded on the turret roller path. The revolving structure of the turret was destroyed. The turret crown was blown upward and hit 'B' gun barrels, knocking them upward to maximum elevation and bending them. Cordite fires started in 'A' turret lobby and the nearby messdecks. At 1050 she was hit by another 500-Kg bomb which penetrated to the lower steering position, where it detonated, killing over 200 people. The explosion was on the crown of the 4-inch magazine, but fortunately all the HE shells had been removed. With her lower steering position out of order, DC Headquarters and telephone exchange destroyed, and no lighting forward of the engine room, *Orion* began to circle and developed an 11 degree list to starboard. 'A' boiler room had to be evacuated because of the smoke from the fires, and her torpedoes were jettisoned to ease the list.

Firefighting in the messdecks was hindered by the large number of dead and wounded - she had 1100 troops embarked- but the fires were extinguished by 1150. By 1200 steam had been raised in 'A' boiler room again, and by 1252 and she was able to make 224 rpm on all shafts. Unfortunately the fuel tanks had been contaminated as a result of the bomb hits, and 'A' and 'B' boiler rooms had to be shut down, with 'C' boiler room providing steam using fuel from the stand by tanks, which were fortunately found to be undamaged. At 1640 she was able to make 180 rpm. She reached Alexandria at 2330 with 10 tons of uncontaminated fuel remaining. She had two rounds of 6-inch HE ammunition remaining. Her forward guns were out of action and the after 6-inch and 4-inch guns could operate in local control only. She had lost over 100 officers and men. Of the troops embarked, 260 were dead and 280 wounded. She had survived 7 hours of continuous high and low level bombing attacks.

She underwent repairs at Simonstown to August 1941, where her aircraft catapult was removed and installed in the *Albatross*. She then sailed to Mare Island for further repairs that lasted to 15 February 1942. She returned to Devonport and there repairs completed on 21 April 1942. She rejoined the Mediterranean Fleet after a work up and escorting a convoy to the Middle East. Her light AA armament then comprised two quadruple 2-pounders (amidships) and seven Oerlikons (on B and X turrets, bridge wings, after control position and after superstructure).

In November and December 1942 she escorted the first convoys into Malta from Alexandria after the siege had been raised by the landings in North Africa. In January she escorted the first convoy to Tripoli to supply the advancing Army. She was at that time part of a striking force operating from Malta with *Cleopatra*, *Euryalus* and 4 destroyers.

She bombarded Pantellaria on 12-13 May, 31 May 1943 and 2-3 June. She was part of the covering force for the assault group which arrived on 10-11 and to which the island surrendered on 11 June. That night she and other cruisers shelled the island of Lampedusa, which surrendered the next morning.

She was in the support force for the landings on Sicily on 10 July 1943 (Op Husky). During this operation she bombarded the Italian destroyer and submarine base at Augusta on 11-12 July. On 25 August she bombarded the Calabrian coast. She carried out a further bombardment of the area on 31 August 1943, with the battleships *Nelson* and *Rodney*, in preparation for the landings there (Op Baytown). She undertook further bombardments in the Messina Strait on 2 and 3 September in support of the Army crossings.

She was in the support group for the Northern attack Force for the Salerno on 9 September 1943 (Operation Avalanche), lying off the coast providing fire support. In October and November she returned to Britain and underwent repairs at Portsmouth, returning to the Mediterranean in November. On 27 November 1943 she and 3 destroyers bombarded enemy positions north of Garigliano River. She carried out further bombardments on 12-13 December in the Gaeta area to prevent enemy re-inforcements to the Cassino area.

After a bombardment with the cruiser *Spartan* and four destroyers in the Terraeina area on 18 January she operated in support of the landings at Anzio (Operation Shingle). She was in the area until March, carrying out various bombardments including some with the Dutch *Soemba* in the Formia area, NW of Naples.

In April she returned to Rosyth in preparation for the Normandy Landings, during which she operated in gunfire support, She helped carry out the opening preliminary bombardment on Gold Beach at 0725 on D-Day. She fired 3358 shells between D-Day and 12 June. She was one of the ships singled out by the Army for special congratulations for their

HMS Orion carrying out a shore bombardment, a task she was often called upon to carry out in World War II.
(Syd Goodman Collection)

supporting fire, being specially mentioned for an intense bombardment at extreme range of enemy positions at Tilly-sur-Seulles. During the operation she had to have her worn out guns replaced.

In July she returned to the Mediterranean. She was in Alpha Gun Support Force for the landings in the South of France (Operation Dragoon) on 15 August as Flagship of Rear-Admiral J M Mansfield.

She then moved east and was part of the British Aegean Force for re-occupation of the Aegean Islands and Greek mainland.24 September - 31 October, being the flagship of Admiral Mansfield for the force entering Athens on 15 October 1944 (Operation Manna). The Navy landed two British brigades to maintain law and order, to establish the Greek government on its return and arrange for Greek relief. She remained at Piraeus and on 7 December landed her Marines to deal with serious sniping at the Navy House in Athens. She left on 19 December and sailed for Malta for repairs, which lasted till March. She then rejoined the 15th Cruiser Squadron at Naples. In April she carried out further bombardments in the Gulf of Genoa and on 12 April 1945 she bombarded San Remo in support of the Army's resumed offensive in Italy. She arrived at Trieste on 11 May and remained there to quell unrest until July.

On 15 May 1946 she and the cruiser *Superb* were fired on by Albanian shore batteries while they were heading south through the Corfu Channel. She was not damaged. Six months later the destroyers *Saumarez* and *Volage* were mined in the same Channel.

She returned to Devonport for refit on 4 July 1946. She was then placed in reserve. In November 1948 she was fitted as a target ships for trials in

Loch Striven. In March to May 1949 she was used for trials and was beached in a sinking condition. On 19 July 1949 she arrived at Troon for breaking up.

She had gained 13 Battle Honours for her name, a total second only to the battleship *Warspite* for the Second World War.

HMS AJAX

HMS Ajax, a pre-war photograph showing her pole foremast and short mainmast. *(Steve Bush Collection)*

The *Ajax* was the fifth of the Leander Class cruisers. She was armed with four twin 6-inch guns and two quadruple torpedo tubes. She also carried an aircraft for spotting and reconnaissance. The 6-inch guns were based on guns that had been fitted as secondary armament on the battleships *Rodney* and *Nelson*, and had elevation of 60 degrees. Their barrels were of the new auto-frettage construction instead of the old wire-wound type. *Ajax* had a standard displacement of 6,985 tons and was 554.5 feet long overall and had a beam of 55.6 feet. Her engines could develop 72,000-shaft-horse-power giving her a maximum speed of 32.5 knots. She had a range of 10,400 miles at 12 knots and 2,300 miles at 31.4 knots. On trials she achieved 33.1 knots. She was built and engined by Vickers-Armstrongs Ltd., Barrow-in-Furness, being laid down on 7 February 1933, launched on 1 March 1934, commissioned for trials on 29 March 1935 and completed on 12 April 1935 – the last of the class. These ships proved good seaboats but their forecastle plating was extended aft and their boats placed a deck higher to combat their wetness amidships.

From completion until the outbreak of war in 1939 she served on the North America and West Indies Station, though she spent the autumn of 1935 and spring of 1936 in the Mediterranean. In May 1936 she escorted *The Viceroy of India* carrying the King of Egypt. In 1936-37 her four single 4-inch AA guns were replaced by twin mountings. In January 1937 she rescued a survey party from the *Discovery II* at the South Shetlands, and in June 1938 she took the body of Governor of Jamaica to sea for burial. In September 1939 she was on patrol off the Rio area of South America. On the 4th she intercepted the German merchant ships *Karl Fritzen* and *Olinda* off the River Plate, both ships scuttling themselves before they could be taken as prizes. On 5 December she intercepted the

Ussukuma which also scuttled herself before capture.

In October *Ajax* and her sister *Achilles* were allocated to join Hunting Group G, comprising the cruisers *Cumberland* and *Exeter* (both armed with 8-inch guns) in the search for the German pocket battleship *Admiral Graf Spee*. They were to search the East Coast of South America. On 13 December she was in company with the cruisers *Exeter* and *Achilles*, operating off the mouth of the River Plate. Commodore H.H. Harwood, flying his flag in the *Ajax*, had anticipated that the *Admiral Graf Spee* would be tempted by the shipping off Rio de Janeiro and the River Plate. He therefore had concentrated his forces there, *Exeter* leaving Port Stanley on 9 December, and *Achilles* being ordered to join him on 10th. The *Cumberland* was covering the Falkland Islands lest the German attempted to take action on the anniversary of the Falklands Battle on 8 December 1914. The three cruisers were together off the River Plate by 0600 on 12th December. 0614 on 13th the enemy battleship was sighted by the *Exeter*. The *Ajax* and *Achilles* remained together as one unit and headed east, whilst *Exeter* parted company to approach the enemy from the west to split the battleship's fire. The *Admiral Graf Spee* concentrated her main armament of 11-inch guns on *Exeter*. By 0650 *Exeter* had been hit heavily, she had a heavy list to starboard, was only able to operate one gun turret in local control and was steering from aft. At 0730 she turned away to the south east to effect repairs. She had 61 killed and 23 wounded. *Ajax* and *Achilles* had been engaged by the battleship's secondary armament of 5.9-inch guns, but these failed to hit the cruisers. At 0630 the German shifted the fire of one main 11-inch turret onto them, straddling *Ajax*. At this point in the action *Ajax* made history by launching her aircraft between 6-inch salvoes. At 0640 *Ajax* was damaged by a shell burst on the waterline, and *Achilles*' gunnery wireless broke down so both ships lost accuracy in their fire. At 0708 they had found the range again, at 16,000 yards, but *Graf Spee* made smoke, making spotting difficult. At 0716 the *Graf Spee* had turned towards *Exeter* as though to finish her off, and the two light cruisers immediately turned towards to distract her. This ploy worked, and the enemy concentrated on *Ajax*, who was hit again at 0725 by 11-inch shells, at 11,000 yards, and both after turrets were put out of action. Shortly afterwards at 0738, when the cruisers had closed to 8,000 yards, she was hit again

HMS Ajax fitted with tripod masts and extra AA guns during the war. *(MoD/Crown Copyright)*

and lost her topmast. *Ajax* and *Achilles* turned away, but the German ship continued to head westwards, so the light cruisers turned back and began to shadow her.

Ajax had lost seven men with 5 wounded. *Achilles* had lost 4 men and was slightly damaged. The badly damaged *Exeter* was detached to the Falklands for repairs. She was so badly damaged that at one time it was planned to leave her at Port Stanley as a permanent battery. However, she returned to Devonport, was refitted, and was finally lost in a battle against overwhelming odds in the Java Sea in March 1942.

Ajax and *Achilles* remained astern of the retiring battleship, which turned occasionally to fire salvoes at them until almost midnight, when it was clear that she was heading for refuge in Montevideo. The light cruisers patrolled the entrance to the River Plate, and were joined the next day by the *Cumberland*. The *Graf Spee* sailed on 17th, but scuttled herself that evening. *Ajax* remained on station until January, then returned to Chatham Dockyard in February for repairs, which took until July 1940. During this refit tripod masts and radar were fitted.

Ajax left Liverpool on 22 August 1940 escorting Convoy AP2 with motor transport and other urgently needed supplies for the Middle East, via the Cape. On reaching Suez towards the end of September, she joined the Mediterranean Fleet, remaining there for most of her war service.

On the night 11/12 October, *Ajax* was covering a convoy from Malta to Alexandria (Operation MB.6). The convoy was attacked by three Italian destroyers, the *Ariel*, *Airone* and *Alcione*. The first two destroyers fired their torpedoes but with no success, and *Airone* obtained three 4-inch hits on *Ajax*, causing some damage, a fire which took 3.5hours to extinguish and casualties. However both destroyers were sunk. Shortly afterwards another enemy destroyer, the *Artiglieri*, accompanied by four others, was engaged and set on fire. She was later sunk by the cruiser *York*. Another enemy destroyer, the *Aviere* was also hit. For *Ajax* this had been her first night shoot after re-commissioning, and her Captain, Captain E. D. B. McCarthy was commended for his skill and resolution.

On 28 October 1940 Italy attacked Greece, and three days later *Ajax* sailed from Alexandria with a battalion of the York and Lancaster Regiment and some AA artillery for Crete. She arrived at Suda Bay on 1 November. Later that month she escorted British troops to Greece, and conveyed a battalion of The Black Watch from Port Said to Suda Bay. On 12 November she took part in a sweep of the Straits of Otranto. On 18 December was with two other cruisers (*Orion* and *Sydney*) and three destroyers (*Janus, Jervis* and *Juno*) on another sweep into the Straits of Otranto, inflicting loss and damage to an enemy convoy off Valona.

She took part in the Battle of Cape Matapan when the British and Italian Fleets met on 28 March 1941. Ajax was part of the light cruiser force (under Vice Admiral Pridham-Whippell) which first encountered Italian heavy cruiser force. The Italian cruisers retired to the cover of the Italian battleship *Vittorio Veneto*. During the ensuring actions the Italian battleship and the cruiser *Pola* were damaged. In a night action that followed the Italians lost three cruisers, *Zara*, *Fiume* and *Pola* and two destroyers, *Alfieri* and *Carducci*, whilst the British Fleet sustained no serious damage or casualties. During the action *Ajax*, being fitted with radar, was able to help clarify the position for the British forces.

On 6 April 1941, the German army invaded Greece and Yugoslavia without any warning. German aircraft made intensive attacks with bombs and mines on Piraeus, putting the port out of action. *Ajax* was amongst the ships present in the port, but Captain McCarthy managed to sail *Ajax* out of the harbour through the smoke and mines. On the night 27/28 April she, with three destroyers, lifted 4,750 troops from Raphtis and Nauplia. The next night she lifted 4,320 troops from Monemvasia.

Continuing on convoy escort and other operations in the Eastern Mediterranean, in the early hours of 8 May the *Ajax* illuminated Benghazi with starshells whilst three destroyers bombarded the harbour at 5,000 yards range. A fortnight later *Ajax* was caught up in the Battle of Crete, which lasted to 1 June. During that she had a successful two and a half hour engagement with an enemy troop convoy

whilst with Admiral Glennie's force on the night of 21-22 May, and sustained slight damage from near-miss bombs. Her stem was bent and forepeak flooded, both port propellers were distorted and her speed was reduced to 25 knots. On 28 May, whilst heading for Crete to assists with further evacuation from Heraklion, her force came under heavy air attacks and she was damaged by bombs, suffered an internal fire, and was detached to Alexandria. The next morning, as the force withdrew with 4000 troops, heavy air attacks began. The destroyer *Imperial* broke down and had to be sunk by *Hotspur*. This delayed the force, and then the destroyer *Hereward* was sunk. The cruisers *Orion* and *Dido* were both badly damaged as the force withdrew to Alexandria, arriving on the evening of 29th with little fuel and ammunition remaining.

From 8 June 1941, the *Ajax*, with the cruisers *Phoebe*, *Coventry* and 8 destroyers took part in the naval operations connected with the campaign in Syria aimed at forestalling a German occupation. She, with *Phoebe* and the destroyers *Kandahar*, *Kimberley*, *Janus* and *Jackal* sailed to cover a commando operation north of Tyre, but the operation had to be abandoned because of the heavy swell. On 9 June she was near missed by a torpedo fired by the French submarine *Caiman*. On 4 July she and the cruiser *Naiad* and 5 destroyers shelled the coast of Syria.

During the summer she was engaged in several convoy and other operations and on the night 20-21 October she bombarded an enemy battery east of Tobruk. In mid November the Mediterranean Fleet put to sea to cover operations by Force K, the cruiser and destroyer striking force operating out of Malta. During this sortie, of which the *Ajax* was a part, the battleship *Barham* was torpedoed and sunk by *U-331* on 25 November with the loss of 862 of her crew.

On 29 November, *Ajax*, together with the cruiser *Neptune* and destroyers *Kimberley* and *Kingston*, sailed for Malta to reinforce Force K. On passage the cruisers and destroyers were attacked by the Italian submarine *Tricheco* without success. The success of Force K in attacks on the supply route to Libya had obliged the enemy to provide cruiser escort for his convoys.

On 30 November Force K sailed to intercept enemy shipping, and sank the passenger ship *Adriatico* which was heading for Benghazi. The destroyer *Da Mosto* was intercepted and sunk as she was rescuing survivors from the tanker *Irido Mantovani*, which had been hit by an air dropped torpedo. Force K was sailed to intercept an Italian convoy off Tripoli, but *Ajax* remained at Malta for that operation. The Force ran onto a minefield on 19 December and *Neptune* and the destroyer *Kandahar* were lost. The cruisers *Penelope* and *Aurora* were damaged.

In support of the advance of the Army of the Nile in the Western Desert, the *Ajax* bombarded enemy headquarters at Bardia on the night of 30-31 December, the Army reporting the results as 'very useful'.

By January 1942 *Ajax* was in need of a thorough refit after her strenuous operations in the Mediterranean, but it was not until 2 March that she could be spared to leave the Station. She arrived at Capetown on 18 and sailed for Freetown, but was recalled to take part in an operation against a Vichy French convoy, which it was believed, was bound, for Madagascar. She sailed again on 27 March and arrived in the Clyde on 14 April. A month later she was taken in hand at Chatham for repairs, which lasted to November. During this refit she was fitted with eleven Oerlikon guns and improved radar, and her aircraft facilities were removed.

After working up at Scapa Flow, *Ajax* sailed from the Clyde on 23 December for Gibraltar to join Force H. Her return to her old station proved unlucky, for on 1 January 1943 she was at Bone, Algeria, during an air raid, and received a direct hit from a 500-Kg bomb, dropped by a Ju 87, which hit the base of her funnel. Both A and B boiler rooms were flooded and she had a 12 x 15 ft hole and 32 ft split in the bottom under the boilers. She was relieved by *Penelope*, which had returned to the station from the USA after being damaged at Malta. She proceeded to Algiers under her own power at 11 knots, arriving on 8 January for temporary repairs. On 23 February she sailed for Bermuda and the USA, where she was under repair in Brooklyn Navy Yard until October. During this period she was fitted with US quadruple 40-mm AA guns and

HMS Ajax showing her after turrets which were put out of action by the *Admiral Graf Spee*'s 11-inch shells. *(Steve Bush Collection)*

her radar was updated. *Ajax* returned to Portsmouth on 12 November, and on 26 December, proceeded to Scapa Flow to work up.

At the end of January 1944, *Ajax* again sailed for the Mediterranean, where she joined the 15th Cruiser Squadron. On the night 2-3 May, she bombarded the town and harbour of Rhodes, in the Dodecanese, firing over 300 rounds into the target area without effective opposition. A week later she left Gibraltar for the United Kingdom to take part in the Normandy landings.

On D-Day, 6 June 1944, *Ajax* was in the bombardment force in support of Assault Force G (Gold) in the landings at Asnelles. The whole support force for Gold comprised 4 cruisers, a Dutch gunboat (*Flores*) and 9 fleet destroyers together with four Hunt class destroyers (one being the Polish *Krakowiak*). They sailed from the Clyde at 1100 on 3 June and arrived in the Eastern Task Force area at 0528 on 6th. *Ajax* opened fire two minutes later. The enemy battery at Longues opened fire at 0557 on the Headquarters ship *Bulolo* but no hits were obtained, The *Ajax* fired 179 rounds of 6-inch at this target. Her gunfire proved to be 'extremely effective', and by 0620 the battery had been silenced.

She returned to Portsmouth on 22 June to replace her worn 6-inch guns, she had fired 2,587 shells during the operation. She was then nominated for the landings on the South of France, and she returned to the Mediterranean in mid-July. On 15 August she took part in the landings, Operation Dragoon, supporting the Third Division in the Bormes area providing gunfire support, firing 116 6-inch shells.

Operation Manna was launched on 15 October to introduce into the area around Athens a British force to maintain law and order, to establish the Greek government and to arrange Greek relief. *Ajax*, together with the cruisers *Aurora*, *Black Prince*, *Orion* and *Sirius* were among the ships which took part, anchoring at Piraeus that day. On 18 October the garrison of Santorin, North of Crete, surrendered to her.

During the Greek Civil War, in December 1944, *Ajax* served as Flagship of Rear Admiral J.M. Mansfield, Commanding the 15th Cruiser Squadron. On 21 December she shelled E.L.A.S. positions near Piraeus. On 26 December a conference was held onboard *Ajax*. Mr Churchill and his Foreign Secretary, Mr. Eden flew out on Christmas Day and boarded her. The Greek Prime Minister M. Papandreou and Archbishop Damaskinos also came onboard - but there was a diplomatic hiatus as they had to share the same boat from the shore to the ship. The two were separated onboard, but the Archbishop became caught up in the sailors' Christmas festivities taking place onboard. All was smoothed over, and it was at this conference that Archbishop Demaskinos was appointed Regent of Greece.

On 4 January 1945, a threatening situation developed at Patras, and *Ajax* proceeded there from Piraeus. A military ultimatum to E.L.A.S. forces to surrender or evacuate the town by 11 January ended the trouble, and the E.L.A.S. troops left the previous night. *Ajax* was able to return to Piraeus on 15th.

When the war in Europe ended on 8 May, *Ajax* was at Taranto. A fortnight later, she was needed at Trieste, where she remained until July.

She refitted at Malta at the end of 1945, and in January 1946 she sailed for South America to escort the *Highland Monarch* to the United Kingdom with German internees from her old adversary *Admiral Graf Spee*. Included in her programme was a visit to Rio de Janeiro as Flagship of Admiral of the Fleet Sir James Somerville for the inauguration of the president of Brazil on 31 January.

She remained on the Mediterranean Station to 1948, returning to Chatham on 16 February 1948 to pay off. By then her armament had become four twin 6-inch, four twin 4-inch, two quadruple pom-poms, four twin Oerlikons and five single Oerlikons and two quadruple sets of torpedo tubes. There was a possibility that she would be sold to Chile, but this did not come to fruition. She was then allocated for ship target trials and was laid up at Falmouth. She was broken up by Cashmore, arriving at Newport on 13 November 1949.

In December 1949 her bell was presented to the Government of Uruguay.

She had gained 9 Battle Honours, bringing the total for her name to 17.

HMS ARETHUSA

HMS Arethusa at Malta in the late 1930's, with national identification marks painted on her B turret. *(Portsmouth Royal Naval Museum)*

The *Arethusa* was the name-ship of a class of four light cruisers. She was authorised under the 1931 programme, and was laid down at Chatham Dockyard on 25 January 1933. These ships were smaller than the earlier Leander class of cruisers in order to conform to current International Treaty limitations on tonnage. Welding was used in her construction to save weight. She displaced 5,220 tons on a hull 506 feet by 51 feet. She was armed with three twin 6-inch turrets, four single 4-inch AA guns and two sets of triple torpedo tubes. She was built to carry two aircraft. The second, an Osprey, was to be stowed on the after superstructure with its wings folded. A stump mast was mounted beside the after funnel in order to move this aircraft to the catapult. During trials this arrangement was found to be unacceptable, and was not fitted in the last two ships of the class. A bullet-proof roof over the bridge was also fitted as an experiment, but this was removed in May, 1937.

Differences between the first two ships of the class (*Arethusa* and *Galatea*) and the second pair (*Aurora* and *Penelope*) were that the later ships were completed with four twin 4-inch AA guns, and had an AA gunnery director abaft the mainmast. The searchlight carried in that position by the first pair was mounted forward of the mainmast in the later ships. *Galatea*'s single AA guns were replaced by twin mountings before the war, but the *Arethusa* was not modified until after the war had started.

The Arethusas had four engines with a boiler room/engine room layout differing from the earlier Leander class cruisers giving them better damage protection. The visible sign of this was their two thin, streamlined funnels. Their appearance was similar to the contemporary Amphion class cruisers, though they lacked the fourth twin 6-inch turret. Their engines developed 64,000-shaft horse power which gave them a speed of 32.5 knots. On trials *Arethusa* achieved 32.6 knots. The class was fitted with cruising turbines, with a fluid flywheel arrangement for transferring between main and cruising turbines. They were designed to have the acceleration and manoeuvrability to lead destroyers, and reports in service confirmed that they met this requirement. They were also, like all cruisers,

HMS Arethusa showing her single after turret arrangement, and the single 4-inch AA gun amidships.
(Syd Goodman Collection)

designed to have a good endurance, and had a range of 8,200 miles at 12 knots, and 1,900 miles at their maximum continuous speed of 30.3 knots.

Arethusa was launched at Chatham on 6 March 1935, by Lady Tyrwhitt, the wife of Admiral Sir Reginald Tyrwhitt. The Admiral had been in command of the previous *Arethusa* (also built at Chatham) in August 1914 when leading the destroyers of the Harwich Force in an action in the Heligoland Bight, when the *Arethusa* had been damaged and had had to be towed home. *Arethusa* commissioned for trials on 26 February 1935, and paid off on 27 March. She was completed on 23 May 1935 and was brought to full complement on 12 June 1935. She then became the flagship of the Third Cruiser squadron in the Mediterranean, relieving *Delhi*. Her arrival at Malta on 20 August was inauspicious as she touched bottom and had to be hauled off by tugs. At first she served in the Eastern Mediterranean, but visited the Western Mediterranean in the next year. In February 1937 she suffered from excessive rolling in bad weather off north-wet Sardinia and had to return to Malta for repairs. Three months later she towed the damaged destroyer *Hunter* to Gibraltar. Afterwards she returned to Sheerness for a refit, and re-commissioned on 2 November 1937, again for the Mediterranean Station, and once more became the flagship of the Third Cruiser Squadron.

At the outbreak of war she was at Alexandria, and in November it was decided that she and the *Penelope* should join the Home Fleet after being relieved by the *Caledon* and *Calypso*. The flag was transferred to *Capetown* on 28 December, and *Arethusa* left Gibraltar on 3 January to join the Home Fleet, where the four ships of her class were to form the Second Cruiser Squadron. This was in accordance with the very desirable plan that cruiser squadrons should be formed of ships of the same class. The First Squadron comprised 8-inch gun cruisers, whilst the 18th comprised vessels of the Southampton class. However, the stress of operations in early 1940 was to destroy the concept almost as son as it had been achieved. *Arethusa* was employed providing close cover to convoys to and from Norway.

'On 14 February she, the *Cossack*, and four other destroyers left Rosyth to sweep the Norwegian coast for enemy shipping, and on 16th they were ordered to search for the German oiler *Altmark*. On 17th, she was the first to sight the German ship off Egero Light. Attempts to board her were frustrated by Norwegian vessels that were escorting her, but shortly afterwards the *Cossack* followed her into Jossing Fjord and carried out a successful boarding. The British merchant seamen being held onboard the tanker were rescued.

In April 1940 she took part in the Norwegian campaign. She was at Rosyth when news of the German movements was received, and she was sailed to join the Home Fleet. On 17th, she, with *Galatea*, *Curacoa* and two destroyers, sailed with 1,000 troops of 148 Infantry Brigade for Namsos, but later they were diverted to Andalsnes, where the troops were landed without loss. She left there on 19th. On 22nd she took stores, light AA guns and an advance party of RAF for a forward airfield to Molde. She stayed there for just 4 hours to land them all. On 30th she was involved in the evacuation of Andalsnes. Four cruisers, two transports and six destroyers managed to pick up 2,200 troops safely and left the harbour before dawn. *Arethusa* was slightly damaged in air attacks during these operations.

In May, when the threat to the Low Countries by the Germans became apparent, she was transferred to the South. She operated off the Dutch coast and on 11 May escorted two bullion ships from Ijmuiden to Southend. On 24 May she, with the *Galatea*, sailed from Portsmouth to bombard concealed batteries off Calais in support of the troops ashore, but could not arrive before nightfall, so went on to Sheerness. She returned on 26th when she carried out the bombardment. Seven destroyers operated with the two cruisers, and the destroyer *Wessex* was lost during these operations. On 16 June she entered Le Verdon, where her Captain (Captain Q.D. Graham) was involved in talks with the British Ambassador, the First Lord of the Admiralty and the First Sea Lord, over the future of the French Fleet. On 19 June the British Embassy Staff from Bordeaux were embarked, and the next day *Arethusa* sailed with the President of Poland and his staff, taking a total of 221 people to Plymouth. She was relieved by the *Galatea* at Le Verdon, where later the destroyer *Fraser* was lost in collision with

HMS Arethusa with her aircraft mounted amidships between her funnels. *(Ken Kelly Collection)*

the cruiser *Calcutta* during the evacuation.

On 28 June she left Portsmouth for Gibraltar wearing the flag of Vice Admiral Somerville, and two days later transferred the flag to the *Hood* on the formation of Force H. She took part in the action against the French Fleet at Mers-el-Kebir. Afterwards she was with Force H during the action off Calabria in July. The next month she helped escort the *Ark Royal* whilst she attacked Cagliari, and the *Argus* whilst she was flying off aircraft to Malta. That month she returned to Sheerness to refit.

On completion of her refit she worked up at Scapa Flow. She was in collision with a merchant ship and had to undergo repairs on the Tyne from 31 October to 23 November. She then rejoined the Second Cruiser Squadron of the Home Fleet and was based at Scapa Flow, covering convoys and patrollnng off Iceland. Some accounts report that she was moored in the Thames to use her guns in the defence of London in November 1940, but official records show her movements as Tyne and Scapa Flow only. She covered minelaying operations off the Norwegian coast, and in May 1941, with *Manchester* and *Birmingham*, patrolled the Iceland-Faroes Gap lest the *Bismarck* and *Prinz Eugen* should break out into the Atlantic through that route. In August 1941 she returned to the Mediterranean to assist in convoys to and from Malta. During Operation Substance, she was part of the cruiser force that escorted the merchant ships right through to Malta, whilst also carrying troops and stores for the island. Four days after their return to Gibraltar, *Arethusa*, together with the *Hermione, Manxman* and two destroyers returned to Malta with more troops who had been unable to sail with the earlier convoy when their troopship, the *Leinster*, had run aground leaving Gibraltar. This dash was supported by Force H, and during the outward journey the *Hermione* rammed and sank the Italian submarine *Tembien*.

She was refitted on the Tyne from 24 August to 1 November 1941, and then rejoined the Home Fleet. In December she led the raid on the Lofotens. It had been planned that this would be the larger of two raids, but one of the two transports had to return to Scapa with defects, reducing the scope of the operation. Troops were landed and a fish factory and a wireless station were destroyed. Two coasters were captured and a patrol boat sunk, while *Arethusa* was damaged by near misses. Because the force had no air cover it had to withdraw when German aircraft were reported to be moving north to intercept it. The force returned to Scapa Flow on 1 January 1942 with prisoners.

In May 1942 she sailed to join the Mediterranean Fleet via the Cape of Good Hope. By this time she had been refitted with tripod masts, radar and extra AA guns. In June she took part in Operation Vigorous, taking 11 ships from the east to Malta. The convoy had a close escort of destroyers, corvettes and minesweepers, and also the old battleship *Centurion*, which had been disarmed between the wars and had recently been fitted with anti-aircraft guns. There was no heavy ship available for cover, and *Centurion* was provided as a dummy battleship. The covering escort comprised eight cruisers and thirteen destroyers. MTBs towed by the merchant ships had to return to harbour because of he bad weather. One merchant ship was damaged by air attacks on 12th, and had to divert to Tobruk. Another merchant ship sent to Tobruk because of engine trouble was sunk in further air attacks. The cruiser *Newcastle* was damaged and destroyer *Hasty* sunk during E-boat attacks off Derna. During air attacks on 15th the cruiser *Birmingham* and two destroyers were damaged, one of the destroyers (*Nestor*) having to be sunk the next day. The force was threatened by the Italian Fleet, which comprised two battleships and heavy cruisers, which approached to within 150 miles of the convoy. As the convoy withdrew to Alexandria, the cruiser *Hermione* was sunk by U-205 south of Crete. *Arethusa* suffered splinter damage during this convoy.

On the night 12-13 August, she, with the *Cleopatra*, and four destroyers, bombarded Rhodes as one of the diversionary actions in support of the Pedestal convoy to Malta. In November 1942, *Arethusa* was part of the escort of the Stoneage Convoy to Malta. The convoy comprised four merchant ships with an escort of the 15th Cruiser Squadron and seven destroyers. The convoy (MW-13) sailed from Port Said to Alexandria on 15th, and the next day, at dusk, the *Euryalus* and eight

HMS Arethusa post war at Malta with broad tripod masts. *(Syd Goodman Collection)*

destroyers joined the escort. At 0700 on 17th the fleet destroyers detached to Alexandria to refuel, whilst the Fifth Destroyer Flotilla joined the escort. At 1330 the 15th Cruiser squadron (*Cleopatra, Dido, Orion* and *Arethusa*) sailed with the 12th and 14th Destroyer flotillas from Alexandria. By daylight the next morning they overtook the convoy and joined the escort. Air attacks by six Ju-88s took place at 1110. There was no damage to the convoy and one aircraft was seen to crash. At 1620 twenty-six Ju-52s with two fighters passed ahead of the convoy, and forty minutes later, at sunset, the Cruiser Squadron and fleet destroyers detached to the north to cover the convoy. There was a Force 5 wind from the west-north-west, and the moon was frequently hidden by low cloud and occasional rain. At 1805 they were attacked by three torpedo bombers, and the second aircraft torpedoed the *Arethusa*. The torpedo hit her on the port side abreast B turret with a track angle of red 170 degrees as the ship was turning to starboard. The explosion from the 400-470 pound warhead blew a hole 53 feet long by 35 feet high in her side. The explosion also went up through four decks. Oil fuel was sprayed over the outside of the ship, and also inside up through the bridge structure, and severe fires started immediately. She was flooded from bulkheads 20 to 61, and communications were lost throughout the ship. She quickly trimmed by the head and took a list of 15 degrees to port.

By daylight the next morning the fires had been brought under control after a major effort. It was found that the flooding arrangements to the forward magazines had been damaged by the explosion, but it was judged that the magazines were either flooded or surrounded by sea, so that the risk of an explosion was minimised. The trim and list were reduced, and *Arethusa* headed eastwards towards Alexandria at 12 knots, escorted by the destroyer *Petard*. *Arethusa* was steering using her mechanical wheel, with the quartermaster using a boat's compass. Communication from the after magnetic compass platform was by a chain of men. There were several air attacks during the day, which were driven off. The destroyer *Janus* and corvette *Gloxinia* joined them at sunset. However, the damaged section of the hull was buckling, and speed was reduced to 8 knots. By the next day she had to stop, and the *Petard* took her in tow stern first. *Arethusa* helped with her main engines, but after four hours one started to overheat and the shaft had to be locked. By midnight she was off Alexandria and during the transfer of the tow she became unmanageable and drifted onto the Outer Buoy. She was in danger of drifting onto a lee shore, and had to use her engines and rudder, which were half out of he water. Helped by four tugs, she kept to seaward. Finally, at 1630, the tug *Respond* took her in tow, with the tug *Brigand* controlling her head, and she entered harbour.

She had lost one officers and 155 men, and had one officer (the Captain- who was badly burnt) and 42 men injured. She had had to travel 450 miles to Alexandria, the last 52 of which had taken 11 hours and been made under tow in heavy weather. It had been a long and gallant struggle. She was the last serious casualty of the 15th Cruiser squadron in their long struggle in the Eastern Mediterranean. All four ships of the Stoneage Convoy reached Malta, relieving the island's siege.

She left Alexandria in February 1943 for Charleston, South Carolina, where she underwent a refit until December. During this refit her after funnel was shortened slightly to save topweight, and quadruple AA guns were mounted between her funnels. She then returned to Britain via Norfolk, Virginia, and Bermuda, and was further refitted at Sheerness until April 1944.

During the Normandy landings she was part of the Eastern Task Force, sailing from the Clyde on 2 June, and arriving off the beaches at 0455 on 6th. She was part of Bombarding Force D, which included the battleships *Warspite* and *Ramillies*, the monitor *Roberts*, four other cruisers and thirteen destroyers. They provided gunfire support for Force S landing at Sword Beach. *Arethusa*'s main task was gunfire support to the Sixth Airborne Division, which had dropped to the east of the River Orne to seize bridges over the river and Caen Canal. For a long time there was difficulty in gaining reliable information as to where the troops were. This caused problems in trying to avoid casualties to friendly forces during their support. She used 392 rounds of 6-inch ammunition by 1600 on the first day. She returned to Portsmouth on 14th.

She sailed again for the beach-head at 0830 on 16th, this time wearing the standard of King George VI. Also embarked were the Allied Naval Commander-in-Chief (Admiral Sir Bertram Ramsay), the First Sea Lord (Admiral of the Fleet Sir Andrew Cunningham), the Chief of the Air Staff (Marshal of the Royal Air Force Sir Charles Portal) and the Chief of Combined Operations (Major General Laycock). She was escorted by the destroyers *Scourge* and *Urania*. The visit to Juno Beach lasted from 1240 to1700, during which time His Majesty landed in a DUKW. *Arethusa* returned to Portsmouth that evening. A week later, on 25 June, she was steaming off the beaches when she was attacked by an aircraft which dropped a mine near her. The mine exploded in her wake, and she suffered internal damage.

Repairs took until November, and in January she sailed for Gibraltar to rejoin the 15th Cruiser Squadron. She remained there until November 1945, when she was relieved by the *Liverpool*. She then returned to the United Kingdom, and was placed in reserve at Chatham. In 1948 she was moved to Portland, then to Falmouth and later to Portsmouth whilst being used for ship target trials.

She was broken up at Troon in May 1950. She had gained three Battle Honours for her name: 'Norway 1940-41', 'Malta Convoys 1941-42' and 'Normandy 1944' bringing the total for the name to nine.

HMS AURORA

HMS Aurora as completed. Note the deckhouse amidships in lieu of an aircraft. *(Maritime Photo Library)*

The *Aurora* was the fourth cruiser of the Arethusa class, authorised by the 1934 programme and laid down at Portsmouth Dockyard on 23 July 1935. She was launched by Lady Fisher on 20 August 1936, and completed on 12 November the next year. She was of 5,270 tons and differed from her sisters in having extra deckhouse accommodation for embarked Flag staff in the catapult space. She did not, therefore, carry any aircraft even though she was designed to carry one. She was nevertheless fitted with the mountings for the catapult lest the deckhouse be removed. She was fitted with a crane to handle aircraft, which was also needed to move her boats. She was armed with four twin 4-inch AA guns amidships, and shelters were provided for the guns' crews. She also carried a gunnery director abaft the mainmast

She was also armed with three twin 6-inch gun turrets and two triple sets of torpedo tubes. Her 506 feet long hull housed four sets of engines developing 64,000-shaft horse power giving her a speed of 32.25 knots. She cost £1,252,915.

She was commissioned for trials on 9 August 1937, and completed to full complement and recommissioned on 9 November as the flagship of Commodore (Destroyers) in the Home Fleet. She spent the spring of 1938 operating on patrols from Gibraltar, but returned to home waters in the summer, when she visited Copenhagen and Malmo. The autumn was passed in Scottish waters. In January 1939 she embarked Rear Admiral (Destroyers) of the Home Fleet and again visited the Mediterranean in the spring before returning to Portland in April. In June she was at Rosyth. When war broke out in September she was with the 18th Cruiser Squadron of the Home Fleet at Scapa Flow. Within a few days

HMS Aurora showing the tripod masts fitted to support radar and extra radio equipment. *(MoD/Crown Copyright)*

of the outbreak of war the Fleet, including *Aurora*, was patrolling off the Norwegian coast to intercept enemy shipping. An intended raid on the Skaggerak by the Second Cruiser Squadron (which then comprised *Southampton, Glasgow, Sheffield* and *Aurora*) and destroyers had to be cancelled when the destroyers *Jersey* and *Javelin* collided enroute. The force returned to Scapa Flow on 23rd, but they sailed two days later to cover the return of the damaged submarine *Spearfish* from off Horn Reef. During the return voyage, the force was attacked by aircraft, and on 26 September *Aurora* came under high level air attacks and received slight damage from near misses.

It was during these attacks that the *Ark Royal* was near missed and claimed as being sunk by the Germans for the first time. In October *Aurora* took part in a sweep for the German battlecruiser *Gneisenau* and her cruiser and destroyer escort, which were reported south of Norway, but no contact was achieved. Later that month she covered a convoy of iron ore ships from Narvik to the Firth of Forth. In November, when the *Scharnhorst* and *Gneisenau* sank the armed merchant cruiser *Rawalpindi*, *Aurora* was with destroyers standing watch off Utsire. On 21 November she stood by the *Belfast*, when the latter had been mined and had to be taken in tow.

On 4 February 1940 cruiser squadrons were reorganised into class units, and *Aurora* became the flagship of the Second Squadron. She was one of the ships that provided extra manpower to the destroyers *Maori* and *Cossack* during their search for the German tanker *Altmark*. In early April she became the flagship of Rear Admiral Sir Edward Evans (of *Broke* fame) and set out for Norwegian waters to control operation R4, which involved laying mines and aimed to forestall German attempts to seize Norwegian ports. Troops were assembled in Rosyth ready to be transported to Trondheim, but the German invasion of Norway occurred on 8 April before the troops could be sent. The plan to

take troops was cancelled, and *Aurora* left Rosyth with six destroyers for Scapa to join the naval operations off the Norwegian coast.

During air attacks off the Norwegian coast, the destroyer *Gurkha* was badly hit, and *Aurora* made an attempt to tow her. However, the destroyer was too badly damaged and had to be abandoned after 190 of her ship's company had been rescued. On 12 April *Aurora* was again at Rosyth, embarking Admiral of the Fleet Lord Cork and Orrery, who had been appointed Flag Officer Narvik, and sailing for Skjel Fjord, where she arrived on 14th. On 18th she entered Rombaks Fjord and engaged some pill boxes, a ferry and a railway bridge. A few days later she hit the railway bridge again, as it had been repaired, also hitting an ammunition train which was crossing the bridge at the time. On 24th she took part in more bombardments of the Narvik area, assisting the battleship *Warspite*, cruisers *Effingham* and *Enterprise*, and the destroyer Zulu.

On 3 May, she, with the battleship *Resolution* and the *Effingham*, bombarded Beisfjord. On 7 May, whilst off the Norwegian coast, she was hit by a bomb from a Heinkel 111, which ripped open B turret, putting it out of action and causing some casualties. On 12-13 May she assisted the *Effingham* in taking two battalions (1,500 troops) of the French Foreign Legion to Bjervik, also carrying out gunfire support. She did not return to Portsmouth for repairs until the end of May. Whilst under repair, her AA armament was enhanced by the fitting of quadruple two pounder pom-poms each side amidships.

On 5 July her repairs were complete and she sailed to join the Humber Force, which had been assembled as an anti-invasion measure. She spent the next few months between the Humber and Sheerness. On 9 September she carried out a bombardment of Boulogne Harbour and concentrations of invasion barges. By November the invasion threat had receded, and *Aurora* returned to join the Home Fleet at Scapa Flow. Her Commanding Officer, Captain L.H.K. Hamilton, was relieved by Captain W.G.Agnew. She arrived at Scapa on 18th, and eight days later she was part of the escort for a minelaying operation in the Denmark Strait. Later she covered minelaying operations off Norway. Christmas Day 1940 was spent at Oban.

In January 1941 she covered the break out of five Norwegian motor vessels from Gothenburg. The ships arrived at Kirkwall safely on 25 March. April found her covering further minelaying operations, this time off the Faroes and Iceland.

In April she had a short refit on the Tyne, which included the fitting of radar. In May she was with the Home Fleet in the search and destruction of the German battleship *Bismarck*. She helped to escort the carrier *Victorious* during her strikes against the battleship. Afterwards she carried out searches for enemy supply ships. On 3 June she, together with the cruiser *Kenya*, found the tanker *Belchen* (6,367 tons) between Greenland and Labrador. The tanker was crippled by gunfire at 16,000 yards range, then sunk by a torpedo from *Aurora*. The tanker had been fuelling *U-93* at the time, and the U-boat rescued 49 survivors. *Aurora* then ran into a blizzard and floating ice on her way back to Reykjavik to land 44 survivors she had found in open boats off Newfoundland during her second day out hunting for the *Belchen*. After landing them she returned to her patrol. In thirty-eight days she spent thirty at sea, and covered 10,500 miles.

With Russia's entry into the war, *Aurora* was allocated to Force A, operating in Northern Waters under Rear Admiral Vian, who had as his flagship the cruiser *Nigeria*. At the end of July, the force, which comprised two cruisers and the destroyers *Punjabi* and *Tartar*, reconnoitered Spitzbergen, with a view to using that port as a base instead of Murmansk. Shortly afterwards the force visited Bear Island, where the Norwegian weather station was evacuated and destroyed. The plan to use Spitzbergen as a base was dropped, but it was decided to carry out a raid to destroy coal installations, evacuate personnel and capture any shipping there. In August troops were taken to Spitzbergen to carry out this operation (Operation Gauntlet). The ships involved were the *Nigeria*, *Aurora*, *Icarus*, *Antelope* and *Anthony* and the troopship *Empress Of Canada*. The Russian inhabitants were taken onboard a transport and taken to Russia, whilst the Norwegians were evacuated to Britain. The coal on the jetty, an estimated 500,000 tons, was set ablaze. Mining machinery and conveyors were destroyed.

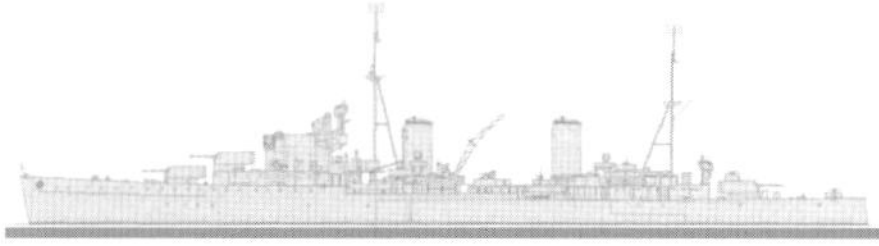

300,000 gallons of petrol and oil fuel were also destroyed, together with two wireless stations. Three colliers, an icebreaker, a tug and two fishing boats were escorted back to the UK.

Whilst the convoy was safely on its way to Scotland, the cruisers in the force made a sortie of the Polar Coast to search for German shipping. On 7 September they met a German convoy off Porshanger Fjord. The *Aurora* and *Nigeria* sank the training ship *Bremse*. Two other escorts of the convoy were damaged, though the two troopships of the convoy escaped. The *Nigeria* was damaged when she rammed a wreck, but the force returned to harbour safely on 10 September.

On 12 October, *Aurora* (still under Captain W.G. Agnew) left Scapa Flow with her sister ship *Penelope* (Captain A.D. Nicholl) and headed south to join the Mediterranean Fleet. They arrived Malta on 21st with two destroyers (*Lance* and *Lively*), whom they had met off Gibraltar. The four ships formed Force K, under Captain Agnew. The force had its first success in the early hours of 9 November when it intercepted an Italian convoy and sank seven merchant ships (39,000 tons) and one destroyer (the *Fulmine*). Two of the other five destroyers of the escort (*Euro* and *Grecale* were damaged. By 1300 that day Force K was back in Malta without damage.

The next day General Rommel reported that transport to North Africa was completely stopped and that only about 8,000 of the 60,000 promised troops had arrived at Benghazi. Five days later the Force intercepted another convoy west of Crete and sank two ships (*Maritza*- 2,910 tons and *Procida* - 1,842 tons) carrying fuel from Greece to Benghazi. Two torpedo boats escorting the convoy escaped. This action deprived the Luftwaffe operating in North Africa of badly needed resources. By now *Aurora* had become known as 'The Silver Phantom', whilst *Penelope* was known as 'The Shadow'.

On the night of 30 November, Force K sank the Italian passenger ship *Adriatica* (1,976 tons), and the next day, off Kerkenah Bank, it came across the

HMS Aurora at speed during the war. *(T. Ferrers-Walker Collection)*

HMS Aurora with additional AA guns mounted on top of B turret. *(MoD/Crown Copyright)*

Italian destroyer *Alvise da Mosta*. The destroyer was rescuing survivors from the tanker *Mantovani*, which had been sunk by air torpedo. The destroyer closed to attack with torpedoes, but was sunk by gunfire. On17 December, Force K was part of the escort covering the passage of the fast auxiliary *Breconshire* from Alexandria to Malta. The convoy came under heavy air attacks but no ships were lost. The operation was hampered by limited shore based air reconnaissance and ran into two Italian battleships with an escort force north-west of Benghazi. The Italian force was covering an Italian convoy. On receiving reports of the British force, the Italians had closed to attack. The British cruisers and destroyers also closed to attack and the Italians opened fire, but withdrew to the north soon afterwards. Neither force of warships was aware of the opposing convoy targets. The *Breconshire* was able to continue her passage to Malta, meeting reinforcements on 18th. This action was called The First Battle of Sirte.

On 19 December, Force K, then supplemented by the cruiser *Neptune* and more destroyers, swept south to the coast off Tripoli to intercept a convoy reported in the area. The Force ran onto a minefield and the *Neptune* and destroyer *Kandahar* were lost, whilst the *Aurora* and *Penelope* were damaged. *Penelope* had her paravanes streamed and a mine blew up clear of the ship's side, and so she escaped with only slight damage. However, a mine exploded close alongside the *Aurora*'s port side abreast A2 oil fuel tank (B turret). She immediately hauled out of line to starboard and reduced speed to 10 knots. She took on a 11 degree list to port, several of her compartments were flooded, and she was slightly down by the head. The list was corrected and she headed back to Malta at 16 knots escorted by the destroyers *Lance* and *Havock*. This disaster marked the end to Force K's operations for a while. By coincidence, a third member of the class, the *Galatea,*

with which Force K had operated less than a week before, had been torpedoed and sunk just five days earlier west of Alexandria.

Repairs at Malta took until March, during which time *Aurora* was further damaged by bombing as she lay in dock. After one raid she was covered with rocks and rubble, her port pom-pom being damaged. She had holes in her hull and the dock flooded. She was floated clear of the dock and loaded with sufficient ammunition for the passage home for further repairs. At the end of March she left Malta with the destroyer *Avon Vale* and, despite an unsuccessful attack by Italian torpedo aircraft south of Sardinia, she reached Gibraltar on 31st. She then steamed on to Liverpool, arriving there on 5 April. Permanent repairs were carried out there, and her AA armament was further supplemented with 20-mm guns. She did not rejoin the Home Fleet until July. At the end of August, after a work up, she escorted a Middle East troop convoy from the Clyde to Freetown, and then returned to Gibraltar in October.

On 28-30 October she was one of the escorts to the carrier *Furious*, which was flying off 29 Spitfires to Malta in Operation Train. She then escorted Convoy KMF-1, bound for Oran, during Operation Torch, the North African landings. Afterwards she covered landings at Oran, supporting the two ex American coast guard cutters *Walney* and *Hartland*, which were to enter the harbour to prevent the French scuttling their ships and destroying the port installations. Both the coast guard cutters were sunk by heavy fire from ashore. Whilst this action was taking place, French destroyers came out of the harbour to attack the transports. *Aurora* helped sink one (the *Tornade*) and then drove another (*Tramontane*) ashore. A third destroyer (*Typhon*) was forced to return to harbour. Admiral Cunningham‘s despatch said that ‘ *Aurora* polished off her opponents with practised ease’. On 11 November she took Commodore Troubridge, on a tour of X and Y beach-heads, and on 26th embarked Admiral Cunningham ,the Naval Commander of the Expeditionary Force, and his staff at Gibraltar and took them to Algiers where their new headquarters was to be established.

She then joined Force H at Algiers and became its flagship. At the end of the month she was allocated to the striking force of the 12th Cruiser Squadron and destroyers, known as Force Q. She was the flagship of Rear Admiral Cecil Harcourt and was paired with the *Argonaut* based at Bone They worked opposite the *Dido* and *Sirius*, and operated against convoys bound for Tunisia. Early on 2 December Force Q intercepted a convoy off Cape Bon and sank four merchant ships and the destroyer *Folgore*. Two other destroyers (*Da Recco* and *Procione*) were damaged in the action. On the return passage from this action the destroyer *Quentin* was sunk in an air attack. When the *Argonaut* was torpedoed in December, she was replaced by *Aurora*'s old partner *Penelope*. On 23 January the Force, with other cruisers and destroyers, bombarded Zuara in Libya. In March 1943, during one of the Force's sorties, the destroyer *Lightning* was lost to E-boat attack.

Aurora remained flagship of Force Q until October 1943, with Commodore Agnew relieving Admiral Harcourt in May 1943. On 7 June she embarked Admiral Sir Andrew Cunningham and General Eisenhower (The Allied Commander-in-Chief) prior to assisting with the bombardment of Pantellaria the next day. The island surrender on 11th. That night *Aurora* and two destroyers bombarded the north coast of Lampedusa, which surrendered on 12th. Also in that month she carried King George VI from Tripoli to Malta, escorted by the destroyers *Lookout, Jervis, Nubian* and *Eskimo*. At Malta the King received a tumultuous welcome from the people of that much-besieged island. After the visit, the King re-embarked in *Aurora* and was taken back to Tripoli.

The next month she was in the covering force for Operation Husky, the landings in Sicily. Afterwards she bombarded Cotrone bridges south of Locri, targets at Castellamare and other targets. In August she bombarded Vibo Valentia, Calabria. She also took part in the landings at Salerno (Operation Avalanche) in September. She was one of the ships involved in Operation Slapstick, when the 12th Cruiser Squadron with the fast minelayer *Abdiel* and the US cruiser *Boise* landed the First British Airborne Division in Taranto. Later she lay off the assault areas at Salerno to provide gunfire support.

In one particular shoot on her third day there, she fired nine rounds of 6-inch, which destroyed seven armoured cars of a column she was engaging.

In October she transferred to the Levant to take part in operations in the Aegean. On 7 October she carried out a sweep of the Aegean with the *Dido, Sirius* and *Penelope* and the 8th Destroyer Flotilla, during which they sank an ammunition ship and five ferry barges. On 21st, she and the Greek destroyer *Miaoulis* bombarded Rhodes. On 30th, she, with three destroyers (*Petard*, *Belvoir* and *Beaufort*) embarked troops and equipment for Leros. The force was bombed four times off Kastelorizo. The second attack took place at about 1600, while the force was 1.5 miles off the coast in Turkish territorial waters, and comprised a formation of thirteen Ju-87s escorted by Me.109s. Beaufighters escorting the ships made contact, but with no effect, and the ships opened fire at a range of seven miles. During dive-bombing, a bomb believed to be 500 Kg. struck *Aurora* between her after funnel and mainmast, and she was near missed by several others. The bomb hit her after conning position and exploded at once, killing nearly everyone on the 4-inch gun-decks and starting a fire, which set off the ready-use ammunition.

Three of her 4-inch gun mountings were put out of action, as was her port quadruple two-pounder pom-pom and three Oerlikons. The fourth 4-inch mounting was damaged but workable. However, there were insufficient survivors to man it. She lost 47 men killed and 30 wounded. The fire was soon brought under control. Speed was restricted to 22 knots to prevent the collapse of the after funnel. *Aurora* was in no condition to defend herself against further attacks, but fortunately the subsequent air attacks were directed against the destroyers. The *Beaufort* escorted her to Alexandria at 19 knots, where they arrived on 31st, whilst the other two destroyers continued with the operation. *Aurora* was later taken to Taranto for repairs, which lasted till April 1944.

HMS Aurora post war with some light AA guns removed. *(Portsmouth Royal Naval Museum)*

During these repairs four of her single Oerlikons were replaced by two twin 20-mm AA guns. She rejoined the Mediterranean Fleet as part of the 15th Cruiser Squadron. On 15 August she took part in Operation Dragoon, the landings in the South of France, providing fire-power support. Five days later she, together with the cruiser *Black Prince* and American and French ships, bombarded Toulon prior to its entry by French troops.

She returned to the Aegean in September, helping to blockade Crete and Milos and carrying out bombardments. On 5 October she, with the destroyer *Catterick*, captured the island of Levitha in the Dodecanese. Ten days later she was part of the force which occupied Athens (Operation Manna) helping to establish the Greek Government there and arranging relief. On 25-26 October she, with the destroyers *Tetcott* and *Tyrian*, bombarded Milos.

On 4 December she, with the destroyers *Marne, Meteor* and *Musketeer*, bombarded shipping targets at Rhodes to prevent German sorties assisting the German held islands. When the Greek civil war broke out in November, she was at Salonika.

She was at Genoa in May 1945 when the war in Europe ended. Five months later it was announced that *Aurora* was to be transferred on loan to the Chinese Navy. She was refitted at Malta from June to October 1945, when her AA armament was again modified, with an extra twin 20-mm gun replacing three single Oerlikons. She then operated from Alexandria in the Eastern Mediterranean until March 1946. She then headed west for Trieste and Malta prior to returning to Portsmouth on 17 April. There she reduced to reserve and was refitted ready for her transfer to Nationalist China in 1948 as the *Chungking*.

In February 1949 she deserted from the Nationalists to the Communists, and was renamed *Tchounking*. She was bombed at Hulutao (Taku Harbour) on 18,19 and 20 March and was sunk. She was salvaged in 1951 and re-commissioned as the *Hsuang Ho*. Later she was renamed the *Pei Ching*. She became a hulk in 1955, and was again renamed the *Kuang Chou*. It is believed that she was broken up in 1960.

She had gained nine battle honours for her name.

Southampton Class Cruisers

This class of cruisers was built prior to the Second World War, and represented a step forwards in the armament race. These ships were not considered as powerful as their contemporary ships being built by the Germans, Americans and Japanese and were much criticised in the Press. Nevertheless, they were armed with four triple six- inch turrets, twice the fire-power of the preceding light Arethusas, and were also fast, at 32 knots. They were built to comply with the then current inter-war treaty limits of 10,000 tons, being of 9,100 tons standard displacement. It was this compliance with the strict treaty rules that gave British naval architects problems in striking the balance between firepower, speed and protection and the need to provide a ship capable of operating both in Home waters and abroad. Nevertheless, the end result was a balanced class of warship, with reasonable firepower, endurance and speed, and suitable for worldwide operations (as the war was to prove).

The first group of this class comprised five ships (*Southampton, Newcastle, Sheffield, Glasgow* and *Birmingham*), and these were followed by a further three of a slightly improved design (*Manchester, Gloucester* and *Liverpool*). Later two further ships of a larger design with extra AA guns (*Belfast* and *Edinburgh*) were built.

The first group displaced 9,100 tons, and were 591.5 feet long with a beam of 61.66 ft. To supplement their main armament of four triple 6-inch turrets, they carried four twin 4-inch guns, two four barreled 2-pounders, and two four barreled machine guns, all against the threat of air attack. This looked a substantial AA armament when fitted, but time was to show that these ships would have to operate in a far more hostile air environment than had ever been envisaged when they were designed. Also carried were two triple torpedo tubes, one on each side amidships. They were also given hangars for two Walrus aircraft, together with an athwartships catapult. These aircraft were to be the ships' long range eyes in those pre-radar days. The hangars, being fitted abreast the forefunnel, caused that funnel to be raised and be taller than the after funnel. Experience with funnel fumes in the first two ships of the class caused the forefunnel to be raised by a further 10 feet. Both funnels and masts were raked, a reversion to World War I style, the earlier light cruisers of the mid-30s having been given upright funnels and vertical masts. The rake was a further effort to reduce problems with funnel fumes around the bridge area. They were fitted with tripod masts to give larger clear arcs for anti-aircraft fire. The end result was ships of a handsome and powerful looking appearance, making them very popular ships with both the public and their crews. They had complements of 700 - rising to 930 in time of wartime. *Glasgow* and *Southampton* were also fitted with ASDIC sets as a trial to determine the policy of such fittings in cruisers. Experience was to dictate that these sets were necessary.

Their four boilers provided steam for four sets of turbines, laid out in two separate machinery units for damage control purposes, developing 75,000-shaft horsepower giving them a speed of 32 knots, with 31.5 knots at deep load. They had an endurance of 12,400 miles at 10 knots; 7,200 miles at 20 knots and 2,800 miles at their maximum continuous speed

Southampton was lost to air attack in the Mediterranean in January 1941. *Gloucester* was sunk by air attack off Crete in May 1941. *Edinburgh* was lost on an Arctic Convoy in May 1942, and *Manchester* was scuttled after being severely damaged during a Malta Convoy in August 1942.

HMS NEWCASTLE

HMS Newcastle, as completed, at speed, showing her fine lines. *(Syd Goodman Collection)*

The cruiser *Newcastle* was the first of the Southampton class cruisers to be laid down. She was built by Vickers Armstrong on the Tyne, being laid down on 4 October 1934, launched on 23 January 1936, and was completed on 5 March 1937. She was originally to have been called *Minotaur*, but the class names were altered from the Mythological to towns, probably in an attempt to gain a more public profile for the Navy. *Glasgow* on her trials reached 32.8 knots.

She initially served in the Home Fleet and she was refitting at Devonport when war broke out. She sailed on 12 September to rejoin the Fleet at Scapa Flow. Later that month she was part of the contingent from the Home Fleet that covered the return of the damaged submarine *Spearfish* from Horns Reef. In October and November she covered convoys in the Western Approaches. On 12 November she intercepted the German ship *Darana* in the Denmark Strait. The German ship scuttled herself to avoid capture.

On 23 November she was patrolling the North Atlantic when the armed merchant cruiser *Rawalpindi* was sunk by the German battlecruiser *Scharnhorst*. She closed the position, and sighted the darkened shapes of the *Scharnhorst* and *Gneisenau*, and tried to shadow them. However, she lost touch with them in poor visibility and rain squalls. At this stage in the war she was not fitted with radar. In January 1940 she sank the derelict German freighter *Bahia Blanca* which had struck an iceberg in the Denmark Strait. She was at sea on 88 days of the first 120 days of the war. She refitted on the Tyne between March and May 1940, returned to Scapa Flow on 3 June. She helped escort troopships and storeships from Harstad on 10 June.

The next month she was despatched to Devonport to cover any possible invasion by German forces. On 11 October she was one of three cruisers and six destroyers providing an escort to the battleship *Revenge*, destroyers and MTBs on a bombardment of Cherbourg. A week later, she, the cruiser *Emerald* and five destroyers chased four enemy destroyers, which had sailed from Brest. Even though she reached 32.5 knots during the chase, with paravanes streamed against mines, she could not close nearer than 12 miles to the enemy destroyers. During this action she sustained damage from the blast of her forward turrets.

On 9 September she sailed south from Plymouth with 200 RAF personnel and important stores for Malta. She was to join Force H at Gibraltar. Eight days later she sailed from Gibraltar, arriving at Malta on 19th. She remained there for seven days, then sailed to join forces covering reinforcements heading from Gibraltar for Malta and Alexandria (Operation Collar). *Newcastle* joined the force sent from Alexandria, which joined up with the main force the next day. As the forces were joining, two groups of Italian ships closed the convoy. The Italian forces, which included two battleships, five heavy cruisers and twelve destroyers withdrew as the British escort closed and engaged them. The cruiser *Berwick* suffered two hits, but an Italian cruiser and destroyer were damaged. The British force sent strikes from the carrier *Ark Royal* but could not slow the retreating Italians and so ceased the chase and returned to cover the safe passage of the convoy.

On 1 December 1940 she transferred to the South Atlantic Station and patrolled the River Plate area, escorting troop convoys. On 25 July in the South Atlantic she intercepted the German *Erlangen*, which scuttled herself. She refitted in Boston from September to December, 1941, when she was fitted with nine Oerlikons in place of her multiple machine-gun. She then crossed the Atlantic for a month at Devonport prior to working up at Scapa Flow. She then joined the Eastern Fleet in February 1942.

On her passage she flew the Flag of rear Admiral W.G. Tennant as Flag Officer Commanding China Force, and escorted a troop convoy. She arrived at Freetown on 1 March, and because of the current threat to Ceylon, she was transferred to the command of the Eastern Fleet. She reached Mombasa

HMS Newcastle post war with new bridgework and lattice foremast. Note the modern AA gunnery directors. *(Steve Bush Collection)*

on 10 May, when Admiral Tennant became Flag Officer 4th Cruiser Squadron, Eastern Fleet.

In June she was among ships lent to the Mediterranean Fleet to support a convoy to Malta (Operation Vigorous). This convoy was to be sailed from the East, whilst another convoy (Operation Harpoon) was to attempt a simultaneous re-supply of the island from the West. She was one of seven cruisers in the escort that sailed from Alexandria on 13 June. The convoy came under attacks by aircraft, submarines and E-boats and was threatened by Italian surface forces, which included battleships. The convoy expended so much time, fuel and ammunition in attacks and diversions that it was forced to return to Alexandria with a loss of a cruiser (*Hermione*), three destroyers and two merchant ships. During this operation the *Newcastle* was torpedoed 90 miles north west of Derna. At 0400 of 15 June, the bow wave of the E-boat was seen at close quarters, and, as *Newcastle* closed to investigate, the E-boat fired two torpedoes at 500 yards range. One torpedo passed ahead and the other hit her under the bow and then exploded. *Newcastle* was making 15 knots and immediately slowed to 6, but was later able to increase to 12 knots and remain with the convoy. Luckily the fuel tanks near the seat of the explosion were filled with fresh water and there was no fire. Her forward turret was put out of action, and her speed reduced, but she had no casualties. After returning to Alexandria, she headed for Mombasa for repairs, but on leaving Aden she ran into severe weather which caused plates to spring in the damaged area. She had to return to Aden, and after emergency repairs, proceeded to Bombay where she underwent temporary repairs before steaming to New York where full repairs were carried out. These took until December. She then returned to Devonport for further work, which completed in March 1943. By this time the number of Oerlikons with which she was fitted had risen to 19.

She worked up at Scapa Flow again, and then rejoined the 4th Cruiser Squadron of the Eastern Fleet, escorting a troop convoy on her way to the East. During 1944 she escorted carriers during their raids on Sabang in April, Sourabaya in May, and the oil installations at Belawan Deli in November and December; as well as carrying out operations against blockade-runners.

In January 1945 she was present at the landings to capture Akyab, and on 26 January she took part in the landings on Cheduba Island.

She left the East Indies Station in April 1945 and reached Devonport on 23 May. She then refitted on the Tyne until November, during which period her X turret was removed. Then she carried out a trooping run to Simonstown, returning to Portsmouth in December before making another trooping trip to Malta, Port Said, Aden and Colombo in January and February 1946.

She underwent a long refit in Devonport 1946-47 and then joined the 1st Cruiser Squadron in the Mediterranean. She paid off in December 1949, and underwent a major refit in Devonport from 1950 to May 1952, when her bridge was modified, a lattice foremast fitted and she was given improved fire control for her secondary armament. She emerged from that refit with three triple 6-inch guns, four twin 4-inch guns, and 18 40-mm guns (six twin and six single), together with her six torpedo tubes. One improvement for her crew's accommodation was the installation of air conditioning.

She worked up in the Mediterranean and relieved the cruiser *Ceylon* in the Far East in July 1952, and started her first patrol off Korea on 23 July, returning fire from shore batteries in the Choda area. Six days later she was relieved by *Belfast*, who came under fire and suffered some casualties. On 29 August she provided gunfire support for guerrilla operations in the Pengyong do area. That winter on patrol was bitterly cold, with blizzards and ice floes. *Birmingham* and *Newcastle* alternated as the Commander of the Task Unit in the Choda area. On 6 January 1953 she and *Birmingham* bombarded targets in the Pengyong do area and on 19 March she visited Inchon with the Flag Officer, Second in Command, Far East Station embarked, who witnessed the bombardment of enemy troop and gun positions in the Pengyong do area on 26th.

On 25 May she accompanied the battleship USS *New Jersey* to the Choda area, where the frigate *Morcombe Bay* and an LSL had been fired upon and the latter hit. *New Jersey* fired 32 rounds of 16-inch at Amgak, whilst *Newcastle*, closer inshore, neutralised two enemy batteries with her 6-inch guns, whilst her 4-inch stood by to engage any aircraft that threatened the battleship's spotting aircraft. The next day she again engaged targets in the Pengyong do area and two days later carried out a concentrated bombardment of a particularly active battery sited in caves ashore. In June the signing of an armistice agreement was imminent, and she finally left the area in July for a refit in Singapore.

In May 1954 she visited Pearl Harbour on her way back to Portsmouth. She re-commissioned at Portsmouth in June 1954 and returned to Singapore in August 1954. In January 1955 she took part in a bombardment of terrorist positions at Kuala Lumpur. Again in May she bombarded terrorist positions in South East Johore. At the end of August she sailed south to visit Australia and New Zealand, and exchanged crews by air in November 1955- the first RN ship to carry out this type of exchange. She visited Korea and Japan as Flagship of the Flag Officer, Second-in-Command, Far East in July 1956. In November of that year she was part of the RN Squadron which visited Australia for the Olympic Games. In January 1957 she was detached to the East Indies Station, visiting Karachi, Bombay and the Persian Gulf. In December 1957 she carried out a further bombardment against terrorist positions in South East Johore. In February 1958 she was at Rangoon for the unveiling of the Commonwealth Land Forces War memorial at Taukkyan, again flying the Flag of the Flag Officer, Second-in-Command, Far East. In June 1958 she left the Station, returning to the United Kingdom via Pearl Harbour Vancouver, San Francisco and the Panama Canal. On 15 July she was at Esquimalt for the first full dress Naval Review of the Royal Canadian Navy by Her Royal Highness Princess Margaret.

She arrived at Portsmouth on 25 August 1958, and a month later approval was given for her to be broken up. She arrived at Faslane on 19 August 1959.

She had gained three Battle Honours for her name, Spartivento 1940, Burma 1944-45 and Korea 1952-53.

HMS GLASGOW

HMS Glasgow showing her triple 6-inch gun turrets and the aircraft hangar amidships.
(Portsmouth Royal Naval Museum)

The *Glasgow* was the fourth ship of the Southampton Class. She was ordered from Scotts' Shipbuilding and Engineering Co Ltd, Greenock on 17 December 1934, and was laid down on 16 April 1935. She was launched on 20 June of the next year by Mrs. Stanley Baldwin, wife of the then Prime Minister, and completed on 9 September 1937, though she had to wait till December to have her HA control system table and director fitted. On trials *Glasgow* achieved 32.8 knots.

Throughout the time she was building the war clouds had loomed larger and larger, but she was commissioned in time of peace, and joined the Second Cruiser Squadron of the Home Fleet. In October 1937 she grounded off Weymouth, and in June 1938 she visited the Clyde in connection with the Empire Exhibition at Glasgow. During the Munich crisis in that September her squadron patrolled off south west Norway. In May the next year she, and her sister ship *Southampton*, escorted the *Empress of Australia* carrying King George VI on his state visit to Canada. The battlecruiser *Repulse*, which was to have carried the King, had been retained in Home Waters as the threat of war grew. *Glasgow* 's escort duties took her to Quebec, New York and Halifax. She sailed from Conception Bay, Newfoundland on 18 June escorting the *Empress of Britain*, with HM the King embarked. The liner went to Southampton, and the *Glasgow* then went on to Portsmouth, where she had a short refit before rejoining her Squadron.

When war was declared the Squadron was at Scapa Flow, and was immediately detailed as part of the Humber Force. The next day *Glasgow* and *Southampton* were with destroyers off Norway when the destroyer *Jersey* intercepted the German merchant ship *Johannes Molken Buhr*, which scuttled itself to avoid capture. Such control duties became her routine, though in late September she, with *Sheffield*, *Southampton*, *Aurora* and destroyers, set out from Rosyth to raid the Skagerrak. However, two of the destroyers collided and so the force had to return to Rosyth. Soon afterwards the

same force sailed from Rosyth to escort the damaged submarine *Spearfish* from Horns Reef to Rosyth. They came under air attack on 26 September, but arrived safely at Rosyth later that day.

In October she escorted the battlecruisers *Hood* and *Repulse* in a search off the south coast of Norway for the *Gneisenau, Koln* and 9 destroyers. A few days later she and the *Newcastle* met a valuable convoy of 19 oil tankers from the West Indies and escorted it to Lands End. In November she left Rosyth with two destroyers to intercept the liner *Bremen*, believed to be on passage from Murmansk to Germany, but the *Bremen* eluded them, and with the loss of the *Rawalpindi* the force headed north to search for the *Scharnhorst* and *Gneisenau*. For the next few months she was engaged in escorting convoys, and in February 1940 she relieved the *Southampton* on Norwegian coast patrol, capturing the German trawler *Herrlichkeit* off Tromso on 12th.

She underwent a short refit at Belfast, docking and fitting degaussing equipment, and returned to the Fleet at the end of March. She was one of a force of cruisers and destroyers which embarked troops at Rosyth ready to be landed in Norway. However, the Germans invaded that country first, and so the troops were disembarked and *Glasgow* sailed to join the Home Fleet. She was with a force detached to cruise off Bergen, when part of the Home Fleet came into action on 9 April with the *Scharnhorst* and *Gneisenau* off Bergen. The German ships escaped in the mist and snow. The detached force came under air attack whilst returning to join the main body of the Fleet. *Glasgow* received minor damage from near misses, 'A' turret being damaged and her speed reduced, and she had one man killed and four injured. The destroyer *Gurkha* was sunk during these attacks.

She carried out repairs at sea. On 14th she landed a force of seamen and marines at Namsos (Operation Harry) - this was the first allied landing on Norwegian soil, and on 23rd she was part of the force that landed troops at Molde and Aandalsnes (Sickle Force). At the end of the month took part in the successful evacuation of Aandalsnes. On the first night - 29/30th she went alongside the quay with fire hoses playing in a scene lit by the fires in the town, embarked King Olav, the Crown Prince and members of the Norwegian Government together with gold reserves and took them to Tromso.

The next month she and the cruiser *Berwick* landed a Royal Marine Battalion at Reykjavik, a move to offset the loss of bases in Norway (Operation Fork). After a search of the eastern fjords of Iceland, *Glasgow* returned to the UK with German consular staff, which included three women, and 20 prisoners. She then called at Liverpool to carry out repairs, including the renewal of her ASDIC unit. Whilst there, on the day war was declared on Italy, a party from the *Glasgow* captured the Italian ship *Gabiamo* which was also lying in Liverpool.

In July, having been fitted with air warning radar and two AA rocket launchers, she rejoined the Fleet, and sailed in a group of cruisers and destroyers to intercept German ships believed to be making a sortie into the North Sea. The German ships returned to harbour, and the British force made for the Pentland Firth, where they encountered thick fog. Eight miles south east of Duncansby Head, at 2355 on 17th, *Glasgow* collided with the destroyer *Imogen*, and both ships caught fire. The destroyer exploded and sank a few minutes later. *Glasgow* was able to rescue about 120 of the destroyer's crew. *Glasgow* was left with a six-foot gash on her side extending for 60 feet, luckily all above the waterline, and she returned to Liverpool for repairs. These took till October 1940, when she called at Rosyth for fitting with Type 286 radar and for modifications to her paravane equipment. She then sailed with the battleship *Barham*, cruiser *Berwick* and four destroyers together with carrier *Ark Royal*, for the Mediterranean. They arrived at Gibraltar on 6 November. The force then sailed for Alexandria, and during the passage covered the raid on Taranto. *Glasgow* reached Alexandria on 14th, and later the same day sailed with the cruisers *Berwick*, *York* and *HMAS Sydney* carrying troops for Piraeus.

She then covered convoys to Gibraltar and Malta, and on 3 December was attacked by two Italian S79 torpedo bombers whilst lying at anchor in Suda Bay, Crete. She was hit by two torpedoes, one of which blew a hole 22 feet square on her starboard

HMS Glasgow astern of a sistership showing her cruiser stern. *(Ken Kelly Collection)*

side forward with an explosion that caused a column of smoke and flame 60 feet high. The other torpedo made a hole 22 x 16 feet on the starboard side aft 90 seconds later. She suffered structural damage, fires and flooding and her two inner propeller shafts were bent and the propellers damaged. The ship suffered whip damage and white smoke spread towards the midships section. 'X','Y' and the 4 inch magazines were sprayed. Nevertheless, because of the danger of further attacks in the area, two hours later she got under way, and sailed for Alexandria, steering by main engines. By 0300 the next morning her steering gear had been repaired, but the weather deteriorated, reaching Force 5 on the first night. During the passage the damaged shafts had to be trailed, and one broke and was lost on the second night. At Alexandria some repairs were carried out. However, the damage to her two inner propeller shafts could not be rectified, and she was then limited to 24 knots. As a result she was transferred to the East Indies Station, passing through Suez on 15 February 1941.

In the East Indies she was used for troop convoy escort duties. The German pocket battleship *Admiral Scheer* was operating in the Indian Ocean at that time, and *Glasgow* took part in a search for her. Her aircraft sighted the German ship on 22 February, but had to return for fuel and so lost contact. *Glasgow* was 140 miles away and was unable to regain contact. In March 1941 she was the Senior Officer's ship for the landings in British Somaliland (Operation Appearance). *Glasgow* carried out a bombardment and the Italian resistance ashore soon crumbled. The rest of the year was spent patrolling the Indian Ocean, searching for raiders and escorting convoys. She visited Singapore and Trincomalee. On the night of 9 December she encountered what she thought was a Japanese submarine of the surface and opened fire, only to sink the RIN patrol vessel *Prabhavati* which had two lighters in tow alongside her. She rescued survivors and landed them at Bombay.

In May 1942 she sailed for New York for a refit which lasted until August. During this period she

HMS Glasgow - note the aircraft homing beacon abaft the after funnel. *(Portsmouth Royal Naval Museum)*

HMS Glasgow post war with X turret removed. She was never as fully modernised as her sisters. *(Syd Goodman Collection)*

had her quadruple machine guns removed and nine 20 mm added. She was also given a comprehensive radar outfit. She then returned to Portsmouth, joining the 10th Cruiser Squadron of the Home Fleet after a work up at Scapa Flow. In January 1943 she covered convoy JW 52 to Russia and convoy RA 52 back to the United Kingdom, returning 8 February. In March she was on patrol in the Denmark Strait when she intercepted the German blockade runner *Regensburg* (8068 tons), which was returning to Germany from Rangoon. The German scuttled herself and *Glasgow* rescued one officer and five men.

In May 1943 *Glasgow* joined the Plymouth Command. And carried out patrols of the Bay of Biscay. In October 1943 she carried the ashes of Admiral of the Fleet Sir Dudley Pound to sea for burial. In that month she was refitted at Devonport, her aircraft and catapult being removed, and her AA armament and radar fit was enhanced and three barrage director control towers were fitted. In December she, and the cruiser *Enterprise*, were despatched to intercept the blockade runner *Alsterufer* due from Japan. The blockade runner was sighted by aircraft and although the two cruisers were directed towards her position, she was sunk before they arrived. The two cruisers then turned their attentions on the waiting German escort of five destroyers and six torpedo boats. The Germans have a superiority of firepower (25 x 15-cm and 24 x 10.5-cm guns against the British 19 x 6-inch and 13 x 4-inch). The two forces came into action at 1313 on 28th, and after a failed pincer attack, the German vessels fled back towards the safety of air cover. During the action, in which *Glasgow* was damaged by splinters, three German vessels (*Z27, T25* and *T26*) were sunk. *Glasgow* and *Enterprise* left off the chase once the German air activity became too intense. They came under attack from conventional bombers and glider bombs. After rescuing 64 German survivors (a further 168 were rescued by an Irish steamer, 6 by Spanish destroyers and 55 by U-boats), they returned to Plymouth on 29th.

Glasgow remained with the Plymouth command until D-Day. During the Normandy landings she provided fire-power support, being part of Bombarding Force C with the US battleship *Texas*, shelling targets inshore of Omaha beach. She then joined Bombarding Group 1 for the assault on Cherbourg. At 1342 on 25 June she was hit by two

heavy shells, the first hitting the hangar and the second the main deck abreast her after HA/DCT. Fires started, and a third shell near missed her aft, causing splinter damage. Her fires were brought under control though she was left with a 10 feet square hole in her hangar, splinter damage to her funnels and her after high angle director was damaged. That evening the Task Force Commander and captains of the Group One ships "spliced the mainbrace" in *Glasgow*. She went to the Tyne for repairs, going west via Devonport and Belfast, arriving on 3 July. Repairs took until 29 June 1945.

The opportunity was taken during this refit to modernise her, and she was fitted with an aircraft homing beacon for use in the Far East, where it had been found necessary to monitor flights of aircraft returning to the carriers for any Japanese that infiltrated the Allied groups of aircraft. Ships carrying out this "delousing" were prime targets for enemy action, and so her next deployment was expected by many probably to be her last. She also had her X turret removed, her armament then comprising 9 x 6 inch, 8 x 4 inch, 28 x 2-pdr (6 quadruple and 4 single), 19 x 20-mm (6 twin and 7 single) and 6 torpedo tubes. Her barrage DCTs were removed and her radar outfit upgraded. On 22 August she sailed for the East Indies with *Jamaica* to relieve the *Phoebe* and *Ceylon*, arriving at Colombo on 5 October, after VJ Day, and so avoided an unpleasant fate.

She spent two years in the Far East, returning to Portsmouth in August 1947, going into reserve prior to a refit in May 1948. In October 1948 she sailed for the America and West Indies Station to relieve the *Sheffield* and in August 1949 attended the bicentenary celebrations at Halifax Nova Scotia. She returned to Portsmouth in October 1950. She was refitted at Chatham in 1951, her close range armament being reduced to 24 x 2-pounders (6 quadruple mountings), and 8 single 40-mm guns, and then joined the Mediterranean Fleet. In June 1952 she was visited by Marshal Tito during a visit to Yugoslavia, and in March 1953, at Phaleron, she hoisted the flag of King Paul of Greece, who had just been appointed an Honorary Admiral in the Royal Navy.

In June 1953 she flew the flag of Admiral Lord Mountbatten, Commander-in-Chef Mediterranean, at the Coronation Review of the Fleet at Spithead. In 1954 she escorted the Royal Yacht *Britannia* from Malta to the UK as HM The Queen and HRH The Duke of Edinburgh returned from their Commonwealth Tour.

In April 1955 she rejoined the Home Fleet and relieved the *Bermuda* as Flagship of Flag Officer Flotillas Home Fleet, taking part in Exercise Long Swell in the Atlantic. In the summer she took part in the Home Fleet cruise, visiting Gdynia in July. She was visited by the Prime Minister, Sir Anthony Eden at Invergordon in September, and the next month visited Kiel. She paid off in November 1956 and was put in extended reserve at Portsmouth. On 4 July 1958 she was handed over to the British Iron and Steel Corporation to be broken up at Blyth. She had gained four Battle Honours for her name, Norway 1940, Arctic 1943, Biscay 1943 and Normandy 1944. A further Honour was to be gained by the next ship of the name, a destroyer, during the Falklands War of 1982, bringing the total for the name to ten.

HMS LIVERPOOL

HMS Liverpool in camouflage with extra AA guns mounted on B and X turrets. *(T. Ferrers-Walker Collection)*

Liverpool was the in the third group of the Southampton class cruisers. She was built by Fairfield Shipbuilding and Engineering Co. Ltd., Govan. She had been ordered on 11 November 1935. This group of the class were slightly heavier than earlier groups, having a 6-inch greater beam and slightly thicker armour over their mazazines. They also had a rounded bridge, which made them readily identifiable from their half sisters. Their 4-inch guns had shelters for the crews, and they carried a director control tower aft as well as one forward. This led to their after AA director being mounted higher still. Their power output was raised from 75,000 to 82,500 shaft horsepower to enable them to maintain the same speed. In fact they were rated slightly faster, at 32.3 knots. On trials *Liverpool* developed 83,386 shaft horsepower on her four shafts, and reached 33 knots. She could steam for 12,000 miles at 12 knots, and 2,600 miles at her continuous full speed of 31.5 knots. She displaced 9,400 tons and was 591.5 feet long, with a beam of 62.33 feet.

She was laid down on 17 February 1936 (her predecessor, a light cruiser, had been laid down on 17 February 1909) and was launched by Mrs. Montagu C. Norman (wife of the Governor of the Bank of England) on 24 March 1937. Mrs. Norman was presented with a rope of fine jade beads in a silver casket as a momento of the ceremony. *Liverpool* was completed on 25 October and handed over on 2 November 1938. She commissioned under Captain A.D.Read with a complement of 765 officers and men on 8 November. A handsome ship, she had a secondary armament of four twin 4-inch HA/LA guns backed by two quadruple two-pounders and two quadruple machine-guns. She was also equipped with two triple torpedo tubes and two Walrus aircraft (although designed to carry three). Her armament was completed by a depth charge rail and six depth charges.

Two months after completion she paid a visit to her name city prior to sailing to the East Indies Station to join the Fourth Cruiser Squadron. At Liverpool she berthed at Gladstone Dock and was

presented with three pairs of silver candlesticks, a silver cup and two bugles, all suitably inscribed by the Corporation. She also received the silver bell and silver plate presented to her predecessor in 1912. She was also presented with a silk White Ensign and Union Flag by the Liverpool Women's Service Bureau.

She called at Malta and remained there for several months undergoing repairs before transitting the Suez Canal. She arrived at Colombo on 14 May 1939, relieving the *Emerald* and in time to join the East Indies Station summer cruise. Hence the outbreak of war found her in the Indian Ocean, where she was employed on trade protection duties. Her complement was increased from 765 to 945. In mid November 1939, she transferred to the China Station to join the Fifth Cruiser Squadron. She carried the flag of the Commander-in-Chief (Admiral Sir Percy Noble) and visited Hong Kong. Later she carried out several patrols off Japan. During one of these patrols, on 21 December, she intercepted the Japanese liner *Asama Maru*, 35 miles off the Japanese coast. She took off her twenty-one German officers and men who were survivors from the German liner SS *Columbus* (32,581 tons) which had been intercepted by the destroyer *Hyperion* off the Florida coast on 19 December, and which had been scuttled. The crew had been on passage to Germany.

The *Liverpool* docked at Hong Kong prior to sailing for Aden in April 1940, where she became the flagship of the Red Sea Force under Rear Admiral A.J.L. Murray. On 20 May 1940, shortly after escorting the Second Australian Troop convoy (US-2) up the Red Sea, she was transferred to the Mediterranean Station, joining the 7th Cruiser Squadron. She was soon in action, being employed on offensive sweeps against Italian shipping and escorting convoys between Egypt, Malta and Greece. On the night 11-12 June, she, and her sister *Gloucester*, with four destroyers, was shelling Tobruk, when the force met four auxiliary Italian minesweepers. One of the minesweepers (*Giovanni Berta*) was sunk, and, although the floating battery *San Giorgio* engaged the cruisers, neither was hit. They also cut some mines with their paravanes.

Sixteen days later the two cruisers, with the cruisers *Neptune*, ORION and Australian SYDNEY, took part in a long-range action with three Italian destroyers sixty miles west of Cape Matapan. The destroyers were carrying supplies from Taranto to Tobruk. One destroyer, the *Espero*, was sunk, whilst the other two (*Ostro* and *Zeffiro*) escaped to Benghazi. *Liverpool* was struck by a 4.7-inch shell, which fortunately hit her armour plate, causing little damage. However, her degaussing cable was broken. This and other recent actions highlighted the shortage of ammunition in the Fleet, there being only eight hundred 6-inch shells still available.

Eleven days afterwards, *Liverpool* was with the Mediterranean Fleet during the action off Calabria, when two Italian battleships supported by ten cruisers and thirty-two destroyers were kept clear of two convoys running between Malta and Alexandria. This was the first capital ship action with the Italian Fleet and during it Admiral Cunningham's force damaged one battleship at long range.

On 29 July *Liverpool* was hit by a 250 pound bomb whilst escorting an Aegean convoy. The delayed action bomb struck the bridge front and went through B gun deck and forecastle and then stopped without exploding. There was minor damage and one man was killed.

In August and September she took part in Operation Hats, a convoy to Malta which also passed reinforcements to the Fleet from Gibraltar. In September she and the *Gloucester* carried troops to Malta.

In October she was in the Fleet covering a convoy of four steamers from Alexandria to Malta, and later she covered a Fleet Air Arm attack on Leros, carried out by Swordfish bombers from the carriers *Eagle* and *Illustrious*. Whilst returning with the Fleet to Alexandria from this operation, she was attacked by aircraft south-east of Crete. The aircraft was heard first and five minutes later was sighted. *Liverpool* increased speed from 17 to 25 knots as the aircraft approached from the starboard bow. She then altered course towards the aircraft and increased speed again, and a torpedo was seen to pass clear astern. However, 10-15 seconds later a second torpedo, which had not been seen, hit her starboard bow and exploded.

Immediately the ship was stopped and, although the decks were found not to be damaged, there were

HMS Liverpool looking forward at the damage to her bows caused by a torpedo hit received whilst escorting a convoy to Malta in October 1940. *(Syd Goodman Collection)*

heavy fumes of aviation fuel forward from a ruptured tank. The forward magazines were flooded as a precaution. The fumes leaked out in the forward areas, where they were exploded by a spark from damaged cabling about 25 minutes after the initial torpedo hit. This violent explosion caused the whole fore end forward of A turret to rise bodily, the ship's sides bent out and a tremendous flame shot over the whole fore part and rose 100 feet in the air. There was much damage to the bows and the roof of A turret was blown off and overboard. After the explosion the fierce flame continued and fire could be seen on the waters to starboard. *Liverpool* went astern to reduce the pressure on the bulkheads forward and to assist the fire parties in their work, but controlling her steering was found to be difficult because of the plating projecting from the damage forward. The fire was fought all night and the bulkheads cooled by hoses. The cruiser *Orion* took her in tow, stern first, and headed for Alexandria, with the *Liverpool* using her maximum astern power to assist.

Initially *Liverpool* was hard to steer, but during the forenoon on 15th the tow parted and whilst manoeuvres were taking place to clear the tow, the damaged section of her bows fell off, which made her easier to handle. She reached Alexandria at noon on 16th, two days after being hit.

After temporary repairs, which lasted to May 1941, *Liverpool* sailed from Alexandria without her hangar pom-poms, and multiple machine-gins, which had been landed to other ships of the Fleet. She sailed via Singapore and Manilla for the Mare Island Navy Yard, San Francisco, where she underwent more repairs until mid November. She then returned to the Clyde via the West Coast, Panama and Bermuda for final repair work, arriving on 5 December, The work, which included the refitting of her pom-poms and the fitting of radar, was completed by 27 January 1942.

She then carried a light AA armament of eight two-pounders (two quadruple), eighteen 20-mm Oerlikons (seven twin and four single) and her aircraft had been landed. She then completed a work up prior to joining the 18th Cruiser Squadron of the Home Fleet. She was then employed escorting Russian Convoys. Her first was QP-10, which sailed on 10 April. *Liverpool* led the close escort of five destroyers, a minesweeper and two A/S trawlers. She stayed close to the convoy in daylight to provide extra AA protection, but stood clear in the few hours of twilight when aircraft could not attack. Two merchant ships were lost to air attacks and two to submarines, while one had to return to Murmansk. Eleven reached Reykjavik safely. In May she was part of the cruiser force sent to escort the damaged cruiser *Trinidad* back from Russia, but the *Trinidad* was sunk before she could reach their protection.

Her next convoy, Convoy PQ-16, was very eventful. *Liverpool* operated under Rear Admiral H.M.Burrough with the *Nigeria*, *Norfolk* and *Kent* and three destroyers. The cruisers were close cover for the convoy against the possibility of German pocket battleships attacking. On 25 June, four days after PQ-16 had sailed, the cruiser force joined the close escort, the cruisers being placed in pairs between the convoy columns, and the destroyers joining the screen. The first German shadowing aircraft arrived soon afterwards and the convoy was then closely monitored by aircraft for the next five days.

On the afternoon of 25th, PQ-16 passed the westbound convoy, and soon afterwards the first air attacks developed. The aircraft were torpedo bombers (He.111s) alternating with dive-bombers (Ju-88s), but the first convoy loss was to a U-boat the next morning. The fire-power of the escorts drove off the air attackers, but on 26th the cruiser force had to withdraw, and on 27th heavy air attacks took place. 108 aircraft attacked that day. Four merchant ships were sunk and two other, and the Polish destroyer Garland, were damaged. Two more ships were lost that evening and another damaged. One damaged ship sank the next day, but, despite further attacks, the convoy fought through to Russia.

On 4 June 1942, she sailed southwards from the UK escorting four ships for Gibraltar, and joined Force H, which was not up to strength as some ships had not yet returned from the assault on Madagascar. These moves were part of the plan to provide an escort for a convoy of six merchant ships sailing from the west to re-supply Malta (Operation Harpoon). At the same time eleven merchant ships were to sail to Malta from the west (Operation Vigorous). The Harpoon convoy had a heavy main escort covering force of the battleship *Malaya*, carriers *Eagle* and *Argus*, and the cruisers *Kenya* (wearing the flag of Vice Admiral A.T.B. Curteis), *Charybdis* and *Liverpool* together with eight destroyers. This escort was to take the convoy to the Narrows between Sicily and Tunisia. A close escort, comprising the cruiser *Cairo*, nine more destroyers and four fleet minesweepers, was to take the convoy through to Malta. Six minesweeping motor launches were also included in the convoy to clear the passage at the approaches to Malta.

By 12 June the convoy was well into the Mediterranean, and the smaller escorts fuelled from the *Liverpool* and the oiler *Brown Ranger*. Air attacks began at 1030 on 14th. It was a fine, sunny, clear day, with what little wind there was blowing from astern, making the carriers' task of flying off aircraft difficult. The first attacks were by dive-bombers, but later torpedo bombers and high level bombers appeared. At about 1120 on 14th *Liverpool* was leading the starboard column of the convoy. The convoy had been under attack for about half an hour when about thirty Italian Savoia S79K torpedo bombers, which were escorted by twenty fighters, closed to attack. They approached in two waves, the first of which went round the stern of the convoy and came in from the starboard (southern) side. The other closed from the port side. The *Liverpool* was singled out for attention by the first group in their attack, during which a merchant ship, the Dutch Tanimbar, was sunk.

Liverpool turned to starboard and increased speed to avoid the group attacking from the port side, but was then attacked by the starboard group. Two torpedoes passed ahead, and one astern, but a fourth, running well at shallow depth, hit her on the starboard side abreast the after engine room. She was immediately put out of control, the starboard telegraphs were jammed and the port engines were put to stop. She reduced speed to three knots in three minutes. She was left with a large hole (twenty four by nineteen feet) in her outer bottom, and her lower deck was lifted three feet. The after machinery spaces flooded and she took a seven degree list. Counter-flooding of A and B magazines and shell rooms corrected the list, but she had three shafts out of action and her steering gear was jammed. Only her port forward shaft was in working order. She continued to turn to starboard until her port engine was put astern. Soon afterwards emergency leads were run to her steering motors so that she could steam slowly at three knots on her one remaining shaft. X and Y turrets had lost power, so could not train. Unnecessary top-weight was jettisoned, which included the Walrus aircraft on the catapult, boats, starboard torpedoes, depth charges and spare ropes and derricks.

The destroyer *Antelope* took her in tow at 1300, but the tow parted at 1630 and shortly afterwards the pair came under further air attack. Two 100 Kg. delayed action bombs exploded within fifteen feet of *Liverpool*'s starboard side, starting more flooding. She took on a list of 9.5 degrees and settled by the stern.

Liverpool's main armament was out of action. Her 4-inch magazines were suffering from leading oil fuel, and her list reduced her rate of ammunition supply. Two Oerlikon guns had been put out of action by cannon shell-fire from attacking aircraft. *Antelope* recovered the tow and, despite continuous air attacks, during which *Liverpool* was credited with shooting down five aircraft, they reached Gibraltar on 17 June. There temporary repairs were carried out. *Liverpool* had lost 12 men in the after engine room. One member of a damage control party was killed, and two other men were killed by aircraft cannon fire, making a total of 15 dead.

Two of the six ships of the convoy reached Malta for the loss of two destroyers (*Bedouin* and *Kujawiak*), with *Liverpool*, three destroyers and a minesweeper being badly damaged.

The next month *Liverpool* sailed to Rosyth for more permanent repairs. Repairs were completed on 22 July 1945, but this period included a spell in care and maintenance from May 1944. Some modifica-

HMS Liverpool showing the flag bridge that distinguished this later group of the class. In this post war photograph it can be seen that X turret was replaced by extra AA guns. *(Syd Goodman Collection)*

tion work was also carried out. X turret was replaced by quadruple two-pounder AA guns, gaining top-weight to permit the fitting of more AA guns, radar and associated equipment. She carried out trials, and in July embarked the Tripartite Commission on their journey to inspect German warships of all classes. She did not complete to full complement until October 1945, when she sailed for the Mediterranean to relieve *Arethusa* in the 15th Cruiser Squadron. By then she was armed with nine 6-inch guns, eight 4-inch guns, twenty-eight two-pounders (six quadruple and four single), nineteen 20-mm AA guns (six twin and seven single) and six torpedo tubes. By 1949 she carried twenty-six two-pounders (six quadruple and two single), six single 40-mm and four 20-mm (two twin) AA guns. Her aircraft and equipment had been landed.

In January 1946 she was the flagship of Admiral Sir John H.D.Cunningham (Commander-in-Chief Mediterranean) for visits to Naples, Algiers, Tangier and Casablanca. In October 1946, in a gale, she escorted the stern first tow of the destroyer *Saumarez* to Malta. The destroyer had been badly damaged by a mine. In 1947 she was again flagship of the Commander-in-Chief (then Admiral Sir Algernon Hugh Willis GCB, KCB, DSO) on the first post war summer cruise of the Fleet, which comprised twenty-four ships. Visits by the Fleet included Turkey, Russia and Greece.

After this she returned to Chatham to pay off and re-commission for the Mediterranean Fleet. Her AA armament for her last commission was twenty-six two pounders and eight 40-mm guns. On October 1951 she was in Egypt whilst there was strike trouble in the Suez Canal, and on 24th of that month she took the Grenadier Guards from Tripoli to Tobruk. She returned to Malta in February 1952, and returned to the UK two months later. She paid off at Portsmouth and was placed in reserve. She was used as an accommodation ship from December 1953 and was relieved as Senior Officer's ship in the Reserve Fleet in November 1956 by the battleship *Vanguard*. She was approved for scrapping in March 1958, and on 27 June 1958 she was handed over to the British Iron and Steel Corporation. She was towed from Portsmouth and arrived at Bo'ness on 2 July 1958. She was broken up there over the next eighteen months. Her dolphin shaped bracket supporting the quarterdeck bell and her name-plate were secured for the Liverpool Museums.

She had gained four battle honours for her name: 'Mediterranean 1940', Calabria 1940', Arctic 1942' and Malta Convoys 1942'. Both her sister ships (*Gloucester* and *Manchester*) had been lost in the Mediterranean, where she herself had been so hard hit.

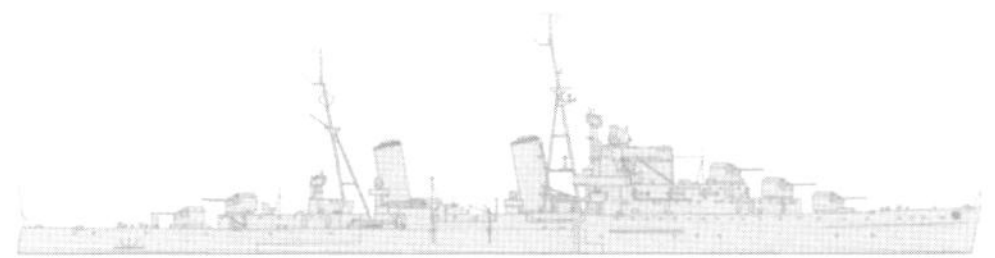

Dido Class Cruisers

The Dido class cruisers were introduced just prior to the outbreak of World War II as a compromise between providing an anti-aircraft vessel but retaining a sufficiently heavy gun armament for use in surface engagements. Eleven of the class were ordered. The supply of the 5.25-inch main armament became a problem, and some ships were completed without their full outfit of five twin turrets, and two vessels (*Scylla* and *Charybdis*) were completed with four twin 4.5-inch guns in lieu of the 5.25-inch. A further five (*Bellona, Black Prince, Spartan, Diadem* and *Royalist*) were ordered to a modified four turret design.

These ships were virtually on the same size hull as the earlier Arethusa Class of light cruisers, with a designed standard displacement of 5,450 tons, a length of 512 feet and a beam of 50.5 feet. They were designed to carry five twin 5.25-inch guns as their main armament, with two quadruple 2-pounders, two multiple machine guns and two triple torpedo tubes. They had four boilers developing 62,000 shaft horsepower, driving four sets of turbines and four propellers. They had a designed speed of 32.25 knots, and an endurance of 3,800 miles at 20 knots. They also had cruising turbines to give them extra endurance, which, at 16 knots, was 4,600 miles, 500 miles further than if they used their HP (high pressure) turbines. They also carried two sets of triple torpedo tubes.

Bonaventure was sunk by torpedo South of Crete in March 1941, and *Naiad* was lost by torpedo attack, also South of Crete, in March 1942. *Hermione* was sunk off Tobruk in June 1942. *Charybdis* was lost in the Channel in October 1943. *Spartan* was lost off Anzio in January 1944. Others suffered damage from torpedo and air attacks and their Battle Honour record shows how busy these handy ships were kept during the war.

HMS DIDO

HMS Dido - an early photograph of her with a single 4-inch gun in Q position. *(Syd Goodman Collection)*

The *Dido*, name-ship of the class, was ordered in the 1936 programme, being laid down at Cammell Laird's at Birkenhead on 20 October 1937. She was launched on 18 July1939 and was completed on 30 September 1940. The war had already started and, because of supply difficulty, she was completed with just four twin 5.25-inch gun turrets. A single 4-inch gun was mounted in Q positon, just forward of the bridge. *Dido* was adopted by the City of Bolton, which raised a million pounds for her in five days. She joined the Home Fleet in October 1940. A month later, she, with her sisters *Naiad* and *Phoebe*, blockaded the approaches to the Bay of Biscay after the *Jervis Bay* had been sunk by the German battleship *Admiral Scheer*. One of *Dido*'s first operations was to escort a troop convoy to Gibraltar and then go on to Takoradi escorting the carrier *Furious*. She returned to Scapa Flow on 14 December.

In April 1941, she, with the fast minelayer *Abdiel* and five destroyers, took reinforcements to Malta.
On completion, she, the *Abdiel* and three of the destroyers sailed on to Alexandria to join the Mediterranean Fleet. A few days later she was part of the cover force for two convoys, one of which was slow and comprised two tankers, the other being a fast convoy of four freighters to Malta from Alexandria. Just afterwards she became involved in the evacuation of Greece. On the night of 21 May, she, with the cruisers *Ajax* and *Orion* and four destroyers, was 18 miles north of Canea in Crete. The force intercepted a small fleet of 20 small craft ferrying troops to Crete, escorted by Italian torpedo boats. In a two and a half-hour action ten of the small craft and one escort were sunk. The British ships then withdrew, being short of anti-aircraft ammunition. Seven days later *Dido* headed for Crete again in company with the same two cruisers together with six destroyers. Their task was to embark troops from Heraklion. On the outward passage they came under air attack and two ships were damaged. At Heraklion two destroyers went into the harbour to ferry troops out to the cruisers. The force sailed at 3.20 in the morning of 29th with the entire garrison of 4,000 men. As they left the area, the destroyer *Imperial*, which had suffered a near miss on the out-

ward voyage, had a steering gear breakdown. The destroyer *Hotspur* was sent to sink her. The *Hotspur* rejoined, crowded with 900 men. However, the force was, by then, well behind its return schedule and the Sun had risen before they passed through the Kaso Strait. The force came under heavy air attacks and the destroyer *Hereward* was damaged, fell astern and was lost. The force's speed had been reduced, and the *Orion* and *Dido* were both severely damaged by bombs, with considerable casualties, which included embarked troops. 103 of the 240 Black Watch embarked in *Dido* were killed. The force reached Alexandria with hardly any fuel or ammunition remaining.

The *Dido* was detached to the Red Sea and escorted the British and Indian troops landing at Assab, Eritrea, the last Italian held harbour on the Red Sea on 10 June. She then went on to Brooklyn Navy Yard for repairs, which lasted until December 1941. During this period her fifth (Q) turret was installed, and the single 4-inch removed.

In December she left Gibraltar with the destroyers *Gurkha* and *Nestor* (Royal Australian Navy) to rejoin the Mediterranean Fleet. On the way they escorted a convoy of empty ships from Malta to Alexandria, where they arrived on 20 December.

In January 1942, she was part of the escort to the fast supply ship *Glengyle* on passage to Malta, and then escorted the *Breconshire* from Malta. Her sisters *Naiad* and *Euryalus* were also part of the escort for these tasks. Two more convoys were run in January, and another in February. In March the cruisers sailed from Alexandria as a result of a false report of an Italian cruiser being torpedoed. They came under air attack on passage. On 11th the *Naiad*, Admiral Vian's flagship, was sunk by *U-565* north of Sollum. Admiral Vian transferred his flag to *Dido*. Four days later *Dido* carried out a bombardment of Rhodes.

Later that month the *Dido*, with *Euryalus* and another sister *Cleopatra*, escorted a convoy to Malta from Alexandria. The convoy came under both air and surface attacks. The AA cruiser *Carlisle* with six Hunt class destroyers stood by the convoy during the air attacks, whilst the three light cruisers, joined by the six-inch cruiser *Penelope* from Malta, together with 11 fleet destroyers became heavily engaged driving off two groups of Italian warships. The Italian ships had sailed from Taranto and Messina. The first group comprised three cruisers (two 8-inch and one 6-inch) with four destroyers. The second group, which arrived on the scene shortly afterwards, consisted of a 15-inch battleship (the *Littorio*), and six destroyers. By using bold and aggressive tactics, and deploying a smoke screen through which the British ships were able to close the enemy, Admiral Vian's force drove off the attackers. This action became known as the Second Battle of Sirte. That evening the cruisers withdrew from the convoy, which then dispersed and headed for Malta. One merchant ship was lost and another damaged by air attacks prior to their arrival. Only 5,000 tons of the 25,000 tons carried by the convoy were got ashore.

In July *Dido*, *Euryalus* and four destroyers bombarded Mersa Matruh. In September she and four destroyers bombarded the Daba area of Egypt.

On 27 November 1942, after escorting the Stoneage convoy of four merchant ships from Alexandria to Malta, the first mercantile convoy after the siege, *Dido* and *Euryalus* and four destroyers, under Admiral Power, formed a surface striking force (Force K) to operate from Malta. Force K operated against enemy convoys to Tunisia. On 13 December the force sank three enemy supply ships off North Africa. Shortly afterwards, *Dido* was detached to be part of the surface striking force operating out of Bone. This was known as Force Q and comprised *Aurora* and *Argonaut* with two destroyers operating opposite the *Sirius* and *Dido* and another two destroyers. The *Argonaut* was badly damaged shortly afterwards, and was replaced by the *Penelope*.

On 26 December, *Dido* returned to Gibraltar with Force H, and during the early part of 1943 she covered Mediterranean convoy as part of that force. She detached to England in April for a refit at Liverpool. In June, her refit complete, she returned to Gibraltar. On 10 July she sailed from Bone with *Sirius* to carry out a bombardment of Marsala. This was a diversion for Operation Husky, the landings in Sicily.

She took part in these landings, where she was with the reserve cover force, which included the battleships *King George V* and *Howe*. On 1 August she bombarded a bridge at the mouth of the River Oliva, and also the harbour at Vibo Valentia. On 9th she bombarded targets near Castellamare, and on 14th she bombarded

Vibo Valentia again and also sank a southbound merchant ship and two escort craft, nine miles south of Cape Bonifati.

Whilst taking part in Operation Avalanche, the invasion of Italy and the landings at Salerno, in September, she took part in Operation Slapstick, the improvised landings at Taranto. These latter were a considerable success, marred only by the heavy loss of life, which occurred when the fast minelayer *Abdiel* hit some mines laid in the harbour. Later she took part in operations in the Aegean. During these operations she collided with the *Aurora* south-east of the Kaso Strait and had to be repaired at Alexandria.

In January 1944 she once again supported landings, this time at Anzio. She helped rescue survivors from the cruiser *Spartan*, which was sunk by a glider bomb on 29 January. Until July she operated in support of the army in Italy, and in August she provided fire support for the landings in the South of France.

She remained in the Mediterranean until September, when she returned to the United Kingdom for a refit and modernisation before joining the Home Fleet. She escorted Convoy JW-61 to Russia in October/November 1944. In late November she escorted the carrier *Implacable*, whose aircraft attacked a German southbound convoy north of Namsos. In the first three months of 1945 she was employed in minelaying and minesweeping operations off the Norwegian coast. On 4 April she supported anti-shipping strikes by Home Fleet destroyers off Stavanger. Two weeks later she acted as the anti-aircraft escort to the fast minelayer *Apollo*, which laid a deep minefield in the approaches to the Kola Inlet.

She, with the cruiser *Birmingham* and four destroyers, steamed through a mine barrage off the Skaggerak on 6 May to take the surrender of Copenhagen on 9 May. She remained there until 24th, when she, and the cruiser *Devonshire*, escorted the German cruisers *Prinz Eugen* and *Nurnberg* to Wilhelmshaven.

She was placed in reserve in 1947, and became the flagship of the Reserve Fleet Group at Portsmouth in August 1951 in place of the *Duke of York*. The flag was transferred to *Jamaica* in May 1953, but *Dido* wore the flag at the Coronation Review in June 1953.

HMS Dido showing her after pair of 5.25-inch turrets. Note the degaussing coil fitted along her sides to counter magnetic mines. *(Syd Goodman Collection)*

The Flag Officer Commanding Reserve Fleet was then Vice Admiral Sir Henry McCall, who had commanded *Dido* from first commissioning until October 1942.

Dido arrived at Barrow for breaking up on 16 July 1958. She had gained ten battle honours for her name.

HMS PHOEBE

HMS Phoebe as configured in 1944 *(Syd Goodman Collection)*

HMS *Phoebe* was a cruiser of the Dido class and was laid down by the Fairfield Shipbuilding and Engineering Company, Ltd., Govan on 2 September 1937, being launched on 25 March 1939. She was completed on 30 September 1940. Due to the shortage of turrets, caused by the late decision to fit these turrets as the secondary armament of the new King George V class battleships, she, together with *Dido* and Bonaventure, was completed with just four twin 5.25-inch guns. In her Q position, just forward of the bridge, was mounted a single 4-inch gun instead.

On completion of working up she joined the 15th Cruiser Squadron of the Home Fleet, and among her early operations were the escort of troop convoys on the first stages of their voyages to the Middle East. In November she took part in the unsuccessful search for the heavy cruiser *Admiral Scheer* after the sinking of the Auxiliary Cruiser *Jervis Bay*. During that period in the North Atlantic she suffered weather damage. In December she and the cruiser *Aurora* were detailed to provide anti-aircraft cover at Oban. January 1941 she helped escort Convoy WS 5B, carrying 40,000 troops in 21 ships, heading for North Africa. On 30 March 1941, after accompanying WS 6 to Durban, she was ordered to the Mediterranean, where she joined the 7th Cruiser Squadron in April.

She took part in the evacuation of the Army from Greece. On 28/29 April she was with a force sent to Kalamata to rescue 10,000 troops, but only 450 men could be recovered. In all a total of 50,672 troops were embarked by the Fleet and taken to Crete and to Egypt between 24 and 29 April. In early May she helped escort tankers from Alexandria to Malta.

The Fleet then concentrated on the defence of Crete, and later had to evacuate troops from the island as it came under sustained attack. On 29/30 May she was Rear Admiral King's Flagship of the force (*Phoebe*, HMAS *Perth*, *Glengyle* and 3 destroyers) that rescued 5,981 troops from Sphakia. The force came under attack and the Australian cruiser *Perth* was damaged during the withdrawal. On the night 31 May/1 June she was again the

Flagship of Vice Admiral King (promoted on 30 May) of a force (*Phoebe*, *Abdiel* and 3 destroyers) that evacuated 3,624 troops from Sphakia.

In June she, with *Ajax*, *Coventry* and eight destroyers, provided cover for an expedition to land troops north of Tyre, but the plan had to be abandoned because the swell was too great for the landings. This was part of the operation to support the Army in preventing German infiltration into Syria. During this she bombarded coastal positions. On 3 July 1941 the Italian submarine *Malachite* fired at her whilst she was off Cyrenaica, but the torpedoes missed.

On 27 August 1941, whilst covering the transport of troops to and from Tobruk, she was hit by an aircraft torpedo and damaged. The torpedo blew a hole 28 x 18 feet in her outer bottom and serious flooding followed, but her machinery remained intact. Although able to return to Alexandria under her own steam, she had to leave the Station for repairs in the United States of America (New York), and was out of action for about eight months. During repairs a quadruple 40-mm mounting replaced the single 4-inch in Q position to save topweight, and more Oerlikons were added.

She returned to the United Kingdom in May 1942, and after working up at Scapa Flow, left for Gibraltar in July. In August she took part in the escort of an important convoy to Malta (Operational Pedestal), the last convoy fought through before the relief of the fortress in the following November. There were 13 ships in the convoy and *Phoebe* was part of the strong covering force. Only five ships of the convoy reached Malta, and the escort suffered heavily, losing the carrier *Eagle*, the cruisers *Manchester* and *Cairo* and destroyer *Foresight*. Many of the other escorting ships were damaged in severe attacks by aircraft, submarines and motor torpedo boats.

Her next duty was in South African waters for the interception of Axis shipping south of the Cape of Good Hope, arriving on station in September. On 23 October, while proceeding with her sister ship *Sirius* from the Cape to Pointe Noire, French Equatorial Africa, she was torpedoed by the Type IXC U-boat (*U-161* - Lt. Cdr. Achilles) about four

HMS Phoebe - this aerial view shows the fine lines of this class of cruiser. *(Syd Goodman Collection)*

HMS Phoebe entering Grand Harbour, Malta. Her Q turret has been replaced by light AA guns.
(Author's Collection)

miles from that port. The torpedo hit her port side abreast Q position and blew a hole 40 x 30 feet stretching from her keel upwards. B turret was put out of action and A turret could not be moved due the risk of damage to the structure. Her speed was reduced to six knots and there was extensive flooding. She lost 49 men dead. *U-161* was to be sunk by a USN patrol Squadron aircraft off Pernambuco on 27 September 1943, a month after transferring German Officers to a Japanese submarine off the Azores.

Before *Phoebe* could cross the Atlantic for repairs at New York, her forward turret had to be landed as her keel was broken and the hull would not take the strain imposed by the turret's weight. She sailed on 1 December for the USA. She was out of action for about eight months. At this time her quadruple pom-poms were replaced by US style quadruple 40-mm guns.

She sailed from Norfolk, Virginia on 26 June 1943, for the United Kingdom via Bermuda. She then underwent further repairs in Barrow-in-Furness, where her forward (A) turret was replaced and extra radar was fitted. She was in home waters until the end of September, and then rejoined the Mediterranean Fleet in the 15th Cruiser Squadron. On 15-16 October she and the destroyers *Faulknor* and *Fury* carried out a search for a convoy in the Aegean but were frustrated by air attacks. On 19 October she bombarded Kalimno in the Dodecanese, firing 350 rounds of 5.25-inch, and afterwards took part in other operations in the Aegean. On 19 November she came under attack from 7 Ju-88s, but was not hit. From 30 January 1944, she operated with other cruisers and destroyers, usually working in pairs, providing gunfire support to the Army in the Anzio area, West Italy.

After other operations in the Mediterranean she was transferred in May to the Eastern Fleet. In mid-June she left Trincomalee with other units of that Fleet, including the carrier *Illustrious*, battlecruiser *Renown* and French battleship *Richelieu*, to carry out naval air strike on Port Blair, Andaman Islands (Operation Pedal).

On 25 July she took part in the sea and air strike on Sabang (Operation Crimson), the Japanese held base in Northern Sumatra. For this operation she escorted the carriers *Victorious* and *Illustrious*. She

also took part in the bombardment of Sabang with the battleships *Queen Elizabeth*, *Valiant* and (French) *Richelieu*, battlecruiser *Renown*, five other cruisers and seven destroyers.

Between 17-19 October, she also took part in a similar strike on positions in the Nicobar Islands. This operation (Miller) was a diversion for the imminent US landings at Leyte. During this operation *Phoebe* escorted the carriers *Indomitable* and *Victorious*. The force came under Japanese air attacks but suffered no losses, 7 of the 12 attacking aircraft being shot down by the fighter cover provided by the carriers.

On 3 January 1945, she, with *Newcastle* and *Nigeria* and three destroyers, covered the landing of a military force which next day captured the port of Akyab, the third largest port in Burma. For this operation *Phoebe* acted as the fighter direction ship. She also operated as fighter direction ship for the landings by the 3rd British Commando Brigade on Myebon on 12 January. She was in the same role on 21 January during the amphibious operation for the recovery of Ramree Island, off the Arakan Coast. (Operation Matador) She also, with the battleship *Queen Elizabeth*, destroyers and sloops, took part in the preliminary bombardments. On 26 January she was again the fighter direction ship for the landing of 500 Royal Marines on Cheduba Island, south of Ramree (Operation Sankey), which was cleared of the enemy by the end of the month.

She took part in Operation Dracula, the amphibious assault on Rangoon. She, with her half sister *Royalist*, four escort carriers, four destroyers, eight frigates and two sloops provided cover for the landings on 2 May. The town itself was entered the next day. Between 15 May and 16 June she supported the Indian sloops *Cauvery*, *Narbada*, *Godavari*, *Kistna*, *Sutlej* and *Hindustan* on patrols between the Mergui Archipelago and Port Blair in the Andaman Sea to prevent the evacuation of and the supplies to Japanese troops.

She was at Trincomalee on VJ-Day, 15 August 1945. On 8 September she relieved the cruiser *London* as guardship at Sabang for a week, and afterwards returned home, leaving Colombo on 27 September, and arriving at Sheerness on 23 October. After a refit at Chatham and Plymouth, she hoisted the flag of Rear Admiral (Destroyers) Mediterranean Fleet at Gibraltar on 7 June 1946. From 1947to 1952 she was part of the First Cruiser Squadron Mediterranean, and on 16 October 1950 was in collision with the cruiser *Gambia*, damaging her starboard outer propeller. She remained in the Mediterranean until March 1951, returning to Chatham on 14 March.

After being reduced to reserve at Harwich, she was transferred to the Reserve Fleet at Portsmouth in 1953. She was handed over to the BISC for scrapping on 27 March 1956,and towed away to be broken up by Hughes Bolckow, arriving at Blyth on 1 April 1956. Breaking up was completed by 11 October 1956.

She gained eight battle honours, Greece 1941, Crete 1941, Malta Convoys 1942, Aegean 1943, Mediterranean 1944, Sabang 1944, East Indies 1944 and Burma 1944-45. This brought the total for her name to seventeen.

HMS EURYALUS

HMS Euryalus fuelling from the auxiliary *San Ambrosio* whilst with the British Pacific Fleet.
(Ken Kelly Collection)

The *Euryalus* was one of the first group of Dido Class cruisers, and was laid down at Chatham Dockyard on 21 October 1937. Her engines were built by Hawthorn Leslie and Co.. She was launched on 6 June 1939 and completed on 20 June 1941. Five of her sisters had already joined the fleet, a much needed addition to the strength as they were fitted with a main armament of dual-purpose guns. Originally the King George V Class battleships were to have been fitted with twin 4.5-inch guns as secondary armament. However, the decision to fit these battleships with the 5.25 inch guns, tried in the old battleship *Iron Duke* in 1936, led to a shortage, and so five of the Dido class had to be completed with a reduced main armament. However, *Euryalus* joined the fleet with all five turrets, and also with air warning and gunnery ranging radar.

She worked up at Scapa Flow, and sailed from there on 15 September to be part of the escort for a convoy to Malta and the Eastern Mediterranean in Operation Halberd. By then her AA armament had been upgraded with the replacement of her quadruple machine guns by five single 20-mm guns, and she had also exchanged damaged propellers at Rosyth. At Gibraltar she joined Force H, which was to be part of the escort. The convoy was to emulate Operation Substance, which took place in July, and was to run 9 fast merchant ships to Malta with stores and troops (some of whom were embarked in the escorting ships). The covering force included the battleships *Nelson*, *Rodney* and *Prince of Wales*, together with the carrier *Ark Royal*, 5 cruisers and 18 destroyers. A diversion was to be enacted in the Eastern Mediterranean, and three empty ships were to be run back to Gibraltar from Malta under cover of the operation. On 27th the convoy came under air attack, which was mainly driven off by *Ark Royal*'s aircraft and the destroyers' gunfire, but the *Nelson* was hit by a torpedo and damaged. The Italian fleet was reported to be at sea and the capital ships remained to cover the convoy from the north whilst

it went ahead to the narrows, where a merchant ship was sunk in further air attacks before the convoy reached Malta on 28th. *Euryalus* sailed from Malta on the same day, returning to Gibraltar on 1 October.

From Gibraltar, *Euryalus* steamed around the Cape to join the Mediterranean Fleet at Alexandria, passing through Suez on 10 November. She joined her sister ship Naiad in bombarding enemy positions in the Halfaya area on the night of 18 November in support of the Army of the Nile's advance in Libya. She continued to operate in support of the army during their relief of Tobruk and capture of Derna and Benghazi.

Between 5 and 8 January 1942 she was part of the escort to the special service ship *Glengyle* from Alexandria to Malta and brought back the supply ship *Breconshire*. On 17th she again sailed as escort to a convoy of four ships to Malta. One ship was sunk by enemy aircraft, whilst an escort, the *Gurkha*, was sunk by a submarine. Later in the month she took part in another convoy to Malta, and brought other ships back. The next month there was a further convoy to Malta, but none of the three ships of the convoy reached their destination, two being sunk by air attacks, and the third, damaged in air attacks, had to be escorted to Tobruk.

On 15th March she took part in a bombardment of Rhodes with the *Dido* and 6 destroyers. A week later she was again part of the escort of a convoy to Malta, this time of four ships including the *Breconshire*. The convoy came under attack by a strong Italian surface force, which included the battleship *Littorio*, two heavy cruisers and three light cruisers as well as seven destroyers. The convoy escort of four light cruisers with eleven destroyers engaged the much stronger enemy and drove them clear of the convoy in a fierce action which became known as the Second Battle of Sirte. Whilst this action took place the AA cruiser *Carlisle* and a Hunt class destroyer laid a smoke screen to protect the convoy, and five other Hunt class destroyers remained close to the convoy to fight off air attacks. The next day one of the convoy was lost during further air attacks, and the three other merchant ships reached Malta but were sunk by air attacks before all their cargoes could be landed. Only about one fifth of the cargo which had been loaded in the convoy was delivered.

In June a further attempt was made to resupply Malta from Egypt in Operation Vigorous. The convoy came under heavy air attacks and was threatened by an Italian surface force, which included two battleships. The convoy and escort used up so much fuel in taking avoiding action that they had to return to Alexandria.

On the night 19/20 July she and her sister ship *Dido*, with four destroyers, bombarded shipping and the port installations at Mersa Mutruh. In September and October she was the temporary flagship of the Admiral Commanding the 15th Cruiser Squadron (Rear Admiral A J Power). In the next month she was part of the escort of the first convoy to reach Malta following the landings in North Africa. Four merchant ships sailed from Alexandria on 16th. During the passage the cruiser *Arethusa* was badly damaged in air attacks. However, the merchant ships arrived at Malta three days later and were able to carry out their unloading without being attacked in harbour. After this convoy the *Euryalus* remained overnight in Malta, berthing alongside the battered wharfs in Grand Harbour. This convoy marked the effective relief of Malta. A few days later she left Alexandria with the *Dido* and four destroyers to form a new Force K, a striking force to be based at Malta. This force was very successful in its actions against enemy shipping bound for Libya. In December another similar force (Force Q) was established at Bone. The *Dido* was transferred to that, whilst *Euryalus* operated with the *Cleopatra* and *Orion* from Malta. On 23 January she was with the force when it bombarded the Libyan coast west of Tripoli at Zuarra, which the army occupied on 31st.

On 8 June she was part of the force of cruisers that bombarded Pantellaria. The island was also bombed, and surrendered on 11th. Just before the invasion of Sicily on 10 July, she joined the 12th Cruiser squadron in the Western Mediterranean and provided cover for the landings. Her sister ship *Cleopatra* was torpedoed by an Italian submarine during these operations and *Euryalus* escorted her to Malta. On 20 July she joined Force Q relieving her sister ship *Sirius*. On 1 August she carried out bombardments in support of the army in Sicily in the Gulf of San Eufemia and on the harbour at Vibo Valentia. On the 17th she took part in the bombardment of Scalea in West Italy. On 27th she hoisted the Flag of Admiral Sir Philip Vian who was in command of Force V. Force V comprised five escort carriers and three cruisers and was to provide air cover for the landings at Salerno on 9 September until shore airfields came available to the Allies. On 15th she, with two other cruisers, carried troops to Salerno to supplement the landings.

After the surrender of Taranto, a meeting was held in *Euryalus* attended by Admiral Sir Andrew Cunningham, the Allied Commander-in-Chief, and the Italian Minister of Marine, during which the disposal of the Italian Fleet and Mercantile Marine was settled. *Euryalus* left Bizerta on 29 September and returned to the United Kingdom, and started a refit on the Clyde in October which was to last until mid July 1944. She had been involved in some of the most intense fighting in the Mediterranean and been fortunate to come through undamaged. During her refit her armament was again upgraded. Her Q turret was removed and replaced by an extra quadruple 2-pounder mounting. Her lighter guns then comprised six twin and five single 20-mm guns. Her radar fit was also upgraded during this period.

On completion of her refit she worked up and joined the Home Fleet at Scapa Flow. She was part of a force that carried out an air strike to mine German shipping routes and bomb shipping off the Norwegian coast north of Stadtlandet on 14th October, and she also took part in a carrier aircraft sweep off the south west of Norway in mid November. She then underwent a refit in Rosyth to prepare her for service in the East Indies. She sailed from Liverpool with two destroyers escorting SS *Rimutaka* on 16 December. The merchant ship was taking HRH the Duke of Gloucester to Australia to take up his appointment as Governor General. She escorted the *Rimutaka* to Colombo, passing Suez on 29 December. She joined the 4th Cruiser Squadron of the East Indies Fleet, entering Trincomalee on 11 January 1945. She then took part in the seaborne air strikes on Pladjoe on 24 January, and Suengei Gerong on 29 January- Operation Meridian. These strikes were very successful, the output of the Pladjoe refinery being halved as a result according to Japanese reports, and the Soengei Gerong refinery was completely shut down for two months.

Immediately after these strikes, the British Pacific

HMS Euryalus showing her three turret forward arrangement - she was the first of the class to receive all five turrets. *(Author's Collection)*

Fleet, which included four fleet carriers and the *King George V*, three cruisers and ten destroyers sailed for Australia, arriving at Fremantle on 4 February and Sydney on 11th. On 28th she sailed for Manus in company with the battleship *King George V* and other units of the fleet. On 18 March she left Manus for Ulithi in the Caroline Islands to take part in Operation Iceberg, the Allied assault on Ryukuyu Islands, Japan. The United States Fleet struck at Okinawa whilst the British ships neutralised the Japanese airfields in the Sakishima group, at the south end of the Ryukyus. This operation continued until the last week in May, the battleships, cruisers and some destroyers carrying out bombardments of the islands and airfields and the British force coming under attacks by Kamikaze aircraft during this period. The *Euryalus* returned to Brisbane in June.

She sailed to rejoin the British Pacific Fleet from Manus on 12 July. The Fleet joined the United States Ships in operations against mainland Japan, with carrier borne aircraft attacks and bombardments on mainland Japan. Japan surrendered a month later, and *Euryalus* sailed from Manus on 19 August for Leyte, where she arrived on 22nd. She joined a force under Rear Admiral Cecil Harcourt which left the Philippines on 27 August and entered Hong Kong on 30th to take the Japanese surrender there. After carrier borne aircraft swept the harbour to ensure the safety of the force against attacks by motor boats, *Swiftsure*, carrying the Admiral's flag, accompanied by the *Euryalus* and destroyers *Kempenfelt* and *Tuscan* and other ships entered harbour at 1000 on 30th. The two cruisers landed parties to seize the dockyard and clear it of Japanese and Chinese with negligible opposition. The formal surrender was received in Government House on 16 September.

She remained in the Far East with the British Pacific Fleet until January 1947, when she left for Chatham, arriving there in February. She was placed in reserve at Rosyth until later in the year when she underwent a refit there. She was then allocated to the Mediterranean Fleet, which she joined in March 1948, relieving the *Ajax*. On 14 May 1948 she sailed from Haifa with the last British High Commissioner in Palestine embarked. She returned to Plymouth in May 1950, and recommissioned for service in the Mediterranean. She was sent to the Persian Gulf in May 1951 to relieve the cruiser *Gambia* at a time of unrest in Persia, when the Shah signed a decree nationalising the oilfields of the Anglo-Persian Company. She was there until 7 June. The next month she sailed from Malta again, this time heading for Abadan to relieve the cruiser *Mauritius*. She remained there until September.

In August 1952 she returned to Devonport again to re-commission for the Mediterranean Station. By then her gunnery armament comprised four twin 5.25 inch, three quadruple two-pounders, two single 40-mm, four twin 20-mm and four 3-pounder saluting guns. She finally left the Mediterranean in March 1953, and joined the South Atlantic Station, relieving the *Bermuda* as flagship in April 1953. On 19 August 1954 she arrived at Devonport, paid off and reduced to reserve there. She was placed on the sales list in January 1956, and on 22 October 1958 approval was given for her disposal by scrap. She left for Blyth under tow by the tug *Welshman* on 14 July 1959, the last of her class in commission and the last to be broken up. She had gained six Battle Honours for her name, Malta Convoys 1941-42, Mediterranean 1941-43, Sirte 1942, Sicily 1943, Salerno 1943 and Okinawa 1945. This brought the total awarded to ships of the name to ten.

HMS CLEOPATRA

HMS Cleopatra with her third turret replaced by light AA guns. *(Syd Goodman Collection)*

The *Cleopatra* was in the third (1938) programme of Dido Class cruisers, and was laid down by Messrs.Hawthorn Leslie and Co Ltd, Hebburn on 5 January 1939, launched on 27 March 1940 and completed on 5 December 1941. These cruisers were armed with a dual purpose main armament of five twin 5.25 inch guns, and also had two quadruple pom-poms amidships, two 2-pounders (shortly afterwards replaced by two 20-mm guns) and three 20-mm guns as well as two sets of triple torpedo tubes. Three of the class were ordered in the 1938 programme, but the other two, *Scylla* and *Charybdis*, were completed to a revised design with four twin 4.5 inch guns due to the shortage of the 5.25 inch guns. Designed to be of 5,450 tons displacement, *Cleopatra* was slightly heavier at 5,582 tons, with a full load displacement of 6,975 tons. Her cost was £1,618,469.

On completion she joined the Home Fleet to work up, but transferred to the 15th Cruiser Squadron in the Mediterranean in February 1942, leaving the Clyde on 5th. And arriving at Malta on 11th. As she closed Grand Harbour with the destroyer *Fortune* she came under heavy air attacks. She was hit by a 500 Kg. bomb, which passed through her forecastle and hull before exploding under water, causing flooding and splinter damage. Warheads on her upper deck were set on fire by near misses. She was out of action for a month. Shortly after repairs had been completed at Malta, she sailed with the destroyer *Kingston* to join her sister ship *Naiad*, Flagship of the 15th Cruiser Squadron. Soon afterwards the *Naiad* was torpedoed by *U-565* and sunk. The Flag Officer, Admiral Vian, was rescued and *Cleopatra* became his flagship.

On 20 March she sailed from Alexandria with two other sisters, *Dido* and *Euryalus* together with some destroyers to escort Convoy MW10 to Malta. The convoy was intercepted by Italian surface forces, which comprised a battleship and two heavy and four light cruisers and destroyers. The Italian ships were sighted at 1427 on 22 March. Immediately the British cruisers, now numbering four with the arrival of the *Penelope* from Malta, together with the eleven fleet destroyers of the escort, closed the enemy force. The convoy, meanwhile, turned away under the escort of the AA cruiser *Carlisle* and six Hunt class destroyers, and found itself under air attack. By skilful use of smoke screens and with complete disregard for the enemy's superior fire-power, the cruisers and destroyers forced the enemy, which comprised two heavy cruisers, a light cruiser and four destroyers, to retire. The cruisers and destroyers rejoined the convoy, which had been well protected from the air attacks by the Hunts, but immediately sighted another Italian force, which included the battleship *Littorio*. Again they turned to engage the enemy and made smoke screens to cover the convoy and their approach. The British cruisers and destroyers emerged from the smoke to fire their guns and torpedoes, closing to within 6,000 yards. No appreciable damage was done to the enemy, but the Italians were forced to turn away and retire. The destroyers *Havock* and *Kingston* were damaged by 15-inch shells and had to return to Malta. During the action the *Cleopatra* was hit by a 6-inch shell just two feet above her compass platform deck, causing only minor damage. Unfortunately the next day, as the convoy had been delayed by the attacks on it by the Italian surface forces, the convoy was still out at sea by daylight and came under renewed air attacks. One ship was sunk and another was hit and had to be towed to Marsaxlokk Harbour on the south side of Malta. The other two ships of the convoy reached Grand Harbour, but were both hit in subsequent air attacks on the harbour. On returning to Alexandria Admiral Vian's force received a congratulatory signal from the Prime Minister, stating it had been an action "of the highest distinction".

In June 1942 *Cleopatra* was again Admiral Vian's flagship for Operation Vigorous, another convoy from Alexandria to Malta. This was to run simultaneously with a convoy to Malta from the west (Operation Harpoon). The convoy came under heavy air and E-boat attacks, and was threatened by an Italian surface force, which included two Littorio class battleships. The convoy expended so much ammunition and fuel in attacks and diversions that it was forced to retire to Alexandria.

On 30 June the *Cleopatra* was allocated to a newly formed bombardment force at Haifa. On 12 August this force, comprising the cruisers *Arethusa* and *Cleopatra* and the destroyers *Javelin*, *Kelvin*, *Sikh* and *Zulu*, bombarded Rhodes as a diversionary move for Operation Pedestal, a convoy from the west to Malta. In September she docked at Massawa, where there was a small floating dock. She was docked half at a time, and during this operation she slipped off the blocks and received slight damage.

In November she provided cover for Operation Stoneage, the first convoy to reach Malta after the siege of the island has been raised after the landing in North Africa. Four merchant ships sailed from Port Said on 16 November, and reached Malta on the night 19/20 and were able to unload their cargoes unmolested. Five days later the *Cleopatra* left Alexandria with the *Dido* and *Euryalus* and four destroyers to form Force K, a surface striking force based on Malta. On 12 December, with *Dido*, *Euryalus* and 4 destroyers, she sank three enemy supply ships off Tunisia.

Early in the morning of 23 January 1943 the *Cleopatra* and *Euryalus* and destroyers *Jervis*, *Javelin*, *Nubian* and *Kelvin* bombarded the withdrawal routes of the German and Italian armies on the Libyan Coast at Zuara in support of the 8th Army.

At the end of May 1943, *Cleopatra* transferred from the 15th Cruiser Squadron to the 12th Cruiser Squadron in the Western Mediterranean and joined Force Q, a surface striking force based on Bone.

She took part in Operation Husky, the invasion of Sicily on 10 July, being part of the covering force off Cape Passero. Afterwards she, with other ships, patrolled the East Coast of Sicily and came under air attacks. She left her patrol at dawn on 16 July for Malta, and her crew stood down from action stations at 0540 having been closed up all night. Full damage control watches were closed up. At 0617 she was zig-zagging at 26 knots when she was hit on the starboard side abreast A Boiler Room by a torpedo from the Italian submarine *Dandalo*. There was a violent explosion and a flash of flame and smoke rose to about 50 feet above the waterline. The ship was shaken violently and rolled to starboard, but steadied and returned towards the vertical, but steadied with a 6-degree list to starboard. Her forward Engine and Boiler Rooms were flooded and there was a fire in the workshop flat, which was brought under control in about 45 minutes. She stopped at first, but at 0800 got under weigh at 10-11 knots using her after machinery. Some top-weight, including her torpedoes and depth charges, was jettisoned. Her main armament was out of action and her light armament could only be worked in local control. A 30 x 20-foot hole had been blown in her side. She had 22 killed or missing, and 23 wounded. She was able to make Malta under her own power, arriving at 1738. She was screened from further submarine attack by the destroyers *Quilliam* and *Quail*, and given AA cover by the *Euryalus*. She arrived with a heavy list and being steered by hand. She remained at Malta to October. She then proceeded to Algiers and Gibraltar, leaving Gibraltar on 7 November for Philadelphia. She returned to the Clyde on 26 November 1944 via New York and Bermuda, and underwent further repairs until March 1945. Her armament then comprised four twin 5.25-inch guns, three quadruple 40-mm, six twin 20-mm and four single 20-mm guns and six torpedo tubes.

She then worked up in the Clyde and at Scapa Flow prior to sailing on 3 May for the Mediterranean. She reached Malta on 12 May to complete her work up. It was planned that she then sail for the British Pacific Fleet, but when she arrived at Colombo on 12 July she joined the 5th Cruiser Squadron of the East Indies Fleet.

She was at Colombo on VJ Day, 15 August. On 27 August she sailed as flagship of Commander-in-Chief East Indies, Admiral Sir A J Power, for the occupation of Singapore (Operation Tiderace). Preceded by minesweepers, she and HMIS *Bengal* entered Singapore on 3 September, the first British warships to return to the Base after 3.5 years. The next day the cruiser *Sussex* arrived with a convoy carrying the 5th Indian Division. On 5 September the Commander-in-Chief reported the plan executed without any fighting. On 9th September and for the next three days over 100,000 men were landed

HMS Cleopatra, Admiral Vian's flagship at the Second Battle of Sirte. *(MoD/Crown Copyright)*

at Port Swettenham and Port Dickson in Operation Zipper, and the Japanese observed the surrender punctiliously. The battleships *Nelson* and *Richelieu* led this force, supported by the cruisers *Nigeria*, *Ceylon* and *Cleopatra*, 15 destroyers and the 21st Carrier Squadron comprising the cruiser *Royalist* and the escort carriers *Hunter*, *Stalker*, *Archer*, *Khedive*, *Emperor*, *Pursuer* and *Trumpeter*. *Cleopatra* was the flagship on 12 September at the official surrender of the Japanese forces in South East Asia area, made by General Itagaki in the Singapore Municipal Buildings. On 17 September it was decided that she was no longer required by the British Pacific Fleet, and that she was to remain with the East Indies Fleet. She stayed there till January 1946, sailing from Trincomalee on 7 January 1946 and arriving at Portsmouth on 7 February 1946.

She underwent a refit and then joined the 2nd Cruiser Squadron in the Home Fleet. In November 1947 she was temporarily laid up due to manpower shortages. In October 1950 she visited the Cape Verde Islands, the first HM Ship so to do for 30 years. That month she also visited Dakar. In November 1950 she was guardship at Dover to salute Queen Juliana of the Netherlands on her arrival for a State Visit to Britain.

She reduced to reserve at Chatham in January 1951, but re-commissioned on 30 October after a short refit and on in 29 November she arrived at Malta to relieve the *Phoebe* in the 1st Cruiser Squadron of the Mediterranean Fleet. During her refit at Chatham her quadruple 40-mm guns were replaced by twin 40-mm guns. Her total secondary armament was then eight 40-mm and eight 20-mm guns. She was the only one of the class, apart from the fully modified *Royalist*, to receive the modern twin Mk V Bofors mountings. On 21 January 1952 she visited Beghazi, the first HM Ship to do so since Libyan Independence. In July 1952 she was visiting Istanbul, and had to depart early due to a coup d'etat in Egypt, sailing with other ships of the Mediterranean Fleet to cover the Canal zone.

She returned to Chatham on 10 February 1953. In June she took part in the Coronation Review at Spithead and entered the Reserve Fleet at Chatham in October. In September 1954 she was laid up at Portsmouth, relieving the *Jamaica* as Flagship of the Reserve Fleet. The Flag Officer Commanding Reserve Fleet, transferred to the battleship *Vanguard* on 28 November 1956. *Cleopatra* was sold and towed from Portsmouth 9 December 1958, arrived at Cashmore's Newport for breaking up 15 December 1958. Demolition was completed by 19 August 1959.

She had gained three battle honours for her name, Malta Convoys 1942, Sirte 1942 and Sicily 1943. This brought the name's total to seven.

HMS ARGONAUT

HMS Argonaut, a fine sight at speed. *(Syd Goodman Collection)*

The *Argonaut* was a Dido class cruiser and was laid down at Cammell Laird's, Birkenhead, under the War Programme on 21 November 1939. She was launched on 6 September 1941. Material supply problems after Dunkirk, especially of aluminium, caused the construction of the last six ships of the class to be halted in June 1940. In October 1940 work recommenced, but only *Argonaut*, whose construction was further advanced, was completed to the original design. She was equipped with all five 5.25-inch twin turrets, and was given a full outfit of radar. She was the eleventh of the class, and was of 5,972 tons standard displacement. She was 500 tons over the original designed displacement despite many weight saving measures, which included the shortening of her after funnel by two feet.

She completed on 8 August 1942, and that day sailed for Scapa Flow to work up, joining the 10th Cruiser Squadron of the Home Fleet. She operated with that Squadron until the end of October. On 13 October she, with the destroyers *Intrepid* and *Obdurate* set out on a special trip to North Russia via Spitzbergen (Operation EZ). They landed a medical unit, which the Russian agreed could look after the British sick and wounded. They also collected survivors from earlier convoys to Russia together with 245 officers and men from RAF Hampden and Spitfire aircraft, with their equipment, had been presented to Russia, and also the crews of three British motor minesweepers, which had been handed over to the Russians too. The *Argonaut* and her destroyers arrived at the Kola Inlet on 21st, and sailed again the next day, returning to Seidisfjord on 26th and to Scapa Flow on 28th.

Two days later *Argonaut* left Scapa Flow in company with the battleship *Duke of York* and other ships to join Force E at Gibraltar ready for the landings in North Africa (Operation Torch). After the landings in November, *Argonaut*, with the cruisers *Aurora* and *Sirius* (all part of the newly formed 12th Cruiser Squadron) became Force Q, a striking force operating from Bone to intercept enemy convoys bound for Tunisia. A similar force was established at Malta.

On 2 December, on its first offensive sweep,

Force Q attacked a convoy 40 miles north of Cape Bon. Four merchant ships and three torpedo craft were hit and left as burning wrecks. Later it was confirmed that the four merchant ships had sunk, together with the Italian destroyer *Folgore*. The cruisers had been accompanied by two destroyers (*Quentin* and *Quiberon*), one of which (*Quentin*) was hit and sunk by an aircraft torpedo during an attack which occurred as the Force was returning to harbour.

Dido also joined Force Q, which then split into two sections, *Argonaut* operating with *Aurora*, and the *Sirius* and *Dido* working together. In December sweeps were carried out repeatedly against enemy shipping, and rarely yielded no results.

During a sweep on 11 December, the *Argonaut* shot down an aircraft during a low level bombing attacks. At 0605 on 14 December, Force Q, then comprising *Argonaut*, *Aurora* accompanied by the destroyers *Eskimo* and *Quality*, was returning from one of its regular sweeps in the Tyrrhenian Sea at 25 knots, when *Argonaut* was hit on her starboard side by two torpedoes. One struck the bow, the other her stern. Initially it was thought that they had been dropped by aircraft, as the force was under air attack at the time, but it was later discovered that they had been fired by the Italian submarine *Mocenigo* (Lt. Cdr. Longhi). The forward hit was three feet above the keel at No.7 station, and damaged the first 30 feet of the bow. The damage aft was more severe. It was 8 feet below the waterline and under the steering gear compartment. Damage reached forward for 60 feet. An initial list of 7.5 degrees to port was soon counteracted. Both inner shafts were bent and their A brackets wrecked, and the steering gear and rudders were destroyed. *Argonaut*'s engines had been stopped as soon as she was hit, but were put ahead again 9 minutes later as it was found she could still manoeuvre using her outer shafts. Her guns opened fire a minute later on attacking aircraft and a salvo of bombs fell a few yards from her starboard quarter shortly afterwards, without apparently causing any further damage.

Argonaut was able to steam slowly, and, at first, it was hoped she could achieve 15 knots. However, wreckage from the port side aft caused the ship to steer to port. With the port engine at full power ahead, and the starboard engine being adjusted in speed, sometimes going slowly astern, the ship was able to make a curving zig-zag at 8.5 knots to Algiers. The destroyers *Ashanti* and *Tartar* were despatched to supplement her escort. Further air attacks developed at 2143, but were driven off by her main armament firing in radar control. X turret could still operate in power, but not in hand, whilst Y turret was not used because of the danger of causing further damage to the surrounding structure. She arrived at Algiers at 1500 the next day. Despite having been at full power for 34 hours, the port outer shaft showed no signs of overheating or vibration. All fresh water tanks had been rendered unusable, and baths in the after structure were cleaned and used for fresh water storage. Three people who had been in the tiller flat region were missing, and eight others suffered minor injuries.

On 2 January she sailed for Gibraltar, arriving there on 4th. There she was docked and temporary repairs carried out. She sailed for America for more permanent repairs on 3 April. She carried out an independent crossing of the Atlantic calling at Ponta Delgada and Bermuda before reaching Philadelphia on 30 April. Throughout she had been steering by use of her two outboard shafts, having no steering gear nor rudder. She remained there until 13 November for repairs. By this time she had her single 20-mm guns removed and replaced by twin 20mm mountings, but she still retained her five turrets. She had also had her after funnel reduced by a further few feet to save topweight, giving her a pleasing appearance.

She left America in November 1943, and arrived on the Clyde on 2 December and reached Rosyth two days later. She then proceeded to the Tyne for a refit, which lasted until the end of March 1944. She then rejoined the 10th Cruiser Squadron of the Home Fleet at Scapa Flow. During 1944 her main armament was reduced to four twin mountings, Q turret being replaced by a quadruple two-pounder mounting.

For the Normandy landings she was allocated to Bombarding Force K, comprising the cruisers *Orion, Ajax, Emerald* and *Argonaut* with the Dutch gunboat *Flores* together with 15 destroyers. The Force was supporting Assault Force G under

HMS Argonaut showing the damage to her stern when she was hit by torpedoes both forward and aft.
(Ken Kelly Collection)

Commodore C.E. Douglas-Pennant in the *Bulolo* attacking the Gold Area (Asnelles). She sailed from the Clyde on 3 June and anchored off the Gold Area at 0630 on 6th. This force was amongst the first ships to open fire that day. She and the *Ajax* engaged a battery at Longues that had opened fire after the intial bombardment. *Ajax* fired 150 rounds, two of which entered the battery through the gun openings. *Argonaut* fired 29 rounds. On 10 June she and the *Orion* were specially mentioned by Rear Admiral Vian, who commanded the Eastern Task Force, for their intense bombardment at extreme range of the enemy positions at Tilly-sur-Seulles. She returned to the Solent on 12th, but on 26th supported operations in the Caen area. On 30th *Argonaut* with other ships bombarded two important enemy concentrations in Andre-sur-Orne and Feuguerolles. During this action she was struck on the starboard side of her quarterdeck by a 155-mm shell from a shore battery. Fortunately this did not explode, but passed through a cabin and out of the ship's side above the waterline. It left a hole 16 by 3 inches large, but only caused minor damage. She left the area on 2 July, and was at Plymouth for 12 days whilst changing 5.25-inch gun barrels. She had fired 4,395 shells in 25 days at the Normandy beaches.

On 21 July *Argonaut* was allocated for temporary duty in the Mediterranean, and left the Clyde on 26 July southbound, escorting SS *Stirling Castle*.

On 15 August she took part in the landings in the South of France (Operation Dragoon), when she was the only British cruiser in what was known as the 'Camel Support Force' under American com-

mand. The other ships in the Force were three American and two French cruisers, supported by the battleship *Arkansas*, eleven destroyers and various minesweeper groups. She fired 394 rounds of main armament ammunition on the first day of the landings.

In October *Argonaut* was engaged in operations in the Aegean. On 12th she bombarded Phleva Island, south-east of Greece, to expedite the withdrawal of enemy forces. An armed caique, overloaded with about 200 German troops, was sunk in the northern Aegean on 16th October, and she sank a large landing ship in the Northern Channel on 18th.

In November *Argonaut* left the Mediterranean for the East Indies to join the 4th Cruiser Squadron, passing through the Suez Canal on 30th, reaching Trincomalee on 5th of the next month. She sailed again on 17th with the force that three days later delivered carrier borne air attacks on the north-east coast of Sumatra, especially on the oil refinery at Pangkalan Brandan (Operation Robson). This particular target was found to be completely obscured by cloud, but as an alternative, the warehouses, railway yards, oil installations and harbour works at Balawan Deli were attacked together with fighter airfields in the Sabang area.

In January 1945 *Argonaut* took part in further air strikes on Pangkalan Brandan on 4th, and on Palembang on 24th (Operations Lentil and Meridian). The second operation was conducted as the British Paciific Fleet tansferred from Trincomalee to the Pacific. This was a very successful operation, the oil refineries at Palembang being reduced to working only at one third of their normal output after the raid. The force arrived at Fremantle on 4 February, and at Sydney on 10th prior to moving into the Pacific.

On 23 March 1945 she was with the Fleet when it left Ulithi (Caroline Islands) to neutralise enemy airfields in the Sakishima Group, at the southern end of the Ryukyu Islands (Operation Iceberg), as part of American operations against Okinawa.

Task Group 111.3 comprising the carriers *Colossus*, cruisers *Bermuda* and *Argonaut*, and destroyers *Tyrian, Tumult, Tuscan* and *Quiberon*, was ordered by Admiral Fraser, the Commander-in-Chief, to investigate the situation of Prisoners of War in Formosa. The Group left Leyte on 4 September and arrived at Keelung - the northernmost tip of Formosa- on 6th. The task completed, the group moved to the Shanghai area on 10th, and arrived off Shanghai on 18th. The next day it anchored off Shanghi Bund, where the ships received an enthusiastic welcome.

Argonaut visited Japan in the spring of 1946, and remained with the British Pacific Fleet until May, when she left for home. She arrived at Portsmouth in the first week of June. She was then placed in reserve. By this time some 20-mm guns had been replaced by 40-mm Bofors and Boffins, giving her a total close range armament of three quadruple two-pounders, nine single 40-mm and four single 20-mm guns.

It was approved that she be scrapped in September 1955. She was handed over to the British Iron and Steel Corporation on 16 November. She arrived at Newport on 19 November 1955.

She had gained seven battle honours for her name.

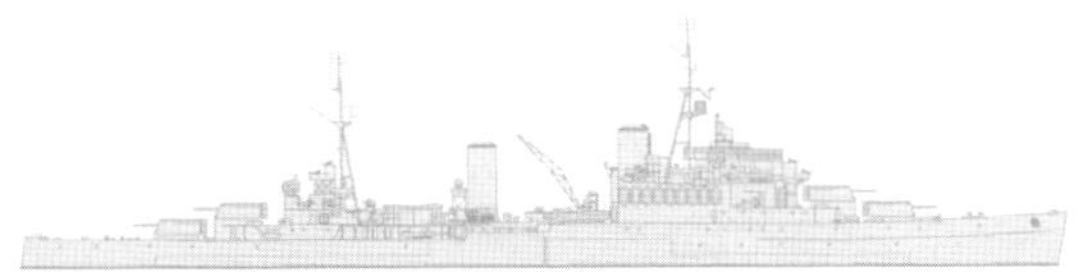

Colony Class Cruisers

A large warship building programme was instituted just prior to the outbreak of World War II. Among the vessels ordered was a class of light cruisers based on the Southampton class, but to an austerity design displacing 1,000 tons less. They had a main armament of four triple 6-inch guns, with four twin 4-inch and six torpedo tubes. Their overall length was 555.5 feet, with a beam of 62 feet. Their engines developed 72,500-shaft horse power giving them a speed of 31.5 knots. Later ships of the class were completed with just three triple 6-inch turrets, the saving in weight being necessary to allow for the addition of extra AA guns, radar and extra personnel.

The class had virtually the same capability as the earlier Southampton class of cruisers, but were 36.5 feet shorter. The savings in length, and in over 1,000 tons displacement, were achieved by mounting the after boilers abreast each other instead of fore and aft, and by the fitting of a transom stern, which reduced vibration and made the after turrets steadier and also improved their speed and manoeuvrability. The 4-inch ammunition supply arrangements were much improved. The main differences, however, were visual, with their two thin vertical funnels giving them a utility look and their smaller hull made them cramped, especially as complements increased as more equipment was added in the war.

Eight of the first group were completed, three of the modified three turret design and three of a later design with an additional twin 4-inch AA gun in X position. Some later vessels were cancelled, but three survived a period of laying-up to be completed in the 1950s with automatic 6-inch and 3-inch guns.

Two of the first group became war losses, *Fiji* in the Mediterranean during the evacuation of Crete in May 1941, and *Trinidad* in the Arctic supporting convoys to Russia in May 1942.

HMS GAMBIA

HMS Gambia at speed in World War II. She served as a New Zealand ship for the latter part of the war.
(MoD/Crown Copyright)

HMS *Gambia* was a Colony Class cruiser ordered under the 1938 estimates. She was laid down on 24 July 1938 at Swan Hunter and Wigham Richardson, Wallsend, and was launched By Lady Hilbery, wife of Mr Justice Hilbery, on 30 November 1940. She was completed on 21 February 1942, having commissioned on 5 February. She displaced 8,000 tons. Her designed armament comprised four triple 6-inch guns, four twin 4-inch guns, two quadruple 2-pounders and two quadruple machine guns, together with two triple 21-inch torpedo tubes. However, as war experience was gained, her light AA armament was amended to two quadruple 2-pounders, two single 2-pounders and 6 single 20-mm. Her engines developed 73,318-shaft horsepower on trials. She had a range of 2,050 miles at 30 knots, and 3,180 miles at 25 knots.

Gambia worked up at Scapa Flow and in April on her way to join the Eastern Fleet she was part of the escort for convoy WS 18 bound for the Middle East. On 15 May 1942, the depot ship *Hecla* in the convoy struck a mine laid by the German *Doggerbank* (Schiff 53) off Cape Agulhas, South Africa. The *Hecla* had 24 dead and 1,000 wounded. *Gambia* stood by the damaged vessel and escorted her to Simonstown. She then sailed for Mombasa, arriving there on 23rd to join the 4th Cruiser Squadron, Eastern Fleet.

In July she helped escort eleven troopships carrying Australian forces from Ceylon to Australia. In September 1942 she was part of a force that covered transports taking a force to occupy Madagascar (Operation Stream), the naval base on that island at Diego Suarez having been captured four months before. The troops were landed on 10th at Majunga. She remained in the area until October supporting the forces ashore. She then visited Bombay to carry out a docking and repairs before returning to ocean escort duties.

In February 1943 she was part of the ocean escort for Convoy Pamphlet, comprising the *Queen Mary*, *Aquitania*, *Ile de France*, *Nieuw Amsterdam* and the *Queen of Bermuda*, carrying 30,000 troops from Suez to Australia. The convoy arrived at Sydney on 27 February without incident. On 8 May she sailed

HMS Gambia showing the sturdy, compact build of this rather utility class of cruiser. *(T. Ferrers-Walker Collection)*

from Kilindini for the UK via the Cape, paying a courtesy visit to the Gambia on the way.

She refitted at Liverpool from June to September 1943. During this refit her aircraft and catapult were removed. She was then commissioned into the Royal New Zealand Navy on 22 September 1943 in place of the *Achilles*, which was undergoing repairs following action damage. At this time her armament comprised four triple 6-inch, four twin 4-inch, two quadruple 2-pounders and ten twin 20-mm guns together with two triple torpedo tubes.

She worked up with the Home Fleet and in December sailed for Plymouth. In December there were reports of the breakthrough of the first blockade runners, and the *Gambia* and the cruiser *Glasgow* were despatched to the Azores to establish a continuous patrol (Operation Stonewall). Refueling was carried out from a tanker at Horta. In December she was involved in the chase of the German blockade-runner *Alsterufer*, which was set on fire by rockets from Liberator Bombers. The cruisers *Glasgow* and *Enterprise* engaged German destroyers sent out to assist the blockade-runner. During the action three German ships were sunk. *Gambia*, with her sister ship *Mauritius*, searched for survivors until 1 January 1944.

The *Gambia* sailed for the Eastern Fleet at the end of January 1944, arriving at Trincomalee on 19 February. She sailed again 3 days later, escorting the carrier *Illustrious* on Operation Sleuth against suspected blockade-runners in the area south west of the Cocos Islands. She left the force on 28th when relieved by the cruiser *Sussex*, and sailed for Fremantle, visiting that port from 2nd to 8th March prior to returning to Colombo on 17 March.

On 21 March she sailed with the Eastern Fleet from Trincomalee to carry out Operation Diplomat. During this operation the British Fleet met the US carrier *Saratoga* and three American destroyers, returning with them to Trincomalee on 2 April.

On 16 April she sailed with the fleet from Trincomalee for Operation Cockpit. On 18 April

she and the cruiser *Ceylon* reinforced Task Force 70 (the battle-cruiser *Renown* and the aircraft carriers *Illustrious* and *Saratoga* together with their escorts) for an air strike against the oil storage tanks at Sabang, an island off the north east tip of Sumatra. This was the first offensive action by the Eastern Fleet for two years. The force also included the French battleship *Richelieu*, and a Dutch cruiser (*Tromp*) and destroyer, as well as Australian and New Zealand ships. Three out of four oil storage tanks were set on fire, 24 Japanese aircraft destroyed on the ground and another three in the air, and the port installations severely damaged. The round trip from Trincomalee involved 7,000 miles of steaming.

On 8 May she became a wholly New Zealand ship when the RN took over the manning of the cruiser *Leander* instead of the RNZN. In May she took part in Operation Transom, an attack by carrier borne aircraft on the oil refineries and harbour at Sourabaya. Twelve aircraft were destroyed on the ground and one freighter sunk.

In July 1944 she took part in the raid on Sabang (Operation Crimson) when she bombarded enemy shore installations. This was the first time the Eastern Fleet had been able to engage enemy shore targets with gunfire. On 25th, the *Gambia* and her sister *Kenya* engaged shore batteries prior to destroying an ammunition dump, whilst capital ships, other cruisers and destroyers carried out other bombardments of harbour installations.

In October she visited Australia and on 4 November arrived at Wellington, New Zealand. She was refitted there to January 1945, and then sailed from Auckland with the battleship *Howe* (Flagship of the Commander-in-Chief, British Pacific Fleet) and other ships on 13 February, heading for Manus in the Admiralty Islands. The British Pacific Fleet had been formed in November 1944 during a re-organisation of the British Eastern Fleet.

In March 1945 the British Pacific Fleet joined Admiral Nimitz's command, and *Gambia* was one of its strength. The British Force was designated Task Force 57 for Operation Iceberg, the assault on

HMS Gambia post war with enclosed bridge and with X turret replaced by light AA guns. *(Steve Bush Collection)*

Japan. The force's task was to neutralise the group of islands known as Sakishima Gunto to prevent them being used as a staging point for air reinforcement from Formosa to Okinawa. The Fleet sailed from Ulithi at dawn on 23 March and refueled from its own tankers two days later. The next day they started attacks on the enemy territory. During the attacks on Okinawa on 1 April the destroyer *Ulster* was damaged by a near miss from a bomb, and had two killed and one wounded. She was unable to steam, and was towed to Leyte by the *Gambia*, escorted by the destroyer *Quiberon*. She returned to reinforce TF 57 with the cruiser *Uganda* and destroyers by 11 April. During attacks on 13 April the *Gambia* accidentally shot down a Hellcat aircraft. The force continued to attack airfields and installations on north Formosa until May.

In May the force again sailed from Leyte to attack targets in the Sakishima-Gunto group. The battleships *King George V* and *Howe* and cruisers with the force shelled the islands and airfields. The force came under Kamikaze attack. The carriers were damaged but were able to continue operations. During this time *Gambia* and *Swiftsure* shelled the Nobara airstrip, *Gambia* firing 230 rounds of 6-inch. In June the *Gambia* called at Sydney for a short refit, sailing again before the end of the month to rejoin the Fleet.

In July the British force joined with US forces in bombardments of Japan, with air strikes against the Tokyo-Yokohama area. In attacks on 17 and 18 July about 1,500 carrier borne aircraft from the combined British and American Fleets raided Tokyo, and during the night the battleship *King George V* with other British and American units shelled the Hitachi area off Honshu.

In August the forces met typhoons which precluded operations for several days, but then attacks on North Honshu and Hokkaido were carried out. On 9 August the *Gambia* and the cruiser *Newfoundland* with the destroyers *Tenacious*, *Termagent* and *Terpischore*, together with US ships shelled Kamaishi Iron Works on Honshu. *Gambia* fired 404 rounds of 6-inch and the target was

HMS Gambia with deck lined carrying out a steam past at speed. *(Syd Goodman Collection)*

severely damaged. During this bombardment the *Gambia* was aided by spotting from American aircraft. On completion of the action, *Gambia* found she still had her guns loaded, and obtained permission to clear them. She thus had the honour of firing the last gun at the Japanese Home Islands. During the return of this group to the main body they came under enemy air attack, the last air attack on the British Pacific Fleet. During the attack the *Gambia*'s pom-pom on the hangar deck was credited with shooting down one of the enemy aircraft.

On 12 August she was part of the small token force of a battleship, two cruisers, a fleet carrier and destroyers led by the battleship *King George V* that did not return to Australia but remained with the American Fleet. On 15th, the combined fleet was attacked by an aircraft. *Gambia* shot it down and was damaged by parts of the aircraft, which fell on her after superstructure. The small British Force was present in Tokyo Bay on 2 September 1945 for the formal surrender of the Japanese by the Japanese Foreign Minister, Mamoru Shigemitsu, and the Chief of the Army General Staff, General Yoshijiro Umezu, onboard the US battleship *Missouri*.

The *Gambia*'s war service had been very busy, at one period she steamed 35,000 miles in 3.5 months. In September she helped in the evacuation of Prisoners of War from Japan. She remained with the Royal New Zealand Navy and returned to New Zealand waters, being at Auckland from October to January. In January 1946 she reduced to one-fifth complement, and shortly afterwards took on a peacetime complement and sailed for the UK, arriving at Sydney 23 February and the UK on 27 March.

On return to Devonport in March 1946 she underwent a refit. The opportunity was taken to remove her X-turret and modernise her light anti-aircraft armament. Most of her class had had their X turrets removed during the war to compensate for the extra radar and other equipment that had been added. She was then armed with three triple 6-inch, four twin 4-inch, five twin and two single 40-mm and two sets of torpedo tubes. She reverted to Royal Naval service on 1 July 1946 and her refit completed in September. She then rejoined the Far East Station, arriving at Singapore 23 November 1946, later becoming the flagship of the 5th Cruiser Squadron. She left Singapore early in December 1947, calling at Aden to assist in preserving order there that month. She arrived at Devonport in January 1948 She then went into reserve 1948-49

She then re-commissioned, leaving Plymouth on 30 March 1950 to relieve the cruiser *Newcastle* on the Mediterranean Station. On 16 October 1950 she damaged her bow in a collision with the cruiser *Phoebe* during a mail transfer. *Phoebe* s stern was dented. In March 1951 she sailed for the Red Sea when there was unrest in the Persian Oilfields, returning in May 1951. In October she visited Port Said owing to unrest in Egypt, being relieved there by the cruiser *Liverpool* in November, She returned to Port Said in January 1952 when the Suez Canal workers went on strike. She was then lent to the East Indies Fleet temporarily until May, when she rejoined the 1st Cruiser Squadron in the Mediterranean. She returned to Devonport at the end July 1951 to pay off and refit, returning to the 1st Cruiser Squadron at Malta on 15 January 1953. In June 1953 she returned to the UK for the Coronation Review of the Fleet at Spithead, where she carried the flag of Rear Admiral F C W Norris DSO, Flag Officer Flotillas Mediterranean Fleet. In August she sailed from Malta for the Greek Island of Zanta with some Marines of 45 Commando to provide relief after an earthquake had struck the island.

In May 1954 she, with other units of the Mediterranean Fleet, escorted the Royal Yacht *Britannia* travelling from Tobruk to Malta at the end of a World Tour by H.M. The Queen and the Duke of Edinburgh. In October 1954 she embarked His Imperial Majesty the Emperor of Ethiopia (Emperor Haille Selassie) and sailed to England escorted by the destroyers *Charity* and *Constance* for a State visit. They arrived at Portsmouth on 14 October. She sailed the next day for Devonport to pay off.

She then underwent repairs at Devonport to March 1955, prior to sailing for the East Indies. She wore the Flag of the Commander-in-Chief East Indies from 1955 until 31 January 1956, when she left Trincomalee to pay off, the first cruiser to com-

plete a General Service Commission in the East Indies. She paid a four-day visit to Massawa before returning home to refit. This not only recalled her duty on the State visit of 1954, but also His Imperial Highness Prince Alexander Desta was serving onboard as a Midshipman at that time. She arrived at Plymouth Sound on 1 March 1956.

Refitted at Rosyth from March 1956 to April 1957, where she was modernised with an enclosed bridge and given radar control for her secondary armament. Her tertiary armament was updated and then comprised a uniform seven twin 40-mm guns. Her torpedo tubes were landed. She then commissioned on 1 May 1957 and joined the Home Fleet at Invergordon for a Review by HM The Queen before proceeding to the East Indies in October 1957 as the last Flagship. She visited Aden in April 1958 because of unrest there. The East Indies Station was abolished on 7 September 1958, and the *Gambia* then returned to Chatham in September, and then onto Rosyth for refit prior to re-commissioning.

She recommissioned on 4 November 1958 based on Rosyth for a General service Commission Home/Mediterranean. In 1959 she damaged her starboard propeller at Copenhagen. After her spell in the Mediterranean she sailed East of Suez to relieve the *Ceylon*, which was being sold to Peru. In February 1960 she was at Male for the signing of an agreement for the use of Gan Island as a base for 30 years. She then took part in 'Jet 60', the tenth and largest in the series of Commonwealth Naval Exercises in South East Asia. The exercise was followed by a fleet regatta in Trincomalee, at which *Gambia* swept the board. She was then diverted to assist Mauritius after a cyclone had hit the island. There were 1,700 casualties and 100,000 buildings had been destroyed or severely damaged. 70,000 of the 600,000 population were in refugee camps and it was estimated that 60 percent of the sugar crop had been lost. After providing much assistance to the island, she visited Singapore and Hong Kong. She then returned to the UK via South Africa and calling in at Bathurst, in the Gambia. Because the new cruiser *Lion* was having engine problems, the *Gambia* remained in commission and headed for Exercise FAIRWIND IV in the Arctic. On 12 October 1960 she was in collision with the oiler *Wave Chief* whilst refueling, but had little damage. She finally paid off at Portsmouth on 7 December 1960 and was then placed in reserve.

She was sold to Thos. Ward on 15 November 1968 and was towed from Portsmouth on 2 December and arrived at Inverkeithing to be broken up on 6 December 1968.

She had gained the following battle honours for her name:

Sabang 1944 (25 July); Okinawa 1945 (26 March – 25 May) and Japan 1945

HMS BERMUDA

HMS Bermuda leaving Grand Harbour Malta, post war, with modernised bridge and new AA fire control systems. *(Syd Goodman Collection)*

HMS *Bermuda* was the last of the first eight Colony Class cruisers. She was ordered under the 1939 estimates, and was laid down on 30 November 1939 by John Brown on Clydebank. She was launched on 11 September 1941 by Viscountess Weir and was completed on 21 August 1942, by which time two of her sisters, *Fiji* and *Trinidad* had been lost in action. Ten Oerlikons were mounted instead of the originally planned multiple machine guns. She was also fitted to carry two aircraft, with hangars abreast the forefunnel and a catapult mounted athwartships between the funnels. Other members of the class which were delayed in building were completed to a modified design with reduced main armament but with better close range protection and radar, benefiting from war experience.

In common with her class, her four boilers powered four sets of turbines, giving her 72,500-shaft horsepower, which could be increased to 80,000-shaft horsepower under overload conditions in war. Her designed speed was 31.5 knots, increased to 32.25 under overload conditions. She had a range of 2.050 miles at 30 knots; 4,900 miles at 20 knots; and 9,800 miles at 12 knots.

Bermuda first commissioned on 5 August 1942, and arrived at Scapa Flow to work up on 26 August. After trials and work up, she sailed on 26 October with the battleships *Duke of York* and *Nelson*, battle-cruiser *Renown* and aircraft carriers *Victorious* and *Formidable* to take part in Operation Torch, the landings in North Africa. She joined Force H under Admiral Syfret on 3 November, sailing with that force into the Mediterranean on 6 November to provide distant cover for the landings at Oran and Algiers. On 8 November, when the landings took place, *Bermuda* was detached to bombard Fort Matafon and Fort D'Estrees. She then joined the cruiser *Sheffield* and that evening the ships came under heavy air attack by 34 torpedo carrying

HE.111s, but she escaped without damage despite the enemy dropping 23 torpedoes and two sticks of bombs. She claimed one 'probable' and one 'damaged' aircraft.

On 14 November *Bermuda* left Force H and then became the Flagship of Rear Admiral C.H. J. Harcourt CBE leading Force Q, a striking force of cruisers and destroyers operating against enemy shipping carrying troops or stores between North Africa and Italy.

She then rejoined the Home Fleet, and was part of the supporting forces for Russian Convoys, starting with JW 51B, which was attacked by the heavy cruiser *Admiral Hipper* and pocket battleship *Lutzow*, which were accompanied by destroyers. The destroyers which were the convoy's close escort held off the superior German until the close cruiser support force was able to close and put the enemy to flight. The escort lost the destroyer *Achates* and minesweeper *Bramble*, whilst the German destroyer *Freidrich Eckholdt* was sunk. All 14 merchant ships of the convoy arrived safely. *Bermuda* was also part of the additional cover for Russian Convoy RA 51 from Murmansk. The whole convoy arrived safely at Loch Ewe on 11 January 1943. In January she, with the *Kent* and *Glasgow*, covered Russian convoy JW 52, and went right through to the Kola Inlet. During this operation she was attacked by *U-625*, but the torpedoes missed her. She returned with the homeward convoy RA 52, which lost one of its eleven ships to U-boat attack.

In March she patrolled the Iceland-Faroes passage with the Canadian destroyer *Athabaskan*, but sighted no German ships. In May she relieved the cruiser *Scylla* which was escorting the RMS *Queen Mary* carrying the Prime Minister (Winston Churchill), to the Trident Conference. At the end of that month, she, with the cruiser *Cumberland*, and destroyers *Athabaskan* and *Eclipse* sailed from Greenock to relieve Spitzbergen. They encountered heavy weather enroute, taking shelter in Akureyri and arriving at Spitzbergen on 10 June, returning to Scapa Flow on 14th.

At the end of June she joined the Plymouth Command, and with *Glasgow* provided cover from surface attack for Escort Group B5 and 2nd Support Group hunting U-boats in the Bay of Biscay. During her first year in commission she had steamed 54,456 miles and spent 189 days at sea. In August she covered convoys OS 53 and SL 134 and then spent till October covering Escort Groups in the Bay of Biscay. During these operations she directed long range fighters against enemy aircraft operating against the escort groups and also against enemy reconnaissance aircraft. During September she had six extra 20-mm guns added to enhance her AA armament.

In November and December she, with the cruisers *Kent* and *Jamaica*, provided the covering cruiser force for the Russian convoys, which were being resumed after an eight-month interval. The convoys would have been too vulnerable to be run in the long, light summer months with enemy airfields, and ports so close to the convoy routes. The cruisers operated in the Barents Sea, covering convoys JW 54A and JW 54B to Russia and the homeward bound RA 54A and RA 54B. From 17-22 December she was on the Clyde having heavy weather damage repaired.

In February she sailed from Scapa Flow as Flagship of the First Cruiser Squadron escorting the carrier *Furious* whose aircraft were to attack enemy shipping in the Norwegian Leads. However the operation was firstly postponed and finally cancelled. In March she was part of the Home Fleet forces deployed to cover a breakout by the German battleship *Tirpitz* from Alten Fjord.

In April and early May 1944 she underwent a refit on the Tyne, when her aircraft were removed, and eight twin and 12 single 20-mm guns were added. On completion she sailed with the Home Fleet to cover air strikes against the *Tirpitz*, but the force was sighted by enemy aircraft and returned to Scapa Flow. The next month she was employed on diversions off the South Coast of Norway, simulating an invasion to distract the enemy from the preparations for the actual invasion in the Normandy region.

Bermuda arrived on the Clyde on 30 June for a refit, which lasted until March 1945. During this refit her X turret was removed to compensate for the extra top weight of radar and light guns being fitted. In April 1945 her armament comprised nine

6-inch, four twin 4-inch, five quadruple 2-pouners, four single 2-pounders, four twin 20-mm and four single 20-mm guns, together with two sets of torpedo tubes.

On completion of the refit she worked up in the Mediterranean, leaving Malta on 6 June for Ceylon, joining the British Pacific Fleet at Sydney on 7 July 1945. She then continued her working up in Jervis Bay, and in August had her armament upgraded. She then carried nine 6-inch, four twin 4-inch, five quadruple 2-pounders, four single 2-pounders, four single 40-mm, two 40-mm Boffins, two twin and two single 20-mm guns and two sets of torpedo tubes.

On VJ Day, 15 August, she sailed from Sydney for Formosa to be part of a British Task group, comprising the carrier *Colossus*, cruiser *Argonaut* and the destroyers *Tumult*, *Tyrian*, *Tuscan* and *Quiberon*, which was formed to occupy the Shanghai area with a US Task Force 95. She called at Manus and Leyte, and from 6-12 September she was employed evacuating Prisoners of War from a hospital at Tahikon to the Hospital Ship *Manganni*. She then sailed for Tsingtao and from 20 September to 8 October helped evacuate internees from Weittsien. She arrived in Shanghai on 11 October, helping to evacuate internees there before heading for Hong Kong to carry out police duties and anti-looting patrols. In January 1946 she sailed for Sydney, and attended the Royal Hobart Regatta, flying the personal standard of the Duke of Gloucester from Hobart on 14 February to Sydney on 16 February. She then returned to Hong Kong for a refit lasting from 11 March to 29 April.

In June she sailed for Shanghai to take part in the Victory Day celebrations, which included the re-hoisting of the flag which had flown over the Consulate until the Japanese had arrived. She then visited Tsingtao, Kure, Chemulpho and Fuknoko, followed by Nagasaki and Yokohama in July. She then called at Hong Kong before heading south to Sydney. In September she called at Melbourne and Adelaide, and in October went north again to visit Hong Kong, Yokohama and Kure.

After a spell of three months in Hong Kong, broken only by a period of four days at sea in December standing by the destroyer *Constance* which was towing the Swedish freighter *Rosebank*, she visited Yokohama, Kure and Shanghai in March and April 1947. On 10 May she sailed from Hong Kong, heading for the UK via the Suez Canal, arriving at Plymouth on 19 June and reducing to reserve at Sheerness from 27 July.

She was refitted at Chatham Dockyard from October 1947 to 12 May 1948, and was then towed to Devonport. On 2 October 1950 she was re-commissioned at Devonport, sailing for Malta on 23 October. She worked up at Malta and then sailed for the South Atlantic to relieve the *Nigeria*, arriving at Simonstown on 18 December, where she became the Flagship of Vice Admiral Sir Herbert Packer KCB.

In February 1951 the carried out brief visits to Port Elizabeth, East London and Durban, and in June carried out a long cruise along the East Coast, returning to Simonstown in August. In September she took part in a regatta in Saldanha Bay and in October, she cruised up the West Coast of Africa to Dakar, calling at Ascension Island and St. Helena before returning to Capetown for Christmas. In June 1952 she carried out an East Coast Cruise and visited Durban, East London and Port Elizabeth. In October she carried out another West Coast cruise.

On 26 January 1953 she sailed north to recommission at Devonport in March prior to joining the Mediterranean Station in an exchange with the cruiser *Euryalus*. She arrived at Malta on 30 March to join the First Cruiser Squadron. From May to October she cruised in the Eastern Mediterranean and then refitted at Malta from August to October. She worked up on passage to Pt. Said before returning to Malta.

In May 1954 she was part of the escort to the Royal Yacht from Tobruk, at the end of HM Queen's World Tour. *Bermuda* spent June and July in the Eastern Mediterranean and Adriatic. On 23 October she sailed from Malta for Plymouth, where she transferred to the Home Fleet on 27 November 1954, becoming the Flagship of Flag Officer Flotillas, Home Fleet.

She took part in the Home Fleet Spring Cruise to Gibraltar and Malta, and the summer cruise to the north including calls at Kiel, Aarhus and Helingsborg. She then paid off, being relieved by the *Kenya*. She was towed to the Tyne in November for an extensive refit at Palmers, Hebburn, which lasted until 24 October 1957. During this period she was modernised, her bridge being enclosed, her secondary armament fitted with radar control and her tertiary armament became seven twin 40-mm guns. Towards the end of her career three of these twin 40-mm guns were landed.

On 24 October 1957 she commissioned for a General Service Commission on the Home and Mediterranean Stations. She worked up in the autumn, arriving at Plymouth on 10 December to join the Home Fleet. In the spring 1958 she visited the West Indies, including a call at Bermuda. In April she joined the First Cruiser Squadron in the Mediterranean. In that June she took a Commando with 4 helicopters from Malta to Cyprus. She also visited ports in the Eastern Mediterranean and Aegean before returning to Malta in December. In the spring of 1959 she visited La Spezia, Benghazi, Cyprus, Beirut and Venice, and then called at Malta prior to rejoining the Home Fleet in April. She then took part in the Home Fleet visits in June and July, which included the Faroes, Greenland and Bermuda. The visit to Bermuda was to mark the 350th anniversary of the island. In June she had become the Flagship of Flag Officer Flotillas Home Fleet again.

In the autumn she called at Hamburg and cruised around the British coast. In January 1960 she sailed for Gibraltar for a short refit which lasted until April. She then returned to the Home Fleet and visited Helsinki for the Trade Fair held there between 20-26 May. After visits to Norway and Denmark she was Cowes Guardship and in August visited Lisbon for the celebrations of the fifth centenary of the death of Prince Henry the Navigator. In September she was at Lagos for the independence celebrations, calling at Freetown and Madeira before returning to Gibraltar on 25 October, where she transferred to the Mediterranean Fleet.

She visited Oran and Toulon before arriving at Malta on 26 November 1960. In February she carried out more visits in the Mediterranean, including Leghorn, Suda and Athens, before returning to Malta, and in March she rejoined the Home Fleet at Gibraltar. She called at Brest on her way to Plymouth, and then visited Freetown and Las Palmas before joining the Home Fleet Summer cruise, when she visited Denmark. Her autumn cruise was spent around the British Isles, with visits to Amsterdam and Antwerp. In February 1962 she again called at Bermuda, spending a month there exercising and calling at Gibraltar on the return passage, arriving at Portsmouth on 6 April. She sailed again the next month for Stockholm, returning to Portsmouth on 2 June. She paid off into reserve on 30 July 1962.

After a spell in unmaintained reserve she was towed away on 23 August 1965 to be broken up at Briton Ferry, arriving there on 26 August. Her silk battle ensign was taken to Bermuda by HMS *Whirlwind* to be laid up in the Cathedral of the Most Holy Trinity there.

She had gained the following battle honours for her name:

North Africa 1942; Atlantic 1943 and Arctic 1943.

HMS NEWFOUNDLAND

HMS Newfoundland a later Colony class built without X turret. *(Author's Collection)*

The *Newfoundland* was one of three Colony Class cruisers (*Ceylon*, *Uganda* and *Newfoundland*) whose building was suspended in 1940. These three ships were later completed to a modified design, allowing for wartime developments and incorporating new equipment (radar) and experience. Their 'X' triple 6-inch turret was never mounted, reducing topweight and permitting more anti-aircraft guns to be fitted. Originally it had been planed to mount an extra twin 4-inch gun in X position, but eventually a quadruple 2-pounder was fitted instead, giving better close range protection. An extra AA control position was fitted and the forward 2-pounders re-sited, improving the ship's AA capability. They also had a larger, square fronted bridge structure.

Newfoundland was laid down on 9 November 1939 by Swan Hunter and Wigham Richardson Ltd., Wallsend-on-Tyne and launched on 19 December 1941. She was commissioned on 31 December 1942, and completed 20 January 1943. She had a designed standard displacement of 8,000 tons, and displaced 11,010 tons when fully loaded. Her engines developed 72,500-shaft horsepower giving her a top speed of 31.5 knots and a maximum sea speed of 30.25 knots. On trials she developed 73,224-shaft horsepower. She was 555.5 ft long and had a beam of 62 ft. She had a range of 9,800 miles at 12 knots and 2,300 miles at maximum continuous sea speed. She was armed with three triple 6-inch guns, four twin 4-inch, three quadruple 2-pounders, six twin and four single 20-mm guns. She also carried six torpedo tubes in two triple mountings.

On completion she joined the 10th Cruiser Squadron of the Home Fleet for working up prior to deploying. On 17 March she and two destroyers were sent to Plymouth to intercept blockade-runners, but did not achieve any success. She was originally allocated to the West African Station, but before sailing south she was re-allocated to the 12th Cruiser Squadron of the Mediterranean Fleet. In April she arrived at Algiers and the next month carried Admiral Cunningham from Algiers to Malta. On 5 June 1943 she and the destroyers *Paladin* and *Troubridge* bombarded Pantellaria. Three days later she, with the cruisers *Euryalus*, *Aurora, Orion*, and *Penelope* and the destroyers *Jervis*, *Laforey*, *Lookout*, *Loyal*, *Nubian Tartar*, *Troubridge* and *Whaddon*, accompanied by *MTBs 73, 77* and *84*, shelled the island again. On the night 10/11 June, the island was bombarded again. The next morning it surrendered to a force which included the *Aurora* with the Allied Commander-in-Chief, General Eisenhower embarked, and the *Newfoundland* flying the flag of Rear Admiral Harcourt. The next day the *Newfoundland*, accompanied by the *Aurora*, *Orion* and *Penelope* and six destroyers bombarded the island of Lampedusa, which led to that island's surrender. On 13 June she and the destroyer *Nubian* accepted the surrender of the island of Linosa.

On 10 July the Allies invaded Sicily (Operation Husky). The *Newfoundland* together with the cruisers *Uganda*, *Mauritius* and the *Orion* and six destroyers sailed from Alexandria to join up with other cruisers and destroyers to form the support force for the Eastern area. On 11th she with the destroyers *Brissenden* and *Blankney* shelled Pozallo in Sicily. On 19 July she and the destroyers *Laforey* and *Lookout* and the Dutch gunboat *Flores* bombarded gun positions at Catania. Two days later she and the monitor *Erebus* repeated the bombardment, and with the destroyers *Lookout* and *Loyal* she bombarded Lentini and Carlentini. Further bombardments in support of the Army ashore took place in the following days, including 17 targets on 19th which including 9 batteries, all on calls for fire by the Army. On 22nd she came under fire from shore batteries but received no hits.

At 1300 23 July 1943 she sailed from Augusta to Malta, wearing the flag of Rear Admiral Force K (15th Cruiser Squadron). She was accompanied by the cruiser *Mauritius* and the destroyers *Laforey*, *Lookout* and *Loyal*. At 1341 the *Newfoundland*, which was zigzagging at 25 knots, was hit right aft by a torpedo, which took off her rudder. The destroyers carried out an immediate search for the enemy submarine, but *Laforey* passed over the attacking U-boat (*U-407*) twice without detecting her. *Laforey* later made contact and attacked with depth charges, forcing the U-boat to go deep to 210 metres. However, after a while *Laforey* decided her contact was a 'non-sub' and moved away to carry out further searches, allowing *U-407* to slip away. Meanwhile, *Laforey* and the destroyer *Eclipse*, which, with other destroyers had joined the search, detected the Italian submarine *Ascianghi*, which fired torpedoes at them. The *Ascianghi* was forced to the surface by depth charges and sunk by gunfire. The Italian survivors, comprising the Commanding Officer, 4 officers and 23 men, reported that they had torpedoed the *Newfoundland*. However, it was later discovered that their torpedoes had missed. Because of the Italians' report, the presence of a second submarine was not considered and the search ended.

Meanwhile the *Newfoundland* was able to continue at 26 knots, steering by main engines, using revolutions for 28 knots on the port engines and for 18-21 knots on the starboard engines. She had lost one seaman, blown overboard by the explosion, which had forced her stern structure for 24 ft below the upper deck upwards and outwards. She had six other men slightly wounded. She reduced speed to 22 knots and at 1730 reached Malta, where emergency repairs were carried out.

She sailed across the Atlantic on two shafts and without a rudder, steering by main engines and underwent repairs at Boston from 22 August 1943 to 19 April 1944. She then sailed for the Clyde, where she underwent further repairs until November 1944. During this period she was fitted with two extra twin and two extra single 20-mm guns. The cruisers *Scylla* and *Charybdis* replaced her and the *Cleopatra*, which had been torpedoed by a submarine seven days previously, in the Mediterranean Fleet. In December 1944 she joined the Home Fleet, and was allocated to the British

Pacific Fleet (BPF) later that month. In January she was on passage to the Far East when a torpedo air vessel exploded onboard. She underwent repairs at Alexandria, which took to March 1945. During this period a quadruple 40mm gun was added forward of her mainmast, and her 20-mm armament reduced to six twin and two single mountings. Experience in the Pacific had shown that a more powerful gun than the 20-mm was required to stop the determined attacks by Kamikaze aircraft.

On 9-10 May 1945 she, with the Australian cruiser *Hobart* and destroyers *Warramunga* and *Arunta*, together with the sloop *Swan* and minesweeping corvette *Colac*, arrived off Wewak in New Guinea for Operation Deluge. They provided gunfire support for the 6th Australian Division, which was advancing along the coast from Aitape in New Guinea. The troops were landed on 14th and captured the airfield, with the ships providing further support, The Wewak peninsula was captured and by 23 May the pockets of Japanese resistance were finally overcome.

In late May *Newfoundland* visited Auckland for docking before joining the British Pacific Fleet at Manus. On 12 June she sailed from Manus with the carriers *Implacable* and *Ruler*, the cruisers *Swiftsure*, *Uganda* and *Achilles* and destroyers *Troubridge*, *Tenacious*, *Termagent*, *Terpischore* and *Teazer* to carry out Operation Inmate, a strike by *Implacable*'s aircraft on Truk Atoll in the Caroline Islands. Overnight 14/15 she and *Troubridge* shelled Uman firing 30 rounds of 6-inch per gun, whilst other ships carried out bombardments at Moen and Dublon. After further air strikes on 15th the force returned to Manus on 17th.

On 28 June she with the *King George V*, *Formidable*, *Uganda Euryalus* and 8 destroyers left Sydney for Manus, arriving on 4 July, They sailed with other ships 2 days later to refuel and then joined with US Naval forces which included the battleships *Iowa*, *Missouri* and *Wisconsin*. The British force included the battleships *King George V* and carriers *Formidable*, *Victorious* and *Implacable*. The combined force carried out an air raid in the Tokyo-Yokohama area on 17-18 July. On 17th to 18th the *King George V*, *Newfoundland*,

HMS Newfoundland after her 1950-52 modernisation, with lattice masts and modern AA directors each side of her bridge. *(Syd Goodman Collection)*

Black Prince, *Quiberon* and *Quality* bombarded Hitachi Engineering Works 50 miles north of Tokyo.

During the subsequent refueling *Newfoundland* took fuel from US tankers owing to shortages in BPF tankers. *Newfoundland* also acted as a relay ship for communications between the British and US Fleets when the distances apart became too large for direct voice-radio exchanges. On 9 August she was part of a combined US/British force that shelled Kamaishi iron works on Honshu Island. The *Newfoundland* and the New Zealand cruiser *Gambia* were helped in this bombardment by American spotting aircraft. During that operation she and the *Gambia*, fired 329 6-inch shells.

On 12 August 1945 she was with the part of the BPF that remained in the area with the US Fleet when the main body of the BPF sailed for Sydney. The remaining ships, forming TF 38.5, comprised the battleship *King George V*, the carrier *Indefatigable*, cruisers *Newfoundland* and *Gambia* (RNZN), destroyers *Barfleur*, *Troubridge*, *Teazer*, *Tenacious*, *Termagent*, *Wakeful*, *Wrangler*, *Napier* (RAN) and *Nizam* (RAN). She entered Japanese waters on 23 August and arrived at Tokyo Bay on 31 August. She was present there on 2 September 1945 for the formal surrender of the Japanese by the Japanese Foreign Minister, Mamoru Shigemitsu, and the Chief of the Army General Staff, General Yoshijiro Umezu, onboard the US battleship *Missouri*.

On 3 September she evacuated allied Prisoners of War to hospital ships and escort carriers off Tokyo. During her war service she had steamed 122,490 miles. In October she visited Wellington, New Zealand, and the next month she refitted at Sydney. In April and May she visited Shanghai and the Yangtse. In June 1946 she refitted at Hong Kong, and then visited Japanese waters. She returned to the UK in November 1946, arriving at Plymouth in December, where she refitted before reducing to reserve in June 1947. She was then used as an accommodation and training ship for the Stokers' Training Establishment (HMS *Raleigh*) at Devonport until July 1950.

She was modernised at Devonport Dockyard in 1950-52. She was fitted with two lattice masts, new secondary armament control system with modern destroyer type (Mk. 6) directors port and starboard and a tertiary armament of five twin and two single 40-mm guns. She was also given a new (not enclosed) bridge. Her torpedo tubes were removed.

She re-commissioned in November 1952, and joined the East Indies Station at the end of February 1953 and in April took part in Exercise Jet in the Indian Ocean. In April 1954 she, wearing the Flag of the Commander-in-Chief East Indies, escorted H.M. The Queen, then in SS *Gothic* as she was returning from her tour in Australia, from the Cocos Islands. During a stay in Colombo HM The Queen visited the ship. *Newfoundland* and accompanied Her Majesty to Aden, arriving on 27 April.

In May 1954 she was lent to the Far East Station for 4 months, bombarding Malayan terrorists 25 miles north of Penang in June. She embarked Flag Officer Second–in-Command of the Far East Station to Japanese waters. She returned to the East Indies after a docking in Singapore in the September. In that December she embarked rulers of the 6 Trucial States for a demonstration exercise in the Persian Gulf, accompanied by the frigate *Loch Insh*.

She returned to Portsmouth in February 1955, sailing the next month for the East Indies, delivering earthquake relief stores to Argostoli in April whilst on passage. She underwent refit at Singapore from May to July 1955 then visited ports in Korea and Japan. In February 1956 she took part in exercise Firmlink in the South China Seas and in April exercised with the carriers *Albion* and *Centaur* in the Commonwealth Exercise Monsoon. In June 1956 she was present at the celebration of Foundation Day Fremantle, Western Australia. The next month she re-commissioned by air at Singapore. On 23 August she bombarded terrorist positions in the Kota Tinga district, firing 101 rounds of 6-inch.

When the Suez crisis developed she was sailed for Aden, arriving on 28 September 1956 to relieve *Kenya*. She was joined by the frigates *Modeste* and *Crane* who had come from Exercise Jet in the Indian Ocean. They formed TF 324 and sailed for the Red Sea on Operation Toreador. On 29 October they made for the Gulf of Suez, joined by the

HMS Newfoundland displaying her modernised bridge, AA directors and close range armament.
(Ken Kelly Collection)

destroyer *Diana* and the tanker RFA *Wave Sovereign*, checking the shipping in the Strait of Gubal. At 0100 on 1 November, *Newfoundland* sighted a darkened ship with just navigation lights. She closed and illuminated her at 7 cables distance. It proved to be the Egyptian frigate *Domiat*, which she ordered to stop. The Egyptian ship then started to train her guns on the *Newfoundland*, who opened fire at 0125 at 1400 yards range, using 6-inch, 4-inch and Bofors guns. At 0128 the frigate turned towards *Newfoundland* as though to ram her. *Newfoundland* turned away, having fired 9 broadsides. Meanwhile the *Diana* had engaged the frigate with her two forward 4.5-inch turrets. The Egyptian ship capsized and sank at 0135. *Diana* picked up survivors, who reported *Domiat* had been carrying mines. During the action *Newfoundland* had been hit by two 4-inch shells. One man (an 'Unofficial Chinese') was killed, one seriously wounded and four others were slightly wounded. *Diana* rescued 55 survivors from the *Domiat*, one of whom died and 13 of whom were wounded. *Newfoundland*'s whaler rescued two others. The *Domiat* had been the British River class frigate *Nith*, transferred to Egypt in 1948. The next evening *Newfoundland* 's radar detected four fast moving contacts closing the ship, which could have been a possible attack by MTBs. She opened fire with 6-inch and 4-inch and the contacts withdrew out of range.

On completion of the Suez operation

Newfoundland returned to Singapore, visiting Hong Kong and Australia in 1957. In January 1958 she re-commissioned at Singapore. In May 1958 she took part in the SEATO Exercise Oceanlink north of Singapore. In August she relieved the cruiser *Gambia* in the Persian Gulf after a coup d'etat in Iraq. She returned to Singapore by the end of September. In April 1959 she sailed for the UK via the Seychelles and South Africa and Freetown. On 24 June 1959 she arrived at Portsmouth and paid off, reducing to reserve in October.

She was sold to Peru on 2 November 1959, being transferred on 30 December as the *Almirante Grau*, and sailing for Peru on 8 January 1960. On 15 May 1973 she was renamed *Capitan Quinones* and was paid off in 1979 to become an alongside training hulk and deleted from their naval lists.

She had gained the following battle honours for her name:

Mediterranean 1943, Sicily 1943 (10 July - 17 August) and Japan 1945.

HMS CEYLON

HMS Ceylon showing her three turret design and the extra high mounting for her gunnery director on the bridge. *(MoD/Crown Copyright)*

The *Ceylon* was ordered in 1938, and was laid down on 27 April 1939 by Alexander Stephen and Sons Ltd. Govan, Clydeside. She was launched on 30 July 1942 and completed on 13 July 1943, having commissioned on 29 June 1943. Her standard displacement was 8,781 tons, and her full load displacement was 11,110 tons. Although ordered and laid down before the last vessel of the earlier Colony Class (*Bermuda*), she was markedly different in that she was not fitted with a 6-inch turret in X position. War experience had shown the need for an increase in close range weapons. Originally her design had been altered so that a twin 4-inch was to be mounted in X position, but this was again altered, and a quadruple 2-pounder mounted instead. The 2-pounders on the hangar deck were mounted further forward and an extra High Angle Fire Control Position was fitted, improving her AA capability considerably. Extra radar was also added. She had a secondary armament of four twin 4-inch guns, and also had three quadruple 2-pounders and 16 Oerlikons. She also carried two triple 21-inch torpedo tubes. She had a designed shaft horsepower of 72,500, to propel her four shafts, giving her a speed of 31.5 knots. She achieved 73,059-shaft-horsepower on trials. She had a range of 10,000 miles at 10 knots, and 2,300 miles at maximum continuous sea speed (30.25 knots). She could be distinguished from the earlier ships of the Colony class by her larger, square fronted bridge structure, with the 6-inch director mounted higher on top to provide clearance for a surface radar mounted forward of it. Her forward AA directors were mounted further aft, abreast the foremast.

On completion in June 1943, she joined the 10th Cruiser Squadron of the Home Fleet to work up at Scapa Flow and Plymouth. She sailed to join the Eastern Fleet on 30 October, but when she reached Gibraltar on 6 November, she was diverted to relieve the cruiser *Glasgow* on the Bay of Biscay patrol. She finally reached Bombay on 27 November 1943.

In March 1944 she was with the Eastern Fleet when it sailed from Trincomalee to meet US Naval vessels which were to operate with the Eastern Fleet (Operation Diplomat). On 2 April the com-

bined fleet arrived at Trincomalee. On 16 April the Eastern Fleet, including *Ceylon* sailed from Trincomalee on Operation Cockpit, a raid by carrier borne aircraft on Sabang. The British Fleet was accompanied by US warships which included the aircraft carrier *Saratoga*. On 19 April aircraft were flown off for the attack on Sabang and surrounding airfields. Thirty tons of bombs were dropped, two merchant ships were hit and 24 bombers destroyed on the ground. Oil tanks and installations were also hit. The Fleet returned to Trincomalee, with Admiral Somerville reporting that he had caught the Japanese commandant 'with his Kimino up'.

On 6 May the combined fleets sailed again from Trincomalee, this time on Operation Transom, a carrier raid on Soerabaya. The *Ceylon* was part of the escort to the *Illustrious* and *Saratoga*. The Fleet replenished in Exmouth Bay on 15 May and attacks were mounted on 17 May, hitting the harbour installations and oil refineries. Twelve aircraft were destroyed on the ground for the loss of one allied aircraft, but the damage achieved was initially overestimated. Only one freighter was sunk. The next day the *Saratoga* left the British Fleet, and as she steamed thorough the British Fleet with her escorting destroyers the British sailors manned ship to cheer them. The Fleet returned to Ceylon on 27 May.

On 19 June *Ceylon* was with the Eastern Fleet on Operation Pedal, a successful carrier raid on Port Blair in the Andaman Islands. On 22nd of the next month the British Eastern Fleet sailed again, this time on Operation Crimson, a carrier raid and bombardment of Sabang, Sumatra. The capital ships accompanied by the cruisers carried out the first bombardment of enemy held territory since the formation of the Eastern Fleet, whilst destroyers entered the harbour to fire torpedoes. In all the British Eastern Fleet fired 294 rounds of 15-inch, 134 of 8-inch, 324 of 6-inch together with over 600 rounds of smaller calibre. The operation was a complete success.

In November 1944 *Ceylon* was allocated to the British Pacific Fleet when it was formed in Ceylon. In January 1945 she took part in Operation Lentil, when the carriers *Victorious*, *Indomitable* and *Indefatigable* carried out a strike against the oil refineries of Pankalan Brandan (Sumatra). In mid January she sailed on Operation Meridian, when the newly formed British Pacific sailed for Sydney. *Ceylon* remained behind to collect mail and radar spares before joining the Fleet the next day. She was detached as escort to the tankers during the refueling of the Task Force. The main fleet then carried out an air strike on the oil refinery at Pladjoe, north of Palembang on 24th. This was to be first of the two largest strikes undertaken by the Fleet Air Arm during World War II. In the first strike 105 aircraft were flown off against the target. Seven were lost to enemy action and another 25 lost in crash landings. On the 26th the Fleet refueled again and then closed the coast to carry out another strike, this time against the oil refinery at Soengei Gerong. 30 Japanese aircraft were shot down and 38 destroyed on the ground for the loss of 16 British aircraft. The Fleet came under attack by Japanese aircraft, but aircraft and gunfire drove off the attackers. The Fleet refueled again on 30 January, and then the tankers, accompanied by *Ceylon*, sailed for Trincomalee, where *Ceylon* joined the East Indies Fleet, becoming part of the 5th Cruiser Squadron.

In April 1945 she was part of Operation Bishop, providing cover for Operation Dracula, the Rangoon landings. The force shelled Car Nicobar and Port Blair on 30 April, 1 May and 2 May. On 3 May *Ceylon* accompanied the French battleship *Richelieu* and cruiser *Cumberland* and the aircraft carriers to make an armed reconnaissance of coastal shipping between Mergui and Victoria Point. On 7 May another air strike was carried out on Car Nicobar airfield, before the force returned to Trincomalee on 9 May, having spliced the mainbrace the day before to celebrate the Victory in Europe. In late May to mid June she supported the Indian sloops on patrol between Mergui Archipelago and Port Blair to prevent supplies reaching Japanese troops or their evacuation.

On 15 August the war with Japan was officially over, but the Fleet had much work to do. On 27 August she was part of a British force led Vice Admiral Walker in the battleship *Nelson* which set out from Rangoon for Penang, arriving on 28 August, for the formal surrender ceremony which took place on 2 September onboard the *Nelson*.

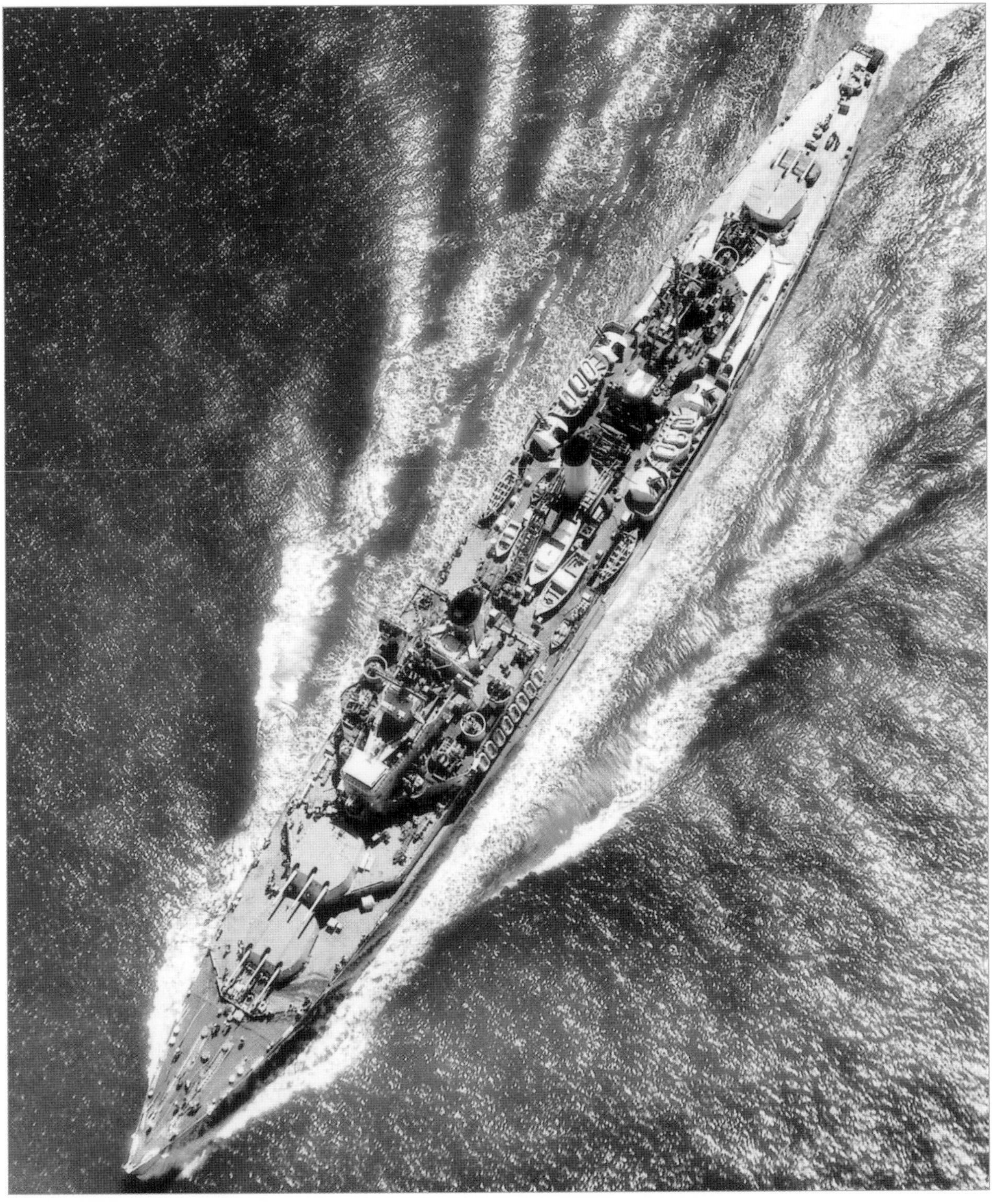

HMS Ceylon a good aerial view of this class of ship showing the transom stern. *(MoD/Crown Copyright)*

On9 September she accompanied the *Nelson* and other ships to Port Swettenham for the occupation of that region. (Operation Zipper). Over 100,000 troops were landed, and fortunately no opposition was experienced. She was at Singapore for the surrender ceremony there on 12 September. Later that month she supported the operations to occupy Western Malaya. She then detached from the Station, arriving at Portsmouth on 25 October.

By then her armament comprised three triple 6-inch, four twin 4-inch, three quadruple 2-pounders, twenty 20-mm Oerlikons in twin power mountings, and eight single 20-mm and two sets of torpedo tubes. During her refit at Portsmouth which lasted to 1947, the eight single 20-mm were replaced by four single 40-mm and two single 20-mm Oerlikons.

After her refit she was placed in reserve at Portsmouth until 1949, when she refitted prior to joining the East Indies Fleet relieving *Birmingham*, becoming Flagship of the Commander-in-Chief, East Indies. She arrived at Trincomalee on 26 June 1950. In June the war in Korea started, and the next month the *Ceylon* and the cruiser *Belfast* were sailed for the Far East. She was at Singapore when she was diverted and embarked 1st Battalion Argyll and Sutherland Highlanders at Kowloon on passage to Japan.

In August 1950 she sailed from Hong Kong with the carrier *Unicorn* and Australian destroyers *Warramunga* and *Bataan* to land the 1st Argylls and 1st Middlesex at Pusan on 29 August. The ships then used Sasebo as their base for operations off Korea, which included patrols of the coast. During these patrols she refueled the destroyers so often she became known as '*Wave Ceylon*'. In September *Ceylon* covered *Triumph* during landings at Inchon by United Nations troops and in early October she was attached to US Naval forces for the assault on Wonsan and bombardments of the main towns on the North Korean coast, including Chongjin. After further patrols she took part in the bombardment of Chinampo in November, and the next month was off Chodo covering transports coming out of the Traedong estuary. 32,428 personnel, 1103 vehicles and 57,741 tons of stores were evacuated from Inchon by 31 December.

She supported the west flank of the 8th Army in

HMS Ceylon refuelling at sea. After modernisation she retained a tripod mainmast, unlike her sistership *Newfoundland*. *(Syd Goodman Collection)*

early January 1951, providing gunfire support with the *Kenya* and Australian destroyers *Warramunga* and *Bataan*, the US heavy cruiser *Rochester* and Dutch destroyer *Evertsen*. 68,913 people, 1404 vehicles and 62,144 tons of stores were taken from Inchon to Taegan and Pusan. In February 1951 she took part in a night bombardment of communist shipping at Inchon. She also landed a Royal Marine detachment in the Chinampo area, who carried out a reconnaissance of the villages. She covered this operation with *Kenya*, both of whom bombarded the area. In May she and *Kenya* landed Royal Marines in support of operations ashore.

In August she and *Warramunga* shelled Haeju. That month, during another operation when she landed her Marines, a sailor from the New Zealand frigate *Rotoiti* was killed. In October she was at Chodoi and aided casualties from the Canadian destroyer *Cayuga*, and helped cover the withdrawal of guerrillas from Simmi Do. In November and December she carried out bombardments and in January 1952 she and the frigate *Mounts Bay* shelled enemy positions on the West Coast. In February she with the frigate *Cardigan Bay* and Canadian destroyer *Nootka* bombarded the Wolsa-Ri batteries. She continued to patrol the West Coast until July. In June she was visited by the Minister of Defence and the Minister of State (Field Marshal Lord Alexander of Tunis and Mr Selwyn Lloyd) at Inchon. She was at this time flagship of the 5th Cruiser Squadron, Far East Fleet In late June and early July she and *Belfast*, the frigate *Amethyst* and Canadian destroyer *Iroquois* shelled the Ongjin peninsula.

She left the area on 4 July for Singapore. She had spent 470 days at sea in the war area, steamed over 80,000 miles and fired nearly 7,000 rounds of 6-inch at enemy positions. She had acquired a reputation for helpfulness and encouragement for any ships of all nations along the West Coast. A farewell signal to her from the Commander-in-Chief of the Far East Station said that she was ‘ a happy and efficient unit to the very end of an extremely long spell in this war, which can be tedious for the cruisers’ ship’s companies’.

After relief by the cruiser *Newcastle*, she was refitted at Singapore, whilst her crew were sent home in the aircraft carrier *Vengeance*. She then became the Flagship of the East Indies Station 1952-54. On 1 January 1953 she was present at the inauguration of the Maldive Islands Republic. On 13 February 1954 she arrived at Hobart, Tasmania to take part in the 150th anniversary of the first settlement of Tasmania and for the visit of H.M. The Queen, who was on her Australasian Tour in SS *Gothic*. In April she escorted the *Gothic* from the Cocos Islands, Her Majesty visited the ship on 9 April. The *Ceylon* returned to the U.K., arriving at Portsmouth on 1 October, and started a long refit, which lasted until 1956.

During this period she was modernised with radar control for her 4-inch guns, and given a tertiary armament of five twin and eight single 40-mm guns. She was given an enclosed bridge and fitted with a lattice foremast.

She recommissioned on 11 September 1956 to serve in the Home Fleet, but in October she left Portland for the Eastern Mediterranean for temporary duty during the Suez crisis. She was present at the Suez operation (Operation Musketeer) in November.

In January 1957 she went to the South Atlantic, relieving *Superb* at Dakar as Flagship of the Commander-in-Chief East Indies. She was present at the Ghana Independence Ceremony on 6 March 1957. On 2 April she was at Simonstown for the handing over of that base to the South African Government. Later that year she joined the East Indies Station and on 15 October was at Trincomalee when the naval base was handed over to Ceylon. She returned to Portsmouth on 5 December 1957.

In the spring 1958 she took part in the Home Fleet cruise to the West Indies with exercises off Halifax, then she sailed to the Mediterranean. In August she took part with the carrier *Eagle* in a combined exercise supporting Marines landing in Libya. In October 1958 she passed through the Suez Canal to Aqaba. On 2 November she, the frigate *Chichester* and LSTs took part in the evacuation of the last of the British troops who had been sent to Jordan to meet the threat of invasion by Iraq. She took officers and men of the First Battalion Cameronians to Mombasa, arriving on 9 November. On completion

of that task she sailed for the Far East.

Early in 1959 she was the Flagship of the Second-in-Command, Far East Station, Rear Admiral V C Begg. She undertook a cruise to New Zealand as Flagship, and was also the Flagship later for a cruise to Colombo, taking part in Exercise Jet with Commonwealth Naval Forces in the Indian Ocean. She was then withdrawn from the Far East, being relieved by the cruiser *Gambia* which was diverted from her Home/Mediterranean commission. *Ceylon* arrived at Portsmouth on 18 December when it was announced that she was being sold to Peru, and she was formally handed over on 9 February 1960 and was renamed *Colonel Bolognesi*. She was deleted in 1982 and broken up in 1985.

She had gained the following battle honours for her name:

Sabang 1944 (25 July), Burma 1945 and Korea 1950-52.

HMS MANXMAN

HMS Manxman with her flush upper deck covering her mine deck, which was also used to carry valuable cargoes. *(Syd Goodman Collection)*

The laying of mines had been exercised in the Great War, using many types of ship. The task was both offensive, for example, when trying to sink enemy warships, and defensive, such as in the protection of shipping routes. The barrage of mines laid across the Straits of Dover had proved very effective in stopping German submarines using that route, forcing them to take the far longer route around the north of Scotland to reach the South West Approaches. Between the wars some of the modern destroyers were designed to carry mines (e.g. *Esk* and *Express*) - landing some of their guns and their torpedo tubes, and using their speed to carry out minelaying operations in the minimum of time on a 'hit and run' basis. One specially designed minelayer was built at Devonport in the 1920s- the *Adventure*. She was of 6,740 tons and could reach 28 knots using her turbine engines. She was fitted with diesel electric engines for cruising. She could carry 340 mines- a substantial quantity. She was the first vessel specifically designed for the minelaying task.

As the threat of the Second World War loomed, the Admiralty decided that further specialist minelayers should be built. Four ships of the Latona class were ordered, *Latona, Welshman, Abdiel* and *Manxman*. These were to be of 2,650 tons and carry 100 mines along a covered deck, or carry 160 mines with a slight penalty on their top speed. These mines would be laid from special ports at their stern. The ships were to be armed with three twin 4-inch, a quadruple two pounder and two quadruple machine guns. These guns were for self-defence, as a vessel carrying that amount of explosive would not wish to become involved in an action. Their main defence, however, was their speed. They were given turbine engines developing 72,000-shaft horsepower, and with their two propellers, were designed to steam at 39.75 knots, with a maximum continuous sea speed of 37.5 knots. With this speed, it was hoped that they could carry out a laying operation under cover of darkness, and be well clear by daylight. On trials *Manxman* achieved 71,873-shaft horsepower. She had an endurance of 3900 miles at 15 knots. Three ships were ordered on 23 December 1938, and the fourth, *Welshman*, on 21 March 1939. *Manxman* was laid down on 24 March 1939 by Alexander Stephen and Sons, Linthouse, Glasgow, launched on 5 September 1940, and completed on 20 June 1941, having been commissioned on 7 June 1941. She was 418 feet long and had a beam of 40 feet.

In 1941 two further vessels of the class were ordered, *Apollo* and *Ariadne*. They were not completed until 1943/4 and carried just two twin 4-inch guns, a different secondary armament and had their mainmast stepped further forward nearer the after of the three funnels. This distinguished them from the first group.

When first commissioned *Manxman* operated as part of the Home Fleet. As part of her working up she laid a dummy field of mines off the Orkneys on 25 June. At that time in the war during the campaign in the Libyan desert it had been realised that the only suitable way of getting stores to Tobruk for the Army was by using fast warships under cover of darkness. Three of the fast minelayers , *Abdiel*, *Latona* and *Manxman* were allocated to the Mediterranean Fleet for this task. The first two were so employed, but the *Manxman* was diverted for other operations.

During the Tobruk task the *Latona* became the first of the class lost, being sunk by aircraft whilst employed supplying the garrison on 25 October 1941. *Latona* and *Abdiel* took 6,600 men and 1,400 tons of stores to Tobruk and brought out 5,000 men in October 1941.

In July *Manxman* was part of the Home Fleet sent to the Mediterranean to re-inforce the convoy escort for Operation Substance, taking vitally needed stores to Malta. The convoy of seven ships left the Clyde on 11 July and reached Gibraltar on 19th. It sailed from Gibraltar on 21st, but the troopship *Leinster* ran aground and had to be left behind. A heavy escort was provided, comprising the carrier *Ark Royal*, the battleship *Nelson*, battlecruiser *Renown*, four cruisers and 16 destroyers together with the *Manxman*. A diversion was carried out by forces in the Eastern Mediterranean and submarines were stationed along the convoy's route. The convoy was attacked by Italian submarines and aircraft,

HMS Manxman showing the ports in her stern for minelaying. *(MoD/Crown Copyright)*

and the cruiser *Manchester* and destroyer *Firedrake* were damaged and the destroyer *Fearless* hit and had to be abandoned. The heavy escort retired on 21 July as the convoy reached the Narrows, but the *Manxman* went through with the convoy and close escort to land the stores it carried on 24th. The next day the escort that had gone ahead to Malta rejoined the heavy escort, bringing with them seven empty merchant ships from Malta. The whole force reached Gibraltar on 27th.

Four days later *Manxman*, with the cruisers *Arethusa* and *Hermione* and two destroyers loaded with 1750 troops and 130 tons of stores landed from the *Leinster*, which had had to retire from the Substance convoy, and dashed to Malta to land them (Operation Style). They were covered by Force H. They arrived on 2 August, unloaded and sailed that afternoon, and returned to Gibraltar at high speed, arriving on 4th. During the passage the *Hermione* rammed and sank the Italian submarine *Tembien* off Tunis.

In August 1941 the *Manxman* carried out Operation Mincemeat, which was a combined operation, with *Manxman* laying mines off Leghorn and aircraft from the carrier *Ark Royal* attacking Northern Sardinia. *Manxman* left England disguised as a French cruiser of the Le Tigre Class. A false bow and stern were rigged and a raked impression given to her masts and funnels. The change was completed in 19 hours. She sailed from Loch Alsh, the base of the First Minelaying Squadron, on 15th, and loaded with mines at Milford Haven on 16th. The next evening she sailed, calling at Gibraltar to collect her operation orders. Once past the Balearic Islands on 22nd, she hoisted the French Tricolour and her crew wore French uniform, heading as though bound for Toulon. On the night of 24 August she rehoisted the White Ensign and carried out her minelaying task in the Gulf of Genoa the next morning, laying 156 mines. She then retired at 37 knots to be clear of the Gulf of Genoa by dawn, when she resumed her disguise. By 0630 on 30th she was back at Loch Alsh, having completed her mission undetected. Meanwhile ten Swordfish from the *Ark Royal* attacked the airfield at Tempio. During these operations the Italian Fleet had deployed to counter the British forces but failed to make contact. However, the submarine *Triumph* torpedoed the Italian cruiser *Bolzano* during the Italian sortie.

During the autumn and winter *Manxman* carried out 17 minelaying operations in the north-west approaches, off the French coast and in the Bay of Biscay. She was also employed carrying depth charges from Milford Haven to Gibraltar and underwent a month's refit at Liverpool.

In February she was allocated to the Plymouth Command during the operations designed to contain the German battlecruisers *Scharnhorst* and *Gneisenau* in Brest.

In April 1942 she was allocated to the East Indies Fleet to relieve the *Abdiel*. She sailed from Plymouth on 18 April, calling at Takoradi, Simonstown, Durban and reaching Kilindini on 15 May.

In August she escorted one of three dummy convoys sailed in the Indian Ocean to indicate to the Japanese landings in the Andaman Islands. She sailed from Madras during daylight on 1 August, and that night reversed course and returned to port.

On 3 September she arrived at Diego Suarez, the French naval base in Madagascar to assist in the operations to extend the Allies hold on the island and to forestall any attempt by the Japanese to occupy the island. One part of these operations was an assault on Majunga (Operation Stream). The *Manxman* was part of the main force, which comprised the carrier *Illustrious*, four cruisers, twelve destroyers, three minesweepers, three anti-submarine whalers as well as the *Erebus*, a netlayer and the headquarters ship (*Albatross*). Pre-operation training (Exercise Touchstone) was carried out and proved very useful. The main landings proved very successful with little opposition from the French, who had no air reconnaissance and hence no warning of the assault. As a diversion for this operation *Manxman* embarked naval boarding parties and Royal Marines from the cruiser *Caradoc* and two platoons of the Pretoria Highlanders, and early on 10 September entered Hellville, Nossi Be Island (Operation Esme(B)). She moored head and stern and carried out a bombardment of known and possible sites for machine gun posts, which could threaten the pier head. She fired 172 rounds of 4 inch at 500 yards range, and then carried out a two minute

HMS Manxman in the Far East as a minesweeper support ship. *(Syd Goodman Collection)*

concentrated sweep of close range weapon fire on the pier head, which included the use of military mortars. Meanwhile, boarding parties had been sent away to capture tugs and powerboats and then a diversionary bombardment was carried out while the Pretoria Highlanders were landed on the pier head. The port was captured with just one casualty.

On 14th the *Manxman* landed a small military force down river from Maromandia in Madagascar. The force then proceeded upstream and caught the retreating French forces who were left with the option of fighting or surrendering. The French surrendered after a short engagement, the town being occupied the next day by a Royal Marine detachment. At dawn on 29th she carried out a reconnaissance of Fort Dauphin where local civilian officials were found to be friendly. An armistice was agreed on 5 November in the island, but the *Manxman* had already been redeployed.

She arrived at Port Said on 30 October. On night 10 November she and six destroyers left Alexandria for Malta with urgently needed stores (350 tons) and 200 naval and Maltese personnel. Her sister, *Welshman*, and submarines carried concentrated food and torpedoes to the island from Gibraltar. All reached the island safely, the *Manxman* arriving on 12th. She was the first surface ship to arrive in the island for 12 weeks. These supplies allowed the island to play its part in Operation Torch, the landings in North Africa.

On 29 November the *Manxman* carried out a lay of 156 mines near Cani near Tunis, embarking the mines that had not been buried in rubble at Malta. She sailed from the island on 25th for Algiers. On the night 29th she sailed from Algiers to conduct the lay. At 2014 she sighted an E-boat that passed too close to fire a torpedo, and which passed down her port side inside her wash and disappeared astern. The minefield was laid without incident.

The next task for the *Manxman* was to carry urgently needed stores from Gibraltar to Malta. On 1 December, while on passage from Algiers to Gibraltar to load for this task, she was torpedoed by the submarine *U-375* (Lt Cdr Konenkamp) off Algiers in position 36.39N 000.15E and badly damaged. Her engines were wrecked and she lost four

men dead. She took on a 12 degree list but remained afloat. She was taken in tow by the destroyer *Pathfinder*. and arrived at Mers-el-Kebir on 2 December. Emergency repairs were carried out so that she could be towed to Gibraltar, leaving on 18 December and arriving on 20th. Temporary repairs were carried out at Gibraltar from then until May 1943. On 23 June she was towed by the tug *Bustler* with convoy MKS 15 to the Tyne to be fully repaired. This took from 9 July 1943 to 18 May 1945.

Whilst she was being repaired, two of her sisters were lost. The *Welshman* was torpedoed by *U-617* whilst on passage from Malta to Alexandria on 1 February 1943 after a minelaying run off Italy. She had carried out five special stores runs to Malta, using her high speed to take essential supplies to the beleaguered garrison. She sank with a heavy loss of life losing 153 officers and men together with some of the military and RAF personnel taking passage. The *Abdiel* was involved in landing troops at Taranto and on night of 9 September 1943 she hit a mine in the harbour and sank with a heavy loss of life. She lost 48 officers and men together with 120 of the 400 military personnel embarked, a further 126 of the crew and troops being wounded.

She recommissioned on 10 April 1945 and sailed for the Far East via Malta and Port Said, and then on to Colombo, arriving in 14 July 1945. She continued eastwards but had just reached Melbourne when Japan capitulated in August. She sailed for the Pacific with supplies for the British prisoners of war being rescued in Japan. Post war, in September, she visited Tokyo, and later Sydney and Shanghai. She remained with the British Pacific Fleet until June 1946. She then returned to the UK for a refit at Sheerness and afterwards returned to the British Pacific Fleet in February 1947 to relieve the cruiser *Euryalus*.

In late 1947 she left the Far East and returned to Sheerness in January 1948, to be laid up in reserve. She underwent a further refit in 1951 when her secondary armament was altered to one twin and four single 40-mm guns. She joined the Mediterranean Fleet in September 1951, and was placed in reserve at Malta in 1953. She was again refitted in 1956,

HMS Manxman in the later years of her career with a dummy forefunnel. *(Syd Goodman Collection)*

when her after gun was removed. She recommissioned in February 1956 as flagship of Flag Officer Flotilla Mediterranean, and in April took part in relief operations when an earthquake hit the Lebanon. Later that year took part in the Suez operations in the headquarters group. In 1957 she was again placed in reserve at Malta and in January the next year was towed to Gibraltar for a refit.

From 17 July 1961-22 February 1963 she underwent a conversion at Chatham Dockyard, and emerged as a minesweeper support ship. During this refit her boiler power was reduced, limiting her speed to 27 knots. She had additional superstructure added, and her remaining two twin 4-inch guns were removed. She retained her forward funnel, though only as a dummy. She grounded in Douglas Bay, Isle of Man on 26 April 1963. In July she took up her role supporting the Sixth Minesweeping Squadron in the Far East.

She returned to Portsmouth on 12 December 1968.

In February 1969 to May 1969 she was converted to be an Engineer Officers' training ship, day running out of Devonport in support of the Royal Naval Engineering College, Manadon. She paid off in September 1970 and was laid up, firstly at Devonport and then at Chatham.

She was sold on 13 September 1972 to John Cashmore and arrived at Newport to be broken up on 6 October 1972. Her two remaining sister ships had been broken up several years before (*Apollo* 1962 and *Ariadne* 1965). The class had proved to be very successful, so much so that their original task of minelaying had been secondary to their very successful high-speed stores passages. They had demonstrated the need for fast surface vessels with a good carrying capacity and with a reasonable self defence capability. The relatively unglamorous task of getting troops and stores to the scene of action is often forgotten by planners more obsessed with cutting costs or the operations ashore during an assault, and too often first line warships (cruisers, fast minelayers and destroyers) had to be diverted to this task.

She had gained the battle honour 'Malta Convoys 1941-1942' for her name.

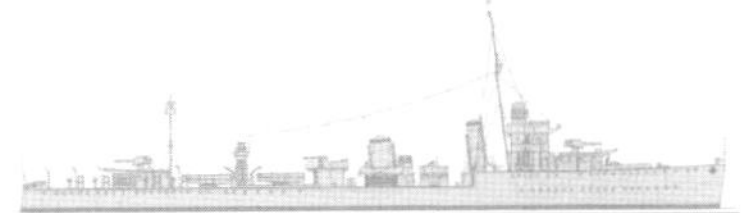

HMS KEPPEL

HMS Keppel in her pre-war leader configuration with five single 4.7-inch guns. *(Portsmouth Royal Naval Museum)*

Keppel was a Thornycroft type destroyer leader of the Shakespeare class. Developed from the successful V and W design, the class displaced 1,480 tons and was 329.25 feet long, with a beam of 32 feet. They were armed with five single 4.7-inch guns (the first destroyers to be fitted with that calibre gun), a single 3-inch (abaft the after funnel) and two two-pounders. They also carried two sets of triple torpedo tubes. Built to lead the V and W destroyers, their machinery was designed for 40,000 shaft horse-power, giving them a speed of 36 knots. However there were reports that they had developed 43,500 shaft horse-power and attained 38.9 knots on trials. Seven of the class were ordered, but two (*Saunders* and *Spragge*) were cancelled in December 1918. *Keppel* was laid down by Tjhornycroft at Southampton in October 1918, was launched on 23 April 1920, and was later towed to Portsmouth Dockyard for completion. However, the final work was carried out at Pembroke Dockyard between December 1923 and February 1925. She commissioned on 28 April 1925. The general design of these ships proved so popular that similar vessels were built for the Spanish, Roumanian and Argentinian Navies.

She served in the Mediterranean from 1925 to September 1926, when she transferred to the China Station, remaining there for two years. In December 1927 she visited Chingwangtao to protect British interests. She then returned to the Mediterranean until June 1931, when she underwent a refit at Devonport. She was allocated to the Reserve Fleet and to replace *Saumarez* for duty with the Royal Naval Engineering College. Instead, however, she re-commissioned in October 1931 for the China Station. In September 1934 she encountered a typhoon in the Inland Sea of Japan, and dragged her anchor. She had to use revolutions for 20 knots, working her engines ahead and astern, to keep head to wind as she got under weigh. She transferred from the Far East to the Mediterranean in 1935, and in the next year she served in Home Waters. She joined the Reserve Fleet in October 1937. In July 1939 she acted as escort for the Royal Yacht during Their Majesties' unofficial visit to Dartmouth. In Late August 1939 she sailed for Gibraltar to take up duties as the leader of 13th Destroyer Flotilla based on Gibraltar. At this time her anti-submarine armament comprised two depth charge throwers, one rail and an outfit of 30 depth charges.

On 24 October 1939 she carried out an unsuccessful attack on a U-boat in the Atlantic west of Gibraltar. On 17 January 1940 she collided with the French light cruiser *Jaguar* about one hundred miles south west of Vigo. She was seriously damaged, and was escorted to Lisbon by the French destroyer *La Railleuse*. She returned to Gibraltar on 20 January, where temporary repairs were effected. On 23/24 June 1940, she, and the destroyer *Velox*, called at Seta and Port Vendres to evacuate British civilians and Czech and Polish troops to Gibraltar.

In July 1940 *Keppel* took part in the operation to prevent the French ships at Oran falling into enemy hands, during which French ships were sunk and damaged. Shortly afterwards she left Gibraltar for Portsmouth, arriving on 18th. On 26 July she sailed for Scapa Flow to join the Home Fleet as a relief for a Hunt class destroyer in the 12th Flotilla. The next month she was detached for convoy escort duties, arriving at Greenock on 7 August. On 16 October she picked up 14 survivors from the SS *Trevisa*, which had been torpedoed and was sinking in the Atlantic.

At the end of October 1940 she rejoined the Home Fleet, and on 10 November sailed from the Faroes with the destroyers *Maori* and *Beagle* to join the Home Fleet in a search for the pocket battleship *Admiral Scheer*. On 26 November she was part of the escort for an operation to lay mines across the Denmark Strait. On 8 December she carried out a similar operation off the south-east coast of Iceland.

On 26 January 1941 she sailed as part of the escort to the battleship *Nelson* to carry out a search for the German battlecruisers *Scharnhorst* and *Gneisenau*. The search was unsuccessful. In February 1941 she transferred from the Home Fleet to the Western Approaches Command to join the 12th Escort Group based on Londonderry. Her duties were mainly escorting convoys in the North Atlantic. On 11 May she rescued the crew of the *Somerset*, which had been sunk by bombing. In July she rescued survivors of the Norwegian MV *Vigrid*, which had been torpedoed and sunk in the previous month.

By September she was leader of the 1st Escort Group and was based on Londonderry. On 12 November she collided with the *Venomous*. Her stem was buckled above and below the waterline and her forepeak flooded. She arrived at Greenock the next day, and repairs were carried out at

HMS Keppel as modernised in the war for anti-submarine duties, with A gun replaced by a Hedgehog A/S mortar and radar on the bridge. *(T. Ferrers-Walker Collection)*

Newport, South Wales. These were completed in mid January 1942. On 18 March she was directed to an area where a U-boat had been detected sending signals. She sighted the surfaced submarine, but it dived before she could close to gun range. *Keppel*, and other destroyers, carried out depth charge attacks until the next day. Although oil was brought to the surface, the submarine escaped. During this attack, *Keppel* used her newly fitted Hedgehog anti-submarine mortar. This was the second operational use of that weapon, and while firing it, five of her charges misfired and fell on her forecastle. On 11 April she met heavy weather, which carried away her topmast and put her radar out of action.

On 27 June 1942 she sailed as part of the escort to Convoy PQ-17 to North Russia. She was then commanded by Commander J.E. Broome, who was senior officer of the escort. The convoy comprised of 36 ships. With the convoy were three oilers. It was planned that the escorts be refueled from the tankers, as the voyage was to be longer than previous convoys because the ice had withdrawn to allow a more northerly track. The first few days were spent quietly in calm weather, and at noon on 2 July the convoy passed a homeward bound convoy, which had not been attacked having been protected by thick weather. That evening the convoy came under air attack, during which one aircraft was shot down with no damage to the convoy. Shortly afterwards the convoy entered thick fog. The next day the convoy was shadowed by aircraft and reports came in that German heavy ships were on the move. U-boats reported that they could not attack owing to the heavy escort. Early on 4 July, one merchant ship was lost to an aircraft torpedo attack. Another air attack took place that evening, but all the bombs and torpedoes fired missed the convoy. Soon after, during another attack, which was pressed home more successfully, one aircraft fired two torpedoes at a merchant ship, and then crashed in flames ahead of the *Keppel*. During this attack three ships were hit, two of which had to be sunk by the escorts. Three enemy aircraft had been shot down. Soon afterwards the convoy received a signal telling it to scatter. This was later the source of much discussion, and had arisen out of a perceived threat to the convoy from German heavy surface ships. The six destroyers of the escort joined the cruisers of the close escort, which were near at hand, and set out with them at speed to engage the German forces, which had not actually put to sea. The other escorts remained to guard the scattered convoy. However, with the scattering, the U-boats and aircraft were able to take a heavy toll of the merchantmen. Only 11 ships arrived safely.

On 30 July *Keppel* left Londonderry for Gibraltar, where she joined the escort for the carrier FURIOUS, which was ferrying aircraft to Malta. Two ferry operations were carried out on 11 and 17 August, and on completion she returned to Londonderry.

On 11 September she sailed from Akureyri, Iceland, as part of the covering force for Convoy PQ-18, returning on 14 September. On 19 September she sailed again as part of the cover for Convoy QP-14, reached Hvalfjord on 22nd. At the end of October she sailed for London, where she underwent a refit, lasting until April 1943. During the war she was modified for escort duties, with A and Y guns removed to allow her to carry the Hedgehog anti-submarine mortar and extra depth charges. She retained her torpedo tubes and was fitted with radar mounted on her bridge. Her after funnel was reduced in height to save top-weight. In April 1943 her armament comprised two 4.7-inch guns, a single 3-inch, two two-pounders and four 20-mm AA guns, with two depth charge rails, four throwers and 140 depth charges. In 1945 she carried just two 4.7-inch guns and five 20-mm guns, four throwers and no torpedo tubes.

On 2 April 1943 she arrived at Greenock to again take up convoy escort duties, this time with Unit B-3. In May she was part of the escort of Convoy HX-239, during which she, with the destroyer *Escapade* closed the submarine *U-752*, which had been damaged by aircraft and was fighting them on the surface. With the approach of the surface escorts the submarine scuttled itself. Survivors were rescued by the *Escapade*. This had been the first successful rocket attack on a U-boat. During June and July *Keppel* escorted convoys in the Mediterranean and South Atlantic. On 6 July she took part in the hunt for a U-boat which had been reported by an aircraft off North West Africa.

On 12 September *Keppel* sailed from Milford Haven with a group of eight ships to escort Convoy ONS-18. The convoy comprised 27 merchantmen. It was overtaken by the fast convoy ON-202 and the convoys merged. Both came under sustained submarine attacks. During the night 20/21 September, *U-229* fired a torpedo at the destroyer *Icarus*. *Icarus* took avoiding action and the torpedo missed. However, in the manoeuvre the destroyer collided with the frigate *Drumheller*. On 22nd the weather was foggy with visibility down to 200 yards. *Keppel* heard a U-boat's radio transmissions and followed the direction. She detected *U-229* on radar at 6,000 yards, and sighted her at 200 yards, opening fire as she did so. *Keppel* then rammed the U-boat, which was sunk. Nineteen U-boats had attacked these two convoys over five days. Six merchant ships were lost together with three escorts, but three U-boats had been sunk and three more damaged.

Convoy escort duties continued until October, when she returned to London for repairs to damage caused by the Atlantic gales. These repairs lasted to January 1944, and on completion she joined the Eighth Escort Group based on Greenock. She took up her new duties in February 1944.

On 20 February *Keppel* sailed from Loch Ewe as part of the escort to Convoy JW-57 to Russia. During this operation, on 24 February, while west of the Lofotens, *Keppel* and the destroyer *Obedient* followed high frequency direction finding (HFDF) detections, and *Keppel* located a submarine by ASDIC at 1,400 yards range. *U-713* broke surface for a moment, and then came under heavy depth charge and Hedgehog attacks from the destroyers, and was sunk.

On 27 March 1944 she sailed from the Clyde to the Faroes to cover Convoy JW-58 to Russia. During this operation she detected *U-360* by radar at 6,800 yards. The submarine dived, but was soon located by ASDIC and came under attack by Hedgehog, which yielded four explosions, followed by several heavy underwater explosions, which brought to the surface oil and debris from the sinking U-boat.

In April she was part of the covering force for the passage of Convoy RA-59 returning to the Clyde in May. Towards the end of that month she sailed to Portland, and on 27th, whilst escorting Convoy WP-528, she attacked a U-boat off Start Point, but without success. During the Normandy landings she escorted Convoy EWC1A from the Solent to the Eastern Task Force area, arriving on 7 June. At the start of July she sailed to Milford Haven enroute to the Clyde for repairs, which lasted to August.

In August 1944 she was again on Arctic Convoy duty, escorting Convoy JW-59. During this convoy, *U-354* was attacked and damaged by a Swordfish aircraft (M/825) from the carrier *Vindex*. The sloops *Mermaid* and *Peacock* and frigate *Loch Dunvegan* with *Keppel* closed and, after attacks lasting from 0313 to 1839 on 24th, they sank the U-boat. Just two days before, the U-boat had torpedoed and damaged the carrier *Nabob* and the escort *Bickerton*. The latter had had to be abandoned. On the return convoy (RA-59A) *Keppel* was able to assist in the sinking of *U-394* two hundred miles west of the Lofoten Islands on 2 September. Other ships involved were the *Mermaid* and *Peacock* and destroyer *Whitehall* together with Swordfish aircraft A/825 from the *Vindex*. The submarine had been attacked by the aircraft and dived later. The *Keppel* gained ASDIC contact as the group closed. Twelve attacks were carried out, including one mass creeping attack by three of the ships, directed by *Peacock*. In this one mass attack 59 depth charges were dropped, and throughout the whole operation 154 depth charges were used as well as Hedgehog mortars. Confirmation of this sinking was obtained from wreckage and human remains that came to the surface.

Keppel continued on Arctic Convoy escort duties until January 1945, when she returned to the Clyde for repairs, which lasted till April. She was then reallocated to the Greenock Coastal Escort Pool, which she joined on 15 May after working up at Tobermory. When the war ended, she sailed to Barrow, where she was reduced to reserve, paying off on 24 June. She was broken up at Barrow in July 1945.

She had gained five battle honours for her name: 'Atlantic 1940-43', Malta Convoys 1942',' Arctic 1942-45', Normandy 1944' and 'English Channel 1944'.

HMS ENCOUNTER

HMS Encounter was typical of the many destroyers built in the 1930's. She withstood much damage in the war but finally succumbed to overwhelming odds in the Java Sea. *(Syd Goodman Collection)*

The *Encounter* was one of the standard destroyers built between 1928 and 1937. They were logical developments from the World War I V and W classes. These ships were 323-329 feet long overall, with a beam of 32.25-33.25 feet. Their armament comprised four single 4.7-inch guns and two banks of torpedo tubes, though in later ships improvements were incorporated, such as the introduction of quintuple instead of quadruple torpedo tubes. Also a marginally better secondary armament was introduced to cope with the ever increasing threat from aircraft. The ships were powered by twin turbines, developing 34,000 to 36,000 shaft horse-power, and giving them a speed of 35-36 knots.

Encounter was in the fifth such class. Each class consisted of eight ships, which formed a flotilla, with a specially built and more heavily armed vessel as the flotilla leader. *Encounter*'s leader was the *Exmouth*. There had been two prototype A class vessels in the Royal Navy, the *Amazon* and *Ambuscade*, built in 1926, whilst two others had been built for the Royal Canadian Navy. Four of the C class had been cancelled as a gesture of unilateral disarmament, and the four remaining C class ships, together with their leader, *Kempenfelt*, were acquired by the Royal Canadian Navy in the late 1930s.

Of the E class, two (*Esk* and *Express*) had tripod mainmasts and had their seaboats mounted a deck higher to facilitate minelaying operations. The class was part of the 1931 programme. *Encounter* was laid down by Hawthorn Leslie on 15 March 1933, launched on 29 March 1934 and completed on 2 November the same year. She had a standard displacement of 1,375 tons, with a length of 329 feet and a beam of 33.25 feet. Her engines developed 36,260-shaft horse-power on trials, giving her a speed of 36.572 knots. She commissioned on 5 November 1934 with a crew from the destroyer *Vortigern*, and, after trials, joined the Fifth Destroyer Flotilla of the Home Fleet.

She spent the spring of 1935 in the West Indies, and afterwards exchanged crews, and port, with her sister ship *Express*. She then re-commissioned and was detached to the Mediterranean. However, she

was damaged in a collision with another sister, the *Escapade*, off Portland in June. In July she took part in the Jubilee Review of the Fleet at Spithead. Two months later she was in the Mediterranean for the Abyssinian Crisis. In 1936 she refitted at Chatham and then rejoined the Home Fleet. In 1937 she was employed in the non-intervention patrols in the Bay of Biscay, and the next spring she operated off the Spanish coast.

In the spring of 1939 she was undertaking Spanish patrols from Gibraltar. She returned to the Nore in July for a refit. She was then scheduled to be placed in reserve. However, the war clouds were looming and she was one of the ships called forward for the King's Review of the Reserve Fleet in Weymouth Bay in August 1939, with a crew of two-fifths active service personnel and three-fifths reservists. After the Review she joined the 12th Destroyer Flotilla of the Home Fleet, mainly operating out of Milford Haven.

That November, her fifth and final Commanding Officer, Lt Cdr E.V.St.J. Morgan, joined. She spent the last part of November in Devonport, having her forecastle repaired after being damaged in rough seas. She then sailed north for Scapa Flow and in March was part of the Rosyth Command, still in the 12th flotilla.

On 9 April 1940 she sailed from Scapa Flow with the destroyer *Grenade*, escorting the *Britsh Lady* to Vestfjord. This was part of Operation R4, a plan to seize Norwegian ports should the Germans retaliate to the laying of minefields by the British. The aim was to stop iron ore traffic from Norway to Germany. This operation was not to be implemented until the German intentions were plain. However, the Germans acted first, and invaded Norway. *Encounter* joined the Home Fleet on 12 April, and was involved in patrols off Otofjord and Narvik during April, being one of the screen that escorted the battleship *Warspite* and three cruisers when they shelled Narvik on 24 April. In May she was part of the carrier *Ark Royal*'s escort. She docked at Rosyth at the end of the month.

In June she, and the Tribal class destroyer *Mashona*, covered the First Minesweeping Squadron whilst they collected buoys from the wreck of the boom carrier *Astronomer*, which had been lost off Kinnaird Head. She was then detailed to assist her sister ship, the *Escort*, search for a German submarine that had been reported to have been bombed by the RAF. Shortly afterwards she grounded and had to be docked in Sheerness for repairs. The opportunity was taken during this period to fit degaussing and undertake repairs to a turbine valve.

On 20 July she sailed for Gibraltar, escorting two troopships (the *Riena Del Pacifico* and *Clan Ferguson*. The next day she stood by the Norwegian *Kollskegg* which was on fire. Three days later she met the carrier *Argus*, and reached Gibraltar six days afterwards. There she joined the 13th Flotilla as part of Force H. The next day she was at sea again as part of the screen to the *Argus*, which was to fly off 12 Hurricanes to Malta (Operation Hurry). The force returned to Gibraltar on 8 August and *Encounter* then sailed as part of the escort to the *Ark Royal*.

Later that month Force H, including the *Encounter*, provided cover for Operation Hats, the reinforcement of the Mediterranean Fleet. The *Ark Royal*'s aircraft struck at Port Elmas in Sardinia before Force H returned to Gibraltar. Two days later she was at sea again with the battlecruiser *Renown* in an attempt to intercept a French Squadron that had sailed from Toulon and which had passed through the Strait of Gibraltar at speed.

In November Force H was covering a convoy 140 miles west of Gibraltar as the German heavy cruiser *Admiral Scheer* had sunk the armed merchant cruiser *Jervis Bay* and some of her convoy (HX-84). The *Encounter* sighted a submarine on the surface in the middle of the convoy, and rammed it. Unfortunately it proved to be HMS *Utmost*. She underwent repairs at Gibraltar.

On 25 November Force H was part of the covering force for a convoy to Alexandria, which was intercepted by an Italian force, which included battleships. After a short engagement the Italian Fleet broke away, believing itself to be faced by a superior force.

The *Encounter* sailed on various missions during the next few months, including a voyage to Freetown with the carrier *Furious* in December. The *Furious* was delivering a large number of RAF

Hurricanes to be flown across Africa to join the Army of the Nile. She returned to Gibraltar on 22 January 1941.

The next month she sailed with Force H, which made a feint to the west before doubling back to join other ships prior to bombarding Genoa on 9 February. On returning to Gibraltar, *Encounter* was allocated to the Mediterranean Fleet, sailing with the destroyer ISIS via the Cape on 24 February. On the way she was temporarily allocated to the Red Sea, but she reached Alexandria on 12 April.

She arrived at Malta on 21 April, where she underwent repairs and docking. At 2200 on 29th, she was damaged by a near miss during an air raid. A 1,000/1,500 kg bomb exploded on the dock steps to starboard, causing 400 holes in her hull, and a greater number in her upperworks. The ship's side in the engine room and No. 3 boiler room was displaced inboard by up to a foot. Three and a half hours later another (50 kg) bomb went through her forecastle and exploded in her anti-submarine directing gear space. A hole 10 by 12 feet was made in her hull and her side was distorted. A fire took hold, fed by oil from a peace tank, and spread to other parts of the ship. These tanks were later removed from destroyers as a result of lessons learnt from this fire.

On 16 May, whilst still under repairs - estimated to take over two months, she was hit by another 50 kg bomb. It passed through the 0.5-inch machine gun platform between the funnels, and exploded in the bilges of No.2 boiler room, making a hole in her

HMS Encounter seen beneath the triple 16-inch guns of the battleship *Rodney*. *(Ken Kelly Collection)*

hull from keel to about 8 feet up her side. Her lower deck was blown upwards, rivets in the ship's side being broken and strained. There was considerable damage throughout the ship.

It was decided that she should go to Gibraltar for repairs, and so she sailed as escort to the empty merchant ships comprising convoy MG-1, which was sent west under cover of an eastbound convoy (Operation Substance). The convoy came under air attack, but the main enemy thrust was against the Substance Convoy, which, despite air attacks, arrived at Malta safely with the loss of only one destroyer (the *Fearless*).

The *Encounter* continued to operate with Force H, escorting reinforcements to Malta, but, in August 1941, again sailed round the Cape to rejoin the Mediterranean Fleet, escorting the battlecruiser *Repulse* to Freetown. She passed through the Suez Canal on 15 October, arriving at Alexandria the next day. That month she took part in the supply runs along the North African coast to Tobruk. On 25/26th she was one of the three destroyers with the fast minelayer *Latona* when they came under attack by Ju-87s. The *Latona* was badly damaged and had to be sunk by *Encounter*, whilst the destroyer *Hero* was also damaged.

Her stay in the Mediterranean was to be short, for in November she was one of the two destroyers ordered from the Mediterranean Fleet to reinforce the Far East. She, and the *Jupiter*, left Alexandria on 15 November, calling at Aden and arriving at Colombo on 28th, where they joined the battleship *Prince of Wales* and the destroyers *Electra* and *Express*. They all sailed the next day, and were joined the following day by the *Repulse*, which had been at Trincomalee since 25th.

The Force (Force Z) arrived at Singapore on 2 December, and *Encounter* was docked for renewal of a stern bush. She did not, therefore, sail with the *Prince of Wales* and *Repulse* on their fateful voyage on 8 December.

On 12th she sailed with a convoy to Sunda Strait, and called at Batavia prior to her return to Singapore on 18th, where shortages in her complement were made up with a few picked men from the survivors of the lost capital ships.

Her next few months were spent escorting shipping in the Java Sea, and she also took the opportunity to boiler clean in Batavia at the end of January. After that she returned to Singapore, and took the destroyer *Isis* in tow for Batavia, from where she was to be taken to Colombo later. The *Isis* had been in dock in Singapore and had been damaged by bombing. It had been decided to remove such ships to a safer harbour for repair. *Encounter* herself had only one main engine operating for part of the tow, due to her propeller fouling the towing wire. The tow had to be completed by *Electra*. Despite her defects, *Encounter* returned to the area as part of the ABDA (American-British-Dutch-Australian) Force. She was kept busy escorting shipping, including the liner *Orcades*, which was carrying 3,400 Australian troops for Sumatra. She also collected RAF personnel, refugees and stores which had reached Pedang from Singapore. These were delivered to Batavia.

On 25th she, together with the cruiser *Exeter* and destroyers *Jupiter* and *Electra*, all of whom were on escort duties in the area, was ordered to Sourabaya. She was at Tanjong Priok that morning during a severe air raid, and left at 1600 in company with *Exeter*, the Australian cruiser *Perth* and the other two destroyers. They arrived at Sourabaya 24 hours later in the middle of an air raid. They fuelled, and by dusk sailed as part of a combined Dutch, American, Australian and British squadron to sweep the north coast of Java. No enemy was sighted by daylight, and the force headed back to Sourabaya to refuel. For most of the forenoon it came under air attack.

At 1430, as the first ships of the force entered the swept channel to the harbour, an enemy sighting report was received, and the force reversed course. *Encounter* was one of the three destroyers scouting five miles ahead of the cruisers. The enemy was sighted at 1600, *Encounter* making her report just as *Electra*'s report was received. A second enemy force was sighted a few minutes later. Action started at 1620, and at 1708 the *Exeter* was hit and fell out of line, causing confusion in the Allied cruisers astern of her. *Exeter* had slowed down, and was being closed by a Japanese force of 2 light cruisers and 14 large destroyers. *Jupiter*, *Encounter* and *Electra* saw the threat to the crippled *Exeter* and

counterattacked the enemy through a smoke screen. Their action has been quoted as 'bravery shown …in countercharging a superior force which exemplified the British style of destroyer training in the best tradition of the Royal Navy'. The *Electra* was overwhelmed and sunk, and *Encounter* fired all her four torpedoes, but did not see any hits. *Encounter* carried out a firefight with one Japanese destroyer at 3,000 yards range, close enough to use her short-range weapons. The Japanese ships then retired and *Exeter* had been saved.

Meanwhile the Dutch destroyer *Kortenaer* had been sunk by a torpedo, the only one of 120 fired by the Japanese at the squadron to have hit. The *Exeter* was detached to Sourabaya with the Dutch destroyer *Witte de With*, and *Jupiter*, *Encounter* and the American destroyers remained as the anti-submarine screen for the other four Allied cruisers. The American destroyers were detached at 2100, and 25 minutes later the *Jupiter* blew up and sank. Thus *Encounter* was the sole destroyer remaining with the Force. The Squadron swept through some men in the water, and the *Perth* ordered *Encounter* to rescue them. These were 116 survivors from the *Kortenaer*, and *Encounter*, low on fuel, returned to Sourabaya with them. That night two of the Allied cruisers were sunk, and the other two headed for Sunda Strait, where they encountered a large landing force. They were overwhelmed and lost after a fierce action.

Encounter reached Sourabaya at 0550 the next morning and fuelled. That evening she sailed with the damaged *Exeter* and with the American destroyer *Pope*. They headed out into the Java Sea, planning to make for the Sunda Strait and then for Colombo. The next morning enemy ships were sighted and course was altered to avoid the superior enemy forces. However, at 0845 enemy destroyers were seen closing from the north, followed by two cruiser forces. *Encounter* made smoke to cover *Exeter* from the southern force, and the *Pope* was engaged by enemy destroyers at 8 miles range. The *Encounter* closed to assist the *Exeter*, which was hit at 1118. *Encounter* turned to cover her with a smoke screen, but came to a stop. She had oil fires in the engine room caused by lubricating oil from pipes, which had been damaged by splinters. Her engine bearings had wiped through lack of lubrication. It was estimated that it would be 20 minutes before the bearings would be cool enough to allow repairs to be started. Meanwhile the enemy, which comprised four heavy cruisers, each with ten 8-inch guns, and at least nine destroyers, continued to close and fire on the Allied ships.

By then the *Encounter*'s engines were out of action, only B gun was working, and that intermittently, and she had used 85 percent of her ammunition. It was therefore decided to abandon her. The order to scuttle was given at about 1125. As the crew left the ship, she started to receive direct hits. Her Captain reported the messdecks clear, engine room flooded and one boiler room on fire, and the ship listing to starboard. She heeled over and sank at about 1210, with two enemy destroyers circling her and firing occasionally. Reports of her last moments are confusing, and include accounts that she was torpedoed by Japanese destroyers, and that the survivors in the whaler were strafed by enemy aircraft.

The USS *Pope* managed to hide in a rain squall, but was attacked by enemy dive bombers and left in a sinking condition before being finished off by two cruisers. *Encounter*'s survivors were picked up the next day. Six men had died in the action, and one died onboard the Japanese destroyer that rescued them. Thirty-seven more were to die in captivity.

The *Encounter* had added a further eight battle honours to her name, bringing the total to twelve.

HMS HERO
Later HMCS CHAUDIERE

HMS Hero, one of two vessels of her class to introduce the new destroyer bridge. *(Syd Goodman Collection)*

The *Hero* was nameship of her class of destroyers. She was built by Vickers-Armstrong Ltd., Walker-on-Tyne and engined by Parsons Marine Steam Turbine Co Ltd, Wallsend-on-Tyne. She was laid down on 28 February 1935, launched on 10 March 1936 and completed on 21 October 1936. She had a standard displacement of 1,340 tons, an overall length of 323 feet and beam of 33 feet. Her engines developed 34,000-shaft-horse-power giving her a maximum speed of 36 knots with an endurance of 5,500 miles at 15 knots and 1,200 miles at full speed. She was armed with four single 4.7-inch guns, two quadruple machine guns and had two quadruple torpedo tubes. In October 1940 a single 4-inch AA gun replaced her after set of torpedo tubes, and by October 1943 she carried three 4.7-inch guns and six 20-mm Oerlikons. Two six pounders were added in April 1944 but removed by April 1945. She also carried two depth charge throwers and one rail. In 1940 her outfit of depth charges was raised from 30 to 44, and in 1944 she was fitted with 4 throwers and two rails and carried 125 depth charges. In April 1944 she was fitted with a Hedgehog ahead throwing anti-submarine mortar. *Hero* and *Hereward* of this class, both built by Vickers-Armstrong Ltd., were fitted with a new design bridge, which was fitted into later destroyers. *Hereward* also carried out the trials of the twin 4.7-inch gun, which was to be fitted into the Tribal class destroyers.

On completion she joined the Second Destroyer Flotilla of the Mediterranean Fleet as a Divisional Leader and at times, from May 1937 onwards, was

detached to the Spanish coast. She returned to the UK for a refit in June 1939. She re-commissioned in July 1939 and rejoined the Third Division of the Second Flotilla of the Mediterranean Fleet. When war broke out she was at Malta. On 5 October she sailed from Gibraltar to undertake patrols in the South Atlantic based on Freetown, and became a unit of raider-hunting group K. She was employed on anti-submarine sweeps and escort duties in the Freetown area for the next two months. In February 1940, she joined a force of British and French ship for Operation V.O. - the interception of some German ships sailing from Vigo. Within a few days the SS *Morea* was captured and taken into Falmouth.

In March the Second Flotilla was then transferred to the Home Fleet, based on Scapa Flow, to augment the destroyer force assembled to forestall the imminent German invasion of Norway. *Hero*, with other destroyers of the 2nd Flotilla, took part in the preliminary Operation Wilfred, the laying mines off Stadlandet, West Fjord, with the aim of forcing coastal shipping outside Norwegian territorial waters. For this operation *Hero* sailed as part of the escort to the battlecruiser *Renown* on 5 April. *Hero* and *Hyperion* were engaged in a diversionary movement, pretending to lay mines off Bud on 8 April. On that day the *Glowworm*, one of *Renown*'s escorts that had detached to look for a man fallen overboard, encountered the German cruiser *Hipper* and was sunk after ramming her.

On 10 April, whilst on anti-submarine patrol north east of Muckle Flugga, *Hero* obtained a firm 'contact' on asdic and in the ensuing engagement sank *U-50* with depth charges. There were no survivors.

On 13 April she was one of 9 destroyers that accompanied the battleship *Warspite* to Narvik to follow up the success of the First Battle of Narvik three days earlier. There were eight German destroyers remaining in the Fjord, three of which were of 2,400 tons and the others of 2,200 tons, and all were armed with five 5-inch guns. All eight were sunk during a close quarters action in which *Hero* boarded the *Hans Lüdemann*, which later had to be sunk by torpedoed. Unfortunately there were insufficient military forces available to take advantage of this action, and Narvik was not to be retaken until 6 weeks later. On 24 April *Hero* was part of the anti-submarine screen for a force that bombarded the town of Narvik.

Hero remained with the forces engaged in the Norwegian campaign until mid-May, when increased tension with Italy necessitated the withdrawal of some ships from Norway to the Mediterranean. *Hero* was one of the ships transferred, sailing from Plymouth on 17 May to join the Mediterranean Fleet based on Alexandria.

It was planned to sail an important convoy from Alexandria on 19 July 1940 to Aegean ports. *Hero*, together with the destroyers *Hyperion*, *Ilex* and *Hasty*, was dispatched ahead to sweep the route through the Kaso Strait, along the North coast of Crete, through the Anti-Kithera Channel and then back to Alexandria. They were to be supported by the Australian cruiser *Sydney* and destroyer *Havock*.

The British force were unaware that two Italian cruisers had left Tripoli on 17 July to raid Allied shipping in the Aegean. At the same time as the four British destroyers were approaching from the eastward towards the Anti-Kithera Channel on the morning of 19th, the two Italian cruisers were approaching from the west. The first sighting report, made by *Hero*, reached the *Sydney* at about 0730 as she was on her way back to Alexandria. *Sydney* turned and steamed at full speed towards the enemy, the *Giovanni Delle Bande Nere* and the *Bartolomeo Colleoni*. At 0830 she opened fire at 20,000 yards range. Both sides, including the destroyers, exchanged fire, although at long range, which made the destroyers' 4.7-inch guns less effective. By 1000 the action had ceased. The *Bartolomeo Colleoni* was stopped and well down by the bows, sinking later. The other Italian cruiser turned to assist her stricken comrade, but then made off at high speed to the south. The British force rescued 525 Italian sailors.

Hero's next task was to join the escorts of a convoy carrying urgently needed military and naval reinforcements to the Middle East (Operation Hats). Four destroyers, *Hero*, *Hostile*, *Mohawk* and *Nubian*, were sent from Alexandria to Gibraltar to augment the escorting forces for the passage

through the Sicilian Narrows. Calling at Malta en route, the destroyers sailed from there on 22 August. Early the next morning *Hostile* struck a mine off Cape Bon and had to be sunk by *Hero*. The *Nubian* had two complete failures in the forced lubrication system of her main engines and returned to Malta. *Hero* and *Mohawk* also returned to Malta with survivors from *Hostile*. Despite the problems, *Hero*, with *Janus*, *Mohawk* and *Nubian* reached Gibraltar to take part in the operation as arranged. Notwithstanding enemy air attacks, the convoy was passed through the Narrows as planned.

Hero was then occupied on routine duties in the Eastern Mediterranean until November 1940, when she went to Malta for a short refit. In early November she helped cover Convoy MW3 comprising five ships for Malta, and she was also part of the escort for the carrier *Illustrious* during the attack on Taranto.

At the end of December 1940, *Hero* joined Force H at Gibraltar. On 25 December, *Berwick*, escorting a troop convoy, reported from about 600 miles west of Cape Finisterre that she was in action with a German cruiser, later identified as *Admiral Hipper*. Force H put to sea immediately to round up and protect the scattered convoy until it could be handed over by Force K who were to escort it to Freetown. *Hero*, with the rest of Force H, returned to Gibraltar on 30 December.

On 1 January 1941, *Hero* was at sea again, with other destroyers of 13th Flotilla, to intercept a French convoy of four merchant ships escorted by an armed trawler off Tres Forcas. The ships were brought safely to Gibraltar.

On 6 January *Hero* left Gibraltar, escorting four merchant ships to join Operation Excess, the passage of eastbound and westbound convoys between Gibraltar and Malta. Severe air attacks on these convoys led to the loss of the cruiser *Southampton*. On completion she rejoined the Mediterranean Fleet. Arriving at Alexandria on 13 January, the next task for *Hero*, together with the destroyer *Decoy*, was to transport the Cyprus Garrison to Kastelogizo. Despite heavy enemy air attacks, the task was accomplished successfully. She also took part in a bombardment of Tobruk by cruisers and destroyers.

At the end of April, the situation of the troops in Greece had become untenable, and the evacuation of Allied troops from Greece and Crete Operation Demon) was started. King George of Greece, his Prime Minister (M. Tsouderos), and the British Minister (Sir Michael Palairet), had already been flown to Crete by the RAF. On the night 22-23 May 1941, *Hero* and *Decoy* took onboard the Greek King and his officials, and conveyed them safely to Alexandria, arriving at 2359 the same day.

Next morning the same two destroyers took onboard 600 special service troops for Selimo Kastelli. The troops were disembarked at night on 26 May at Suda Bay. The withdrawal of the two ships was covered by the battleship *Queen Elizabeth*.

Hero was next dispatched for routine patrol duties along the Syrian coast, where, with *Kimberley* and *Jackal* in company, she remained until late June. During the course of their return to Alexandria, the ships were diverted to intercept the French hospital ship *Canada*.

On 10 July, *Hero* was ordered to disembark torpedoes and take on military stores for Tobruk. She sailed on 11 July and, apart from an unsuccessful attack by a U-boat on 13th, had an uneventful voyage. *Hero* continued to transport stores along the North African coast until September 1941. During this period she was withdrawn temporarily to take part in Operation HALBERD - the passage of Convoy WS11 to Malta. *Hero* acting in company with the battleship *Queen Elizabeth* took part in a diversion as part of the overall operation.

On 25 October *Hero* was with the minelayer *Latona* and destroyers *Hotspur* and *Encounter* on a run to Tobruk when they came under prolonged air attacks about 30 miles north of Bardia. *Latona* was hit and set on fire, and *Hero* went alongside to provide assistance. During this period she was near missed by three bombs from Ju-87s. As a result her side plating and upper deck were distorted and her steering gear damaged. Her speed was reduced to 29 knots and her manoeuvrability impaired. She continued to rescue the crew of the stricken *Latona*, but she had to retire to Alexandria for repairs. After repairs, for the next six months she was re-employed on routine anti-submarine patrols and escort duties in the Eastern Mediterranean.

In January 1942 she helped escort Convoy MW 8A (Operation MF.3) from Alexandria to Malta. On 9 March she sailed with cruisers and other destroyers in a bid to intercept an Italian cruiser force, but the intelligence on the enemy movements proved false. The group met the cruiser *Cleopatra* and destroyer *Kingston* coming from Malta, but on 11 March the cruiser *Naiad* was torpedoed and sunk north of Sollum by *U-565*.

In March 1942, *Hero* was part of the escort of a convoy to Malta from Alexandria. The convoy comprised three merchant ships and the naval supply ship *Breconshire*. The escort was made up of the AA cruiser *Carlisle* and six destroyers, with also three Dido class cruisers and four more destroyers. *Hero* was one of the destroyer escort. Six Hunt class destroyers joined the escort from Tobruk and on 22 March the cruiser *Penelope* and destroyer *Legion* joined the escort from Malta. On that day the convoy was intercepted by Italian warships, comprising two 8-inch cruisers, a 6-inch cruiser and 4 destroyers. The British cruisers and destroyers immediately closed and drove off the enemy, though the *Carlisle* and one Hunt class destroyer made a smoke screen and the other 5 Hunts remained with the convoy to beat off the heavy air attacks that were taking place at the time. Just as the cruisers and destroyers returned to the convoy, a second Italian force comprising the battleship *Littorio*, the three cruisers and seven destroyers approached the convoy. Again the British cruisers and destroyers closed the enemy using smoke screens to allow them to engage at short range. *Hero* was in the division of destroyers closest to the enemy, and *Havock* in that division was hit by a 15-inch shell and had to retire to the convoy. The division closed to within 6000 yards of the enemy. In a second attack on the Italian force with torpedoes, *Lively* of the same division was also hit by a 15-inch shell. By 7pm the enemy turned away and the convoy had been saved. Only the *Penelope* had 6-inch guns, the Dido class cruisers were armed with only 5.25-inch guns, yet they had driven off a 15-inch

HMS Hero's appearance during the war was altered by the addition of radar and A/S weaponry. She had a very successful career in both surface and anti-submarine operations *(Syd Goodman Collection)*

battleship, and 8-inch and 6-inch cruisers. Regrettably the engagement caused delays to the convoy's passage, and in subsequent heavy air attacks one ship was sunk, another badly damaged, and the two that reached Malta safely were both damaged by air attacks whilst in harbour.

On 28 May 1942, while on patrol with *Eridge* and *Hurworth*, north east of Tobruk, concerted depth charge attacks on an underwater contact resulted in the sinking of *U-568* after a 15hr pursuit. 42 survivors were rescued. U-568 had attacked the USS *Kearney* on 17 October 1941 believing her to be a British escort.

In mid June she helped cover convoy MW11 from Alexandria, Port Said and Haifa bound for Malta, running at the same time as a convoy from Gibraltar to Malta (Operation Harpoon). The convoy came under heavy air attacks, was threatened by Italian surface forces and hounded by submarines, and had to retire.

At the end of June 1942, the enemy launched an attack to attempt the capture of Alexandria, and as many service personnel as possible were evacuated from the town. In the course of these operations, the depot ship *Medway* was torpedoed by *U-732* while on passage to Haifa and sank in 15 minutes. *Hero* and *Zulu* picked up 1,105 survivors.

By July, *Hero* was in need of a major refit, but owing to the heavy escort commitments that were becoming increasingly difficult to meet, the Commander-in-Chief, Mediterranean decided that *Hero* could not be released from the Station. Accordingly she continued with her duties at the time of escorting convoys transporting troops to and from Cyprus. In the course of these operations – known under the general title of 'Robertsbridge' - one of the transports, the SS *Princess Marguerite*, was torpedoed and sunk by *U-83*. *Hero* and *Kelvin* picked up, between them, 1,100 survivors.

In October 1942, *Hero* was employed on anti-submarine patrols in the eastern Mediterranean. On 30 October she was in company with four other destroyers (*Pakenham*, *Petard*, *Dulverton* and *Hurworth*) when, with the help of a Wellesley aircraft of 47 Squadron, *U-559* was hunted and brought to the surface about 60 miles north east of Port Said. 40 of the crew were rescued and secret documents were recovered from the submarine before she sank. *U-559* had torpedoed the Australian sloop *Parramatta* off Bardia the previous November.

In December 1942 it became evident that a major refit for *Hero* could be postponed no longer. After some discussion on routing, it was decided she should return to the UK via the Cape. In February she helped provide anti-submarine protection to Convoy 'Pamphlet' with 30,000 men of the 9th Australian Division en route from Suez to Sydney and Melbourne. She covered the passage from Perim to Socotra and then handing the convoy over to an Ocean escort.

Hero was taken in hand for a refit at Portsmouth in April 1943 and it was not completed until the end of the year. Whilst under refit, it was decided she should be handed over to the Royal Canadian Navy, to which she transferred on 15 November 1943. She re-commissioned as HMCS *Chaudiere* the same day. In December she worked up at Scapa Flow.

She was assigned for duties in the North Atlantic as part of Escort Group C-2. On 15 February she sailed from Londonderry to support a section of Convoy ON 224 (outward bound to North America)) on the first stage of the voyage to the rendezvous with other sections of the convoy when escort duties were to be taken over by the ocean escort.

In March 1944, *Chaudiere* was working with Escort Group C2 - a combination of RN and RCN escort destroyers and corvettes. At the beginning of March the Group were escorting Convoy HX 228 (Halifax to UK) and by the morning of 5th had reached a position 480 miles West of Cape Clear (Ireland). At 1000 a submarine asdic contact was obtained by HMCS *Gatineau* and from that moment began a U-boat hunt that was to last 30 hours. Fifteen attacks were made in the next eleven hours by destroyers *Chaudiere*, *Gatineau* and *Icarus*, the frigate *St Catherines*, and the corvettes *Kenilworth Castle*, *Chilliwack* and *Fennel*. After a lull, between 2230 and a few minutes after midnight, three more attacks were made in the next hour, but the U-boat continued to take violent avoiding action. Two more 'Hedgehog' attacks carried out at about 0800 on 6 March were also unsuc-

cessful, as the enemy kept deep, and another creeping attack at 1100 was also avoided.

The Group decided to wait, as asdic condition were good and contact could be maintained, and as it was expected that conditions would compel the U-boat to surface late in the evening. At 1530 their patience and perseverance paid off. The U-boat surfaced unexpectedly, having been forced up by lack of air. It was *U-744*. Making no reply to gunfire from the ships, she was abandoned by her crew and finally dispatched by a torpedo from *Icarus* after codebooks had been recovered.

Early in June 1944 some of the anti-submarine escort groups were withdrawn from their convoy duties to protect the invasion fleet for the Normandy landings (Operation Neptune). *Chaudiere*, with four other Canadian destroyers, formed the 11th Escort Group based on Plymouth. The Group was not actively employed in the invasion itself, but carried out the important duties of anti-submarine patrols to prevent U-boats attacking the convoys carrying troops and stores to the invasion beaches. The Group was mainly operating around the departure areas from the Solent.

At the end of July, Escort Group 11, including *Chaudiere*, left Plymouth for Operation Kinetic - an offensive operation in the Bay of Biscay against enemy convoys passing along the coastal routes close to the West Coast of France. This lasted from 30 July to 6 August but no shipping was found. The Escort group remained in the Biscay area after the completion of this unproductive operation. On 10 August, while on patrol with HMCS *Ottawa*, a submarine contact was made about 40 miles West of Belle Isle. An attack was made but with no success. On 12 August, *Chaudiere* picked up an Austrian Petty Officer, a survivor from *U-981*, which had been sunk that day by Halifax aircraft F/502.

On 19 August while Escort group 11 was patrolling about 60 miles West of La Pallice, a submarine contact was made and an attack mounted. This resulted in the destruction of *U-621*. Then, on 20 August, the Group made another submarine contact West by South of Brest. After three Hedgehog attacks had been made, an underwater explosion was heard. *U-984* had been sunk. *U-984* had earlier escaped after a 30-hour pursuit 30 miles north west of Ushant, and on 25 June had torpedoed and damaged the frigate *Goodson* 40 miles north of Jersey.

In October 1944, *Chaudiere* was detached from the Plymouth Command and sailed for Reykjavik for further service in the North Atlantic. By 26th she had sustained heavy damage from gales - her forepeak was flooded and her oil tanks leaking. Temporary repairs were effected and she sailed for Ireland, arriving at Londonderry with Escort Group 11 in the early hours of 5 November 1944.

On 19 November she left Londonderry for what was to prove to be her last voyage, arriving at Halifax on 29 November. She was taken in hand at Sydney, Cape Breton, for repairs on 22 January, but these were not completed before the war in Europe had ended. She paid off at Sydney on 17 August 1945 and was placed in reserve there. She was purchased for breaking up by the Halifax Shipyards Ltd., Halifax, Nova Scotia in 1948 and but was not broken up till 1950.

She had gained a massive ten battle honours for her name as *Hero*, bringing the total for that name to eighteen. She had gained a further three battle honours for the name *Chaudiere*.

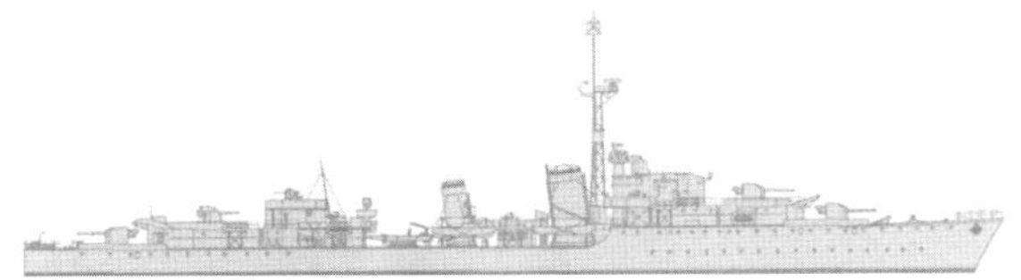

Tribal Class Destroyers

During the late 1930's international tension was mounting, and plans were made for war. Amongst these plans was a programme of shipbuilding, which included many classes of destroyers. In 1936 a new style of destroyer was laid down, the Tribal class. Previous destroyers had followed on from the Great War 'V and W' designs, with single superimposed guns and two sets of torpedo tubes. The Tribals were fitted with twin superimposed guns, giving them a heavy main armament of eight 4.7-inch. To offset the extra weight, they were given just one quadruple torpedo tube mounting. Despite this, they were large by contemporary standards, being of 1,870 tons displacement and 377 ft overall. By comparison, the 'I' class destroyers, building at the same time, were only of 1,370 tons and 323 ft in length. The Tribals had extra boiler power, and their engines developed 44,000-shaft horsepower giving them a speed of 36.5 knots. For anti-aircraft work they were given a quadruple two-pounder and two quadruple machine guns. They also carried two depth charge throwers and one rail with 46 depth charges, as well as one quadruple set of torpedo tubes. They had a complement of 8 officers and 191 men compared to the 'I' Class complement of 7 and 146.

Sixteen Tribals were built for the Royal Navy, and only four survived the war. Eight were built for the Royal Canadian Navy, one of which, *Athabaskan*, was lost in the Channel in April 1944. Three of the class were built for the Royal Australian Navy.

HMS MOHAWK

HMS Mohawk was built with a heavy gun armament of four twin 4.7-inch guns, but lacked an adequate AA armament. *(Portsmouth Royal Naval Museum)*

HMS *Mohawk* was in the first flotilla of Tribals (1935 estimates). She was laid down by Thornycroft on 16 July 1936, was launched on 5 October 1937 and completed on 7 September 1938. She achieved 36.6 knots on trials. In all two flotillas of eight Tribals were built for the Royal Navy.

On completion she joined the Mediterranean Fleet, returning to Home waters in October 1939 and then joining the Rosyth Command. On 16 October whilst in the Firth of Forth, the *Mohawk*, together with the cruisers *Edinburgh* and *Southampton*, was damaged by bombs during an air attack by Ju-88s. She was hit just forward of the bridge and her structure was considerably damaged, but fortunately the bombs failed to explode. Twenty-five of her crew were killed or wounded. Her Commanding Officer, Commander R.F. Jolly, was mortally wounded, but remained on her bridge for the 80 minutes required to bring *Mohawk* ship to safety. He died several hours later. He was posthumously awarded the Empire Gallantry Medal. *Mohawk* went to Hawthorn Leslie on the Tyne for repairs, which completed in December.

In December she sailed from the Tyne with the destroyer *Kelly* which was mined. *Mohawk*'s tiller flat flooded, but she took the *Kelly* in tow back to the Tyne.

In April 1940 she was part of Operation R4, which was a plan to land troops to seize Norwegian ports should the Germans retaliate to British minelaying operations off Norway. Troops were embarked in four cruisers and 8 destroyers at Rosyth. When German ships were detected sailing into the North Sea, it was believed they were breaking out into the Atlantic and the Home Fleet was sailed. The ships involved in Operation R4 landed their troops and sailed to join the Home Fleet. On 9 April 1940, *Mohawk* was part a force of four cruisers and six other destroyers under Vice-Admiral Layton which was detached from the Home Fleet to attack Bergen, where the Germans had just landed. This attack was later cancelled and the opportunity to catch three German cruisers in the harbour was missed. The force turned back to rejoin the Home Fleet. Both the main fleet and detached force came

under air attack, and the Tribal class destroyer *Gurkha* of the detached force dropped astern to gain sea room to manoeuvre to raise the elevation of her guns by heeling over during turns, but was sunk. The cruisers *Glasgow* and *Southampton*, also part of the detached force, were damaged in the air attacks, during which the Fleet used 40 percent of its AA ammunition. The lessons that ships should stay together for mutual support and that AA ammunition expenditure should be controlled during air attacks were to be reinforced throughout the long years ahead in all theatres of the war.

The Fleet then turned away from the Norwegian coast, and returned to Scapa Flow. On 5 May she escorted the SS *Royal Ulsterman* from Mo, where she had landed troops. On 10 May Germany invaded Holland and Belgium. *Mohawk* with the older destroyers *Vivien* and *Windsor*, proceeded to the Hook of Holland on 13 May to embark Dutch Government officials, the British, Belgian and Norwegian Delegations and 400 refugees, whom they to Tilbury. Immediately afterwards *Mohawk* was sailed for the Mediterranean, arriving at Alexandria on 29 May to join 14 Destroyer Flotilla. Italy declared war on 10 June.

In June 1940 she was with cruisers and other destroyers helped escort convoys from the Dardanelles and Greek harbours to Suez. On 9 July 1940 she was part of the escort to the Mediterranean Fleet when it encountered the Italian battlefleet off Calabria. In a long-range fight the Italian flagship (*Giulio Cesare*) was damaged, as was the cruiser *Bolzano*. Attacks by Italian aircraft damaged the cruiser *Gloucester* and caused splinter damage to some of the battleships and the carrier *Ark Royal*. Although inconclusive, the action helped establish the British Fleet's supremacy over the Italian Fleet in the forthcoming years.

In Late August/early September she helped escort convoys in the Gulf of Nauplia. On 22 September 1940 she, with *Janus*, *Jervis* (D14) and *Juno*, bombarded the airfield and troop concentrations at Sidi Barrani. The concentrations were bombarded again on 23 September by the gunboat *Ladybird*, and on 25 September by four destroyers.

In November 1940 she helped escort convoy MW.3 (Op MB.8), comprising five ships bound for Malta. On 11 November, whilst the *Illustrious* car-

HMS Mohawk showing the fine lines for which the Tribals were famous. *(T. Ferrers-Walker Collection)*

ried out the air strike on Taranto, *Mohawk*, with the cruisers *Orion*, *Ajax* and *Sydney*, and the destroyer *Nubian*, carried out a raid on the Strait of Otranto. Off Valona the British force encountered and engaged a convoy of four ships with two escorts, sinking all the ships in the convoy with no damage to the British force.

In early January she sailed with the main Mediterranean Fleet from Alexandria to cover convoy Op Excess from Malta to Piraeus. During this operation, on 10 January 1941, the destroyer *Gallant* was severely damaged by mine. The mine was part of a barrage in the Sicilian Channel laid by Italian cruisers and destroyers in the previous August. *Gallant*'s bow was blown off, and sank later. She had lost 65 killed or missing and had 15 wounded. The destroyer *Griffin* took her injured and the majority of the survivors, whilst *Mohawk* took the damaged destroyer in tow for the 120 miles to Malta. The tow was managed at 6.5 knots, with the cruisers *Bonaventure*, *Gloucester* and *Southampton* providing cover. The *Gallant* was taken in hand at Malta for repairs, but on 5 April 1942 was bombed whilst still under repair. She was then stripped and sunk as a blockship in September 1943.

On 24 February *Mohawk* sailed from Alexandria with the Australian cruiser *Perth* and destroyer *Nubian* to support the monitor *Terror* which was under attack, but the *Terror* was sunk before the ships could reach her.

On 28 March 1941 she was part of the Mediterranean Fleet which had sailed to meet the threat from Italian surface forces to the British convoys to Greece. She was one of the escorts to the British battleships and carrier (*Formidable*). The Fleet engaged Italian forces in a night action, during which the British battleships sank two Italian cruisers (*Fiume* and *Zara*), at close range. Destroyers in company sank the cruiser *Pola*, which had been brought to a standstill by air attacks, and two Italian destroyers (*Alfieri* and *Carducci*)

After further operations with the main Mediterranean Fleet, she and the *Jervis*, *Janus* and *Nubian* arrived at Malta on 11 April to form a striking force to operate against enemy convoys crossing the Mediterranean. On 16 April 1941 she was with the other three destroyers off Sfax, Tunis, when they encountered an axis convoy of five ships (14,398 tons) escorted by three Italian destroyers bound for the German Afrika Corps. The merchant ships were chiefly carrying ammunition, motor transport and German troops. The convoy was sighted at 0213 in moonlight off the Kerkenah Bank, and the British destroyers opened fire at 0220. Two enemy destroyers (*Baleno* and *Luca Tarigo*) and all five ships of the convoy were sunk. The third destroyer (*Lampo*) was forced ashore and left burning. *Mohawk* was torpedoed by the *Luca Tarigo* early in the action but continued to engage the least damaged merchant ship with her forward guns. Whilst still in action, but stopped, she was hit again amidships and heeled over, and had to be sunk by gunfire from the *Janus*. She lost two officers and 39 men.

Of the sixteen Tribals class destroyers built for the Royal Navy, only four were to survive. They had been in the thick of the fighting in all theatres of the war.

Mohawk had gained seven battle honours for her name:-

Norway, 1940; Calabria 1940; Libya 1940; Mediterranean 1940-41, Sfax 1941, Matapan 1941 and Malta Convoys 1941.

HMS TARTAR

HMS Tartar seen early in the war with a tripod foremast. She earned a massive 13 Battle Honours for her name. *(Syd Goodman Collection)*

The *Tartar* was laid down on 26 August 1936 by Swan, Hunter and Wigham Richardson Ltd, and was launched on 21 October the next year. She completed on 10 March 1939. She was one of the Leaders of the class. Previously flotilla leaders had been built to an enlarged design and were usually faster and more heavily armed than the others in their flotilla. With the Tribals, the policy had changed, and leaders were built to the same specifications as the others in the flotilla, but had more compartments for the extra staff and communications to be carried. On trials she achieved a mean speed of 36.4 knots.

On 1 June 1939 she was one of the ships that stood by the stricken submarine *Thetis* in Liverpool Bay. At the outbreak of war she was in Home Waters in the 6th Destroyer Flotilla and operated out of Scapa Flow. She was on convoy duty when the Norwegian campaign started in the spring of 1940, and she was immediately diverted to escort the battleships and cruisers off the Norwegian coast. She took part in the evacuation of troops from Norway on the night 30 Apr - 1May when 2200 troops were lifted from Aandalsnes and Molde, and was one of the force sent to escort the damaged cruiser *Suffolk* back to Scapa Flow after she had been heavily bombed. She later helped blockade Trondheim.

In June she provided A/S cover for Swedish destroyers off the Faeroes. For the rest of the year she took part in patrols and carried out escort duty. In December she carried out trials of Type 74X radar. In January 1941 she escorted the battleship *King George V*, carrying Lord Halifax to the United States as Ambassador. In March of that year she took part in Operation Claymore, which was a commando raid on the Lofoten Islands partly designed to capture intelligence material. Fishery processing installations and merchant shipping were destroyed and many prisoners taken as well as the capture of codes from the trawler *Krebs*.

Two months later she was part of the force deployed to sink the German battleship *Bismarck* which had broken out into the Atlantic. She had

HMS Tartar later in the war with a twin 4-inch AA gun in X position, and with a lattice foremast supporting radar. *(Syd Goodman Collection)*

been escorting the battleship *Rodney* heading for the USA when they were diverted. The *Rodney* was to join the *King George V* for the final engagement. During *Tartar*'s return from the operation, German aircraft attacked her and her sister ship *Mashona*, and the *Mashona* was sunk on 28th. The *Tartar* rescued 14 officers and 215 ratings whom she landed at Greenock.

In June 1941 she took part in Operation 'EC', whose aim was the destruction of the German weather reporting trawler near Jan Mayen Island. The trawler was first sighted by the *Tartar* on 28th. Then *Tartar* with the cruiser *Nigeria* and destroyer *Bedouin*, sank the trawler after recovering vital codebooks. The next month she took part in a reconnaissance of Spitzbergen investigating Russian and Norwegian settlements there, and later evacuating the weather station at Bear Island, followed by anti-shipping strikes off the Norwegian coast.

Tartar was one of the escorts to the battleship *Prince of Wales* as she returned to Scapa Flow with the Prime Minister, Winston Churchill, after his meeting with President Roosevelt in Newfoundland, when the Atlantic Charter was signed. Shortly afterwards she took part in another raid on Spitzbergen.

In January 1942 she was an escort to the covering force for convoy PQ 7B to Russia. The convoy arrived safely, and *Tartar* assisted in covering the return convoy QP 5. In March, she escorted the carrier *Victorious* whose aircraft carried out a strike against the *Tirpitz* in Vestfjord. A few days later convoy PQ12 was threatened by the appearance of the German battleship in the area, and *Tartar* and other destroyers were despatched by the Home Fleet to intercept her. Although contact was not made, the convoy escaped attack.

Tartar was then refitted at Hull, and then in August sailed with the battleship *Nelson* and other ships to cover a convoy to Malta (Operation Pedestal). During the first stages of this convoy's passage through the Mediterranean, it came under heavy air attack, and the destroyer *Foresight* was torpedoed, and the *Tartar* took her in tow for Gibraltar, but the next day the *Tartar* had to sink her. The convoy continued to come under heavy attack from Italian and German aircraft as well

from submarines and E-boats, with heavy losses to the merchantmen and escorts. Only five of the fourteen merchant ships in the convoy made Malta, and the Navy lost the carrier *Eagle* and cruisers *Manchester* and *Cairo* as well as the destroyer *Foresight*. Many other ships were badly damaged.

Later in the month she returned to northern waters and the next month escorted convoy PQ18 to Russia as part of a very heavy fighting escort, comprising the cruiser *Scylla* and sixteen fleet destroyers, designed to cope with the intense attacks which had befallen the previous convoy PQ.17. Three ships were sunk by U-boats and ten by aircraft, but 27 were delivered safely.

In November 1942 she returned to the Mediterranean to join Force H prior to the landings in North Africa. On completion of the landings she was attached to the 6th Flotilla of the Mediterranean Fleet and in December joined Force Q operating from Algiers on anti-shipping strikes as well as on escort duties. In March, 1943, she was ordered to Mers-el-Kabir during an attempted attack by human torpedoes on Force H, but she did not sight anything., and no attack developed. In April she and the destroyer *Laforey* attacked German motor torpedo boats near Marettimo. In early May she and other destroyers engaged small craft off the Cap Bon Peninsula, taking many German prisoners. In June she bombarded shore batteries on the island of Pantellaria, which surrendered three days later. The *Tartar* with two trawlers and six landing craft remained at the island to protect the port until the NOIC was established. She then took the Admiral Commanding the seaborne assault to Djidjelli.

Tartar rescued 200 of the 400 survivors from the hospital ship *Talamba*, which was sunk off Sicily by the Germans during the landings on that island. The next day she sank an ammunition ship (*Baarn*) which was on fire. The day after she towed the *Eskimo*, which had been damaged by bombing in the operation, to Malta. She then operated off the Italian coast until October. On 30th of that month she left Gibraltar for Home Waters and a refit.

After the refit she was allocated to the Plymouth Command. On 10th March she took part in an operation to intercept enemy destroyers believed to be escorting a German submarine to Brest. However, the enemy destroyers stayed too close to the coast to be intercepted. Later that month she took part in

HMS Tartar - this class had only one set of torpedo tubes amidships to compensate for the weight of their gunnery armament. *(MoD/Crown Copyright)*

Operation Tunnel, which was a routine patrol off the French Coast at the western end of the Channel.

During the Normandy landings she was the senior ship of eight destroyers of the 10th Flotilla providing cover against attacks by surface ships upon the invasion force, when they encountered four enemy destroyers off Brest. The British force, led by the *Tartar*, closed to point blank range before opening fire and causing confusion among the enemy. *Tartar* stopped the *ZH1*, but was hit by *Z32*. However, *Ashanti*, with *Tartar* in company, finished off the *ZH1*. The *Z32* was then driven ashore by two (Canadian) destroyers of the force. The *Tartar* was out of action for two weeks. In another action in the same area, on the night 7-8 July she and the *Huron* sank two minesweepers off the Channel Islands, and on the night 14-15 July she, the *Haida* and *Blyskawica* sank two submarine chasers off Lorient.

On 6 August, she was part of a force comprising the cruiser *Bellona* and four Tribals (*Tartar*, *Ashanti*, *Haida* and *Iroquois*) that attacked an enemy convoy 32 miles SSW of St Nazaire. At least seven enemy ships, all four merchant ships and three escorts, were destroyed.

Tartar was again refitted prior to being allocated to the East Indies Station in November. She left the Clyde on 12 March escorting light fleet carriers to the Mediterranean, and reached Aden on 12 April. That month she assisted in the bombardment and air strikes on Car Nicobar airfields and the bombardment of Port Blair. She joined Force 61 to operate in the Andaman Islands area in Operation Dukedom, during which the Japanese cruiser *Hugaro* was sunk in a combined operation by aircraft and destroyers. In June, she and the *Nubian* took part in an anti-shipping strike off Sabang and sank two enemy ships despite enemy air attacks.

On 8 August *Tartar* accompanied the battleship *Nelson* and other ships to Penang, and was there for the Japanese surrender at that port. She left Penang on 7 September heading for Home Waters, arriving at Plymouth on 17 November 1945. She was then placed in reserve. She was handed over to BISCO 21 February 1948, was removed from the Reserve Fleet on 2 March and was towed to Newport for breaking up less than 9 years since her completion.

She had gained a massive 13 Battle Honours for her name, bringing the total to 18.

HM Ships LOOKOUT & LOYAL

HMS Loyal - a handsome and powerful destroyer. *(Syd Goodman Collection)*

The *Lookout* and *Loyal* were two destroyers of the Laforey Class, which, with the follow on M class, were considered by many to be the most handsome destroyers ever built for the Royal Navy. The Laforeys, in common with all the all too few modern fleet destroyers available in the early years of the war, were hard worked and were always in the front line of action. Consequently a heavy toll was taken of these ships and *Lookout* and *Loyal* were the only two out of the eight in the class to survive the war, albeit with *Loyal* badly damaged and out of action. The 'L' and 'M' classes were a development of the 'J' and 'K' classes, repeating the single funnel arrangement. However, they incorporated a new twin 4.7-inch gun mounting which was enclosed and power operated. The guns had a better AA capability, with an elevation of 50 degrees instead of the Javelins' 40 degrees, and they also fired a 62 pound shell, 12 pounds more than the Javelins, and had a range of 19,400 yards instead of 16,700 yards. To compensate for the extra weight, the centre tubes of their quintuple torpedo tube mountings were not fitted.

Their standard displacement was 1920 tons, with a full load of 2,642 tons. They were 362.5 ft. long (14.5 ft shorter than the earlier Tribal class but 6 feet longer than the Javelins), and had a beam of 36.75 ft. (over a foot broader than the Javelins). Their twin turbine engines developed 48,000-shaft horsepower giving them a speed of 36 knots, with a maximum sea speed of 31 knots. *Lookout* achieved 32.43 knots on trials, and *Loyal* 34.1 knots. They had an endurance of 5,400 miles at 15 knots, 3,400 miles at 20 knots and 1,150 miles at maximum continuous sea speed. They were designed to carry three twin 4.7-inch guns with a quadruple pom-pom abaft the funnel. During building two multiple machine guns were added abreast the bridge together with two single (later increased to two twin) 20-mm abreast the searchlight amidships. By October 1944 both *Lookout* and *Loyal* had had their machine guns removed, and their 20-mm armament comprised four twin and two single guns. They also carried two sets of quadruple torpedo tubes. For a period a single 4-inch replaced the after set of torpedo tubes. Because of production delays with the 4.7-

inch guns, four of the class were completed with four twin 4-inch guns instead of three twin 4.7-inch mountings. Two depth charge rails and four throwers were fitted for anti-submarine work, with an outfit of 36 (later increased to 42) depth charges. Six of the L class became war losses, and three of the M class were lost.

Lookout was laid down by Messrs. Scotts Shipbuilding and Engineering Co. Ltd., Glasgow on 23 November 1938, launched on 4 November 1940 and completed on 31 January 1942, commissioning on 7 January. *Loyal* was also built by Scotts, being laid down on the same date, launched on 8 October 1941 and completed on 31 October 1942.

After working up on the Clyde and at Scapa Flow, the *Lookout*'s first task was in March 1942, when she was part of the escort to the battleship *King George V* and aircraft carrier *Victorious* covering Russian convoys PQ 12 and QP 8. The German battleship *Tirpitz* and 4 destroyers sailed to attack the convoy but only achieved the sinking of one straggler. On 23 March, having been allocated to Force H, *Lookout* sailed south, escorting troop convoy WS 17 (Winston Special, with troops for the Middle East). The convoy called at Ponta Delgada on 28th and reached Freetown on 6 April. *Lookout* sailed three days later for Durban to join Operation Ironclad, the landings at Diego Suarez in Madagascar. She was part of the screen to the battleship *Ramillies* for the actual assault on 4 May. After the successful conclusion of that operation, *Lookout* was lent to the East Indies Fleet, escorting convoys to and from Colombo during June and July.

She returned to Gibraltar in August, escorting the aircraft carrier *Formidable*, to rejoin Force H. She was in time to take part in Operation Pedestal, an important supply convoy to Malta. The convoy of 14 ships passed Gibraltar on 10th and the next day the carrier *Eagle* was torpedoed. *Lookout*, which had been escorting the carrier *Furious* which was to fly off Spitfires to Malta, with *Laforey* and the tug *Jaunty* went to *Eagle*'s assistance. Between them the three ships rescued 927 survivors from the stricken carrier, *Lookout* rescuing 48 officers and 438 men. On 12th and 13th the convoy came under heavy air attacks and also overnight E-boats

HMS Lookout with the after set of torpedo tubes replaced by a single 4-inch gun. *(Syd Goodman Collection)*

attacked the convoy and escorts. During the attacks the *Indomitable* was hit, and *Lookout* went alongside to provide firefighting assistance. On 12th the *Lookout* sighted a periscope and the destroyer *Tartar* nearby sighted torpedo tracks. They carried out a joint attack on the Italian submarine *Emo* without damaging her, but keeping her down until the convoy had continued on to a safe distance. Only five of the merchant ships survived the fierce attacks and reached Malta. Besides the *Eagle*, the cruisers *Cairo* and *Manchester* and destroyer *Foresight* were lost. The carrier *Indomitable* and cruisers *Nigeria* and *Kenya* were damaged. *Lookout* arrived back at Gibraltar on 15th, escorting the battleship *Nelson*. She then became part of the Gibraltar escort force, covering Fleet movements and convoys until October, when she escorted the battleship *Malaya* back to the UK.

Lookout returned to Gibraltar, leaving Scapa with the battleship *Rodney* on 23 October. Having rejoined Force H, she was able to take part in Operation Torch, the landings in North Africa on 8 November. On completion of that operation, she resumed her escort duties in the Mediterranean, and carried out patrols off the enemy coast for the next few months.

In December 1942 *Loyal* had arrived in the Mediterranean, coming south as escort to a fast convoy from the Clyde to Algiers. She then joined Force Q, a striking force of cruisers and destroyers (*Lookout*, *Loyal* and (their sister ship) *Lightning*) operating out of Bone. She and the *Lightning* sank one enemy transport 30 miles SE of Cagliari, Sardinia on 18 January. On 16 February 1943 *Lookout* rescued 3 officers and 47 men, survivors from the Canadian corvette *Louisberg*, which had been torpedoed by aircraft off Oran. On 12 March Force Q (*Aurora*, *Sirius*, *Lightning* and *Loyal*) was on a sweep off Galita Island, north of Bizerta, when *Lightning* was torpedoed twice by a German E-boat. The destroyer sank and *Loyal* rescued 181 survivors, including the Captain.

In May 1943, *Loyal*, still with Force Q, took part in the blockade to prevent German forces in North Africa crossing the Mediterranean to Sicily and Sardinia during their retreat. On 9th she and *Tartar* sank two merchant vessels off Cape Bon. Four days later *Lookout* captured 12 Germans in a small boat off Plane Island, and whilst operating off Cape Bon with *Laforey* sank a small supply ship on 23rd.

On 8 June 1943 both *Lookout* and *Loyal* were in the force bombarding the island of Pantellaria. They carried out a further bombardment overnight 10/11 June and on the next day the island surrendered. That evening *Lookout* came under 25 dive bombing attacks but survived without damage. On 20 June, when HM the King arrived in Malta in the cruiser *Aurora*, *Lookout* was one of the four escorting destroyers, *Jervis*, *Eskimo* and *Nubian* being the others.

In July 1943 both ships *Lookout* and *Loyal* were attached to Force K in the Eastern Support Force for Operation Husky, the landings in Sicily on 10 July. Once the landings had started, the destroyers provided gunfire support for the troops ashore, and joined with the cruiser *Newfoundland* and Dutch gunboat *Flores*. Shore targets were engaged on nearly every day from 13th to 21st, the ships responding to calls for fire from the Army ashore. On 19th the *Lookout* and cruiser *Newfoundland* had responded to calls on 17 targets, including 9 shore batteries. On 23 July both destroyers, together with their sister *Laforey*, escorted the cruisers *Newfoundland* (Flagship of Force K) and the *Mauritius* from Augusta at 1250. At 1338 the *Newfoundland* was hit right aft by a torpedo, which removed her rudders. The *Newfoundland* was able to continue to Malta at 22 knots, steering by main engines. The German submarine *U-407* had fired the torpedoes, and was then twice passed over by *Laforey* without being detected. The *Laforey* then detected her on ASDIC and attacked, forcing *U-407* down to 210 metres. However, after several more attacks, the contact was classified 'non sub', and the U-boat was able to slip away to safety. *Laforey* and was joined by other destroyers in her search for the attacker, and the Italian submarine *Ascianghi* fired torpedoes at her and the destroyer *Eclipse*. The two destroyers promptly carried out five attacks, driving her to the surface. The Italian sank by the stern, leaving survivors who claimed that they had fired the torpedoes that had hit the *Newfoundland*. However, their torpedoes had missed.

On 2 and 3 September the *Loyal* accompanied

battleships, monitors and cruisers in bombardments on the coast of Cape Armis, Reggio Calabria, the Messina Strait and Pessaro prior to the landings in Calabria (Operation Baytown). During the landings at Salerno (Operation Avalanche) on 9 September 1943, the *Laforey*, *Lookout* and *Loyal* were in the support group for the northern attack force. They closed the shore astern of the first waves of minesweepers to carry out a bombardment before the landings. After the landing craft had gone in, the destroyers provided gunfire support for the troops ashore. They engaged in duels with German tanks. The *Laforey* was hit five times and had to retire, being replaced close to the beach by *Lookout*. *Lookout* engaged one enemy shore battery at 1,000 yards, stopping only when she saw Allied troops storming it with bayonets. *Loyal* was slightly damaged by near misses from air attacks. On 9th *Loyal* was also hit in the boiler room by a 88-mm shell which put her No. 2 boiler room out of action, fracturing and distorting boiler tubes. She remained in action and left the area for repairs on 10th after firing 1714 rounds. On 12th she returned to the beaches after re-ammunitioning and repairs. On the afternoon of 13th she was near-missed by rocket bomb fired by a Heinkel III aircraft and suffered slight damage. The nearby destroyer *Nubian* was also slightly damaged by a near miss, whilst the cruiser *Uganda* was badly damaged by a hit. *Lookout* was also near missed by a radio-controlled bomb on 16th. She sailed for Malta for repairs before returning to the area on 25th.

On 13 October *Laforey* and *Lookout* and the Dutch gunboat *Flores* bombarded positions north of the Volturna River in conjunction with landing of tanks from LCTs. That afternoon the ships were attacked by 12 fighter-bombers and the *Lookout* suffered damage and casualties from splinters from a near miss by a 250 Kg. bomb. On 13 November *Lookout* arrived at Taranto for a refit, which lasted to 24 July 1944.

In November and December *Loyal* operated off the East Coast of Italy in the Adriatic with *Quilliam*, carrying out bombardments. She was slightly damaged by shore batteries on 19 November while intercepting an enemy convoy. The 3-inch shell left a hole 2ft. by 1ft. in her side but her fighting efficiency was not impaired. On 25 November she shelled Civita Nuova and on 2 December shelled San Benedetto and Ancona. In January 1944 *Loyal* rejoined Force K, then based on Malta. She was part of the support and escort group for Operation Shingle, the landings at Anzio that month. She operated close offshore, providing support to the Army wherever gunfire was required. On 29 January she was near the cruiser *Spartan* when a radio-controlled bomb hit the cruiser. The cruiser sank after about an hour and *Loyal* helped rescue survivors. On 9 February *Loyal* was hit by shore batteries. The shell burst on the upper deck, starboard side forward of the engine room after bulkhead, leaving a 1.5- ft. square hole. Her speed was reduced to 20 knots, and she was forced to return to Naples on one engine. Repairs were carried out at Taranto and took till 30 March. She returned to the Anzio area in May. On the night 9/10 May she at anchor off the beaches when she was straddled by bombs. The damage was not severe, but did involve repairs at Taranto which took several weeks.

On 24 July, *Lookout*'s refit at Taranto being over, she joined the 14th Flotilla for Operation Dragoon, the landings in the South of France on 15 August. She supported the landings on the Islands of Levant and Port Cros. After the landings had been completed successfully, she remained to provide support where required. On 19th she fired 116 rounds in support of the attack on Toulon, spotting being provided by aircraft. On 25th she, with other ships including the battleships *Ramillies* and *Lorraine*, carried out a bombardment of St. Mandrier Peninsula, at the entrance to Toulon, firing 411 rounds. That action forced the Germans there to surrender.

In September *Loyal* with the destroyers and *Undine*, *Urchin* and *Kimberley* and the gunboats *Aphis* and *Scarab* shelled the Rimini coast in support of the 8th Army. *Loyal* and *Urchin* carried out bombardments on 4th and *Loyal* and *Scarab* on 7th. *Lookout* was also in that area and carried out a bombardment on 17th and 18th, when she fired 202 rounds. Further bombardments took place on 20th. On 24th she fired at tanks and troop concentrations north of Rimini. On the night 11/12 October *Lookout* and *Loyal* carried out a bombardment of

HMS Loyal. Although her operational service was cut short in 1944 by mine damage, she continued to serve as a base and accommodation ship. *(MoD/Crown Copyright)*

enemy positions comprising a battery and billets in the Cesenatico area. The following morning the two ships left the area at 20 knots and at 1607 *Loyal* ran over a ground mine which had been laid in 7.5 fathoms. There were no casualties, but her bottom was extensively damaged. The explosion took place ten yards off her starboard side abreast the engine room and gearing room, and her structure was strained and buckled, with 160 ft of side plating being blown in. She started flooding aft in X magazine and her propeller shaft passages. She developed a 7-degree list. All her steam and electrical power failed and she was immobilised. Her main and auxiliary machinery, guns and radar were all extensively damaged. Her after set of torpedo tubes came off its rollers. Only her forward guns could be used in local control. *Lookout* towed her to Ancona. She was later towed to Taranto where she was assessed as a constructive total loss. She paid off to care and maintenance in December and was used as an accommodation ship and base at Malta from 1946 to 1947.

Lookout returned to her escort and bombardment tasks and on 1 January 1945 joined the 3rd Destroyer Flotilla. On 15 January she bombarded San Remo, on 18th the Franco-Italian border and on 19th she fired 84 rounds at an enemy supply dump in the same region. In March 1945 the *Lookout* and her half sister *Meteor* were detailed to search for the destroyer *TA 32 Premuda* (formerly the Yugoslav *Dubrovnik*) and the ex Italian Torpedo Boats *TA 24* (*Arturo*) and *TA 29* (*Eridano*) north of Corsica. At 0300 on 18th they made contact and opened fire using radar control for their guns, and launching torpedoes. In a running fight the British ships sank two torpedo boats, but the *Premuda* escaped using smoke and the cover of a minefield. 244 German sailors were rescued by the destroyers and coastal forces. The British ships were unscathed. This was the last of the large number of destroyer actions in

the Mediterranean during the war. On 23-25 April the *Lookout* accompanied two French cruisers in a bombardment of the German bases on the Italian Riviera.

After the war in Europe was over on 8 May, *Lookout* visited ports in the Mediterranean, finally leaving the area on 19 October, sailing for Plymouth via Gibraltar. On arrival she paid off into reserve.

Lookout was scrapped at Newport, being handed over on 6 January, towed from Devonport on 23 February, and arriving on 29 February 1948. *Loyal*, which had ceased to be used as an accommodation ship, was towed back to the UK in late July by the tug *Earner*. The *Earner* took her on to Milford Haven for breaking up on 5 August 1948.

The destroyers had gained the following battle honours for their names:

Lookout – Diego Suarez 1942; Malta Convoys 1942; Arctic 1942; North Africa 1942-43; Sicily 1943; Salerno 1943; South France 1944; Mediterranean 1943-45

Loyal – Sicily 1943; Salerno 1943; Mediterranean 1943; Anzio 1944; Adriatic 1944

Both were second ships of their names, the first being World War I destroyers.

HMS PETARD

HMS Petard. This class was completed with 4-inch guns because of a shortage of 4.7-inch guns.
(T. Ferrers-Walker Collection)

By the outbreak of the Second World War an emergency building programme of warships had been established, and included in this were many destroyers. The fleet destroyers were designed on the lines of the pre-war J and K classes, but had only single main armament guns instead of twin. The alphabetical sequence was maintained, and the P class, the second emergency war class, commenced building in late 1939 and 1940. *Petard* was laid down at Vickers-Armstrong's Walker Yard on the Tyne on 26 December 1939, and was launched on 27 March 1941,commissioned on 4 June 1942, and completed on 15 June 1942, the next to last of her flotilla to complete. She had originally been named *Persistent.*

She was 345-ft long overall (338.5-ft pp.), and had a beam of 35 ft. Her displacement was 1,540 tons, and she was armed with single 4-inch guns due to the shortage of 4.7-inch. She carried these superimposed fore and aft. She also had a quadruple pompom abaft the funnel and four Oerlikon 20-mm. She was designed to carry two quadruple torpedo tube mountings, with the after set replaced by a fifth 4-inch gun when the aircraft threat warranted. She carried 4 depth charge throwers, two rails and 70 depth charges. The next emergency war design destroyers, the Q class, were 13.75-ft longer with 8-inches more beam - a reversion to almost the original J and K class dimensions, and carried single 4.7-inch guns in square shields.

Her engines developed 40,000-shaft horsepower giving her a designed speed of 36.75 knots, with a maximum continuous sea speed of 30.25 knots. She had an endurance of 4,600 miles at 20 knots, and 1,150 miles at her maximum continuous seagoing speed.

On completion she worked up at Scapa Flow and in July 1942 she sailed from the UK as part of the escort of a troop convoy to the Middle East, routed around the Cape. When she arrived at Port Said on 22 September, she joined the 12th Flotilla of the Mediterranean Fleet.

On 30 October 1942 in the Eastern Mediterranean she, with the *Pakenham*, *Hero*, *Dulverton* and *Hurworth* supported by a Wellington aircraft were diverted to attack a submarine that had been reported by a Sunderland aircraft. Contact was gained and held on and off for 10 hours, with *Petard* carrying out the first depth charge attack at 1257. Three destroyers attacked the submarine, with one standing by and the other keeping the ring. At 2217 *Petard* carried out a final attack with depth charges and at 2240 the submarine (*U-559*) surfaced. In all 150 depth charges had been dropped on the submarine. *Petard* and *Dulverton* opened fire and then sent away boarding parties. *Petard*'s one 4-inch shell, fired before she became too close for her guns to depress, passed through the conning tower and then exploded. She fired 114 pom-pom and 79 Oerlikon rounds at the U-boat, and then went alongside. During the boarding operation that followed her First Lt. (Lt. F A B Fasson) and an AB (C Grazier) managed to recover an M-4 cypher machine and codebooks. Both men were lost when they went down with the U-boat when it sank at 2343. They were awarded posthumous George Crosses. The recovered material helped Bletchley Park break German codes in December. 14 of the submarine's crew were saved.

On 16 November she sailed as part of the escort of convoys to Malta and Tobruk (Operation Stoneage). On 17 November six Italian bombers attacked the convoy and at dusk there was an attack by German torpedo aircraft. At first light the next day there were more attacks by small groups of German and Italian aircraft. Beaufighter cover was provided, but that evening 26 Ju.88s attacked in three groups. They marked the convoy with flares and the cruiser *Arethusa* was hit forward. Her Captain was badly burned and 157 of the crew were killed. She turned stern to wind to assist the fire fighters, but was 10 degrees down by her head and had a list of 15 degrees to port. *Petard* and *Javelin* closed to assist, but *Javelin* was ordered to return to the convoy. *Petard* took *Arethusa* in tow. She managed 10 knots, but the first tow parted and a second tow was passed and speed limited to 5 knots. The next morning the wind rose and there were more bombing attacks. In the rising gale, the tow was slipped and re-rigged on the cruiser's stern, and

HMS Petard was modified during the war and had twin 4-inch guns at B and X positions. *(Syd Goodman Collection)*

Petard took the cruiser in tow stern first at 3 knots. Bombs fell within 15 yards of *Petard*, but she was not hit. On 20 November, the tow was passed to tugs and *Petard* remained in company to guard against submarines until *Arethusa* was safely at Alexandria.

On 15 December 1942 she was on passage from Benghazi to Malta with the Greek destroyer *Queen Olga* south of Malta. The Italian submarine *Varsciek* (*Uarsciek*), was sighted in poor light on the surface at 0405. The destroyers were expecting to sight the British submarine *Ultimatum* at dawn, so challenged the vessel. The submarine had noted the ships, but thought there were four vessels. She was undeterred by the *Petard*'s challenge, which happened to co-incide with the Italian's recognition signal for the day! She was sure they were enemy, and fired her stern tube torpedoes at the destroyers and crash-dived. However, the submarine had lost control and dived to a depth greater than that shown on her depth gauges. Coming up to 70 metres, she again lost trim as *Petard* dropped a ten-charge pattern, and was forced to the surface. The Captain opened the conning tower and looked around, but saw nothing and dived again without having been seen. *Queen Olga* then attacked with depth charges and severely damaged the submarine, which blew her tanks to try to escape surfaced. The destroyers opened fire at once, killing the Captain. Others of the crew jumped overboard or hid. *Petard* then collided with the submarine, which was still under way. They called to the submarine's crew to stop the engines, which they did, and the Italians surrendered. Attempts to scuttle the submarine by her crew failed. The *Petard* took her in tow, but the submarine's rudder had jammed and the tow parted. A further tow was rigged, but, in correcting the submarine's rudder, air leaks were started in compartments aft. The submarine started to settle and, after seven hours she sank. 32 of her crew had been saved. However, charts had been recovered showing the positions of enemy minefields.

She had to undergo repairs at Alexandria for the damage to her bow, set back by four feet, sustained when she collided with the *Uarsciek*. Originally estimated to be in dock for six weeks, she was at sea again after just 11 days.

In February 1943 she helped escort convoy Pamphlet, carrying 30,000 men of the 9th Australian Division from Suez to Sydney and Melbourne. She helped provide anti-submarine cover from Suez as far as Socotra for the five liners, which included the *Queen Mary*. The convoy arrived at Sydney on 27 February without incident.

In May she, with other destroyers of Force K operating from Malta, helped maintain a blockade between Sicily and Sardinia. Early on 4 May she was with the destroyers *Nubian* and *Paladin* when they sank the Italian torpedo boat *Perseo* seven miles east of Kelibia, Tunisia, together with the large merchantman (*Campo Basso* - 3566 tons) carrying munitions which the torpedo boat had been escorting to Tunis.

On 12 and 13 May she accompanied the cruiser *Orion* in a bombardment of Pantellaria, and on 1 June was with the *Penelope* when she bombarded the island. On the night 10-11 June she accompanied the Headquarters ship *Largs* to the island with a landing force of the 1st British Division. The island surrendered on 11 June.

On 18 June she was alongside the mole at Bizerta during an air raid and had three near misses, one on her port quarter, and one either side of her bow. She received considerable minor damage to her hull and fittings, and was out of action for two days.

For the landings in Sicily (Operation Husky) on 10 July 1943, she was part of the escort to the reserve covering force comprising the battleships *King George V* and *Howe* and the cruisers *Dido* and *Sirius*. The force was operating south of Sardinia, and shelled Favignana on the night 11-12 July and Marsala on the West Coast as a diversion. On 21 July she helped shell Cotronei.

She took part in the landings at Salerno (Operation Avalanche - 9 September), during which she was escort to Force H which was covering the landings. Force H included the battleships *Nelson*, *Rodney*, *Warspite* and *Valiant*, and the carriers *Illustrious* and *Formidable*. The force came under air attack the night before the landings and *Warspite* and *Formidable* were narrowly missed.

On 16 September, whilst off the Salerno beaches she was hit by a 6-inch shell from the battleship *Warspite*, which damaged her director, transmitting

HMS Petard in reserve after the war. *(T. Ferrers-Walker Collection)*

station and side plating and also killed and injured several of her crew. *Warspite* was later severely damaged by glider bombs.

On 4 October she transferred to the Levant to assist with a German attack on Kos. On 7 October she, with the cruiser *Carlisle* and destroyer *Panther* sailed from Alexandria and were joined by the destroyers *Aldenham* and *Thermistocles* (Greek) for a night sweep for invasion forces threatening Leros and for any German supply craft. On 8 October the *Aldenham* and *Thermistocles* were relieved by the destroyers *Rockwood* and *Miaoulis* (Greek), and the force sailed north through Scarpento Strait seeking more invasion forces. On completion of their search they turned south for the Strait. At midday the aircraft cover reliefs failed to arrive, but 16 Ju.87s attacked. *Carlisle* was hit by 4 bombs, and came to a stop with only two guns working and 20 dead. *Panther* then was hit twice with further near misses. Her back was broken and she sank rapidly. The force shot down 4 aircraft, and then the air cover appeared and shot down a further 11 enemy aircraft. *Rockwood* took *Carlisle* in tow, stern first, at 12 knots to Alexandria, where the cruiser remained as a base ship for the rest of the war.

Petard and the destroyer *Eclipse* were sent to investigate a minefield off Kalimno where the destroyer *Hurworth* had been sunk and the *Adrias* had her bow blown off. The *Adrias* had been beached in Gurvergenik Bay. The *Eclipse* hit a mine and sank at 0050 on 24 October. *Petard* rescued 44 of her crew. On 30 October she was slightly damaged by a near miss astern, and the next day came under sustained air attacks during which the cruiser *Aurora* was hit and had to return to Alexandria, and the destroyer *Belvoir* was hit by a bomb that failed to explode.

On the night 9-10 November she, *Rockwood* and *Krakowiak* (Polish) found two caiques and a landing craft 10 miles from Levitha. The craft were loaded with troops and the destroyers sank them with gunfire. The next evening they bombarded

Levitha harbour and Port Kalimno during the battle for Leros and Samos in the Dodecanese. They sank a merchant ship (SS *Trapani*) in Kalimno during the bombardment. On the morning of 11 November, at 0020, during the return passage from this operation the destroyer *Rockwood* was hit by a glider bomb, which hit her gearing room but did not explode. Though damaged, *Rockwood* could still steam at 12 knots. However, *Petard* took her in tow so that they could clear the area quickly as they were still under air attack. She towed her for seven hours to the Bay of Losta, in the Gulf of Doris, in Turkish waters, where they anchored. The *Petard* escaped damage during the attacks. On 19th the destroyer *Blencathra* towed the *Rockwood* to safety. Despite the Naval support, the German forces forced the surrender of the British garrison later in the month after heavy fighting.

In January 1944 she transferred to the Eastern Fleet, passing through the Suez Canal on 15 January and sailing for Colombo from Aden on 21 January with the battleships *Valiant* and *Queen Elizabeth*. In February, *Petard*, her sister *Paladin* and the cruiser *Hawkins*, escorted a convoy of five ships from Kilindini to Colombo. On 12th whilst they were off the Maldives, the Japanese submarine *I-27* torpedoed the troopship *Khedive Ismail* (7513 tons) with 1318 passengers (including 19 WRNS and 54 QARNNS) and 188 crew onboard. The troopship sank in 3 minutes leaving 1,000 survivors in the water. *Petard* and *Paladin* remained in the area whilst the rest of the convoy steamed clear escorted by the *Hawkins*. The destroyers detected the submarine hiding under the many survivors from the torpedoed ship. *Petard* attacked the submarine with depth charges whilst *Paladin* rescued survivors, some of whom had got onto floats and rafts. After three depth charge attacks the submarine surfaced to continue the action. The submarine was large, 1,950 tons and was powerfully armed with a 5.5-inch gun and two 25-mm guns. The destroyers' gunfire damaged the submarine, putting her big gun out of action, but *Paladin* was also damaged when she tried to ram. Her side was cut open by the submarine's hydro-plane and she came to a stop. The destroyers had no semi-armour piercing ammunition to inflict fatal damage to the submarine, so *Petard* fired her torpedoes. Her seventh torpedo hit and *I-27* sank. *Petard* then took onboard the survivors from the troopship and submarine, and half of *Paladin*'s crew, before taking her in tow to Addu Atoll, 100 miles away, arriving the next morning at 1000. They had rescued only 214 survivors from the troopship and one crew member of *I-27*.

Petard sailed from Trincomalee on 16 April with the forces supporting a carrier strike on Sabang (Operation Cockpit). They arrived off Sabang on 19th. Aircraft from *Illustrious* and USS *Saratoga* achieved complete surprise and destroyed and damaged oil tanks and port installations. 24 enemy aircraft were destroyed on the ground and only one allied aircraft was shot down, the pilot being rescued by the submarine *Tactician*.

Petard returned through the Suez Canal on 2 August June 1944 and paid off for a refit at Portsmouth. She was re-armed with twin 4-inch guns in B and X position, four 2-pounder pom-poms in a mounting abaft her funnel, two twin 20-mm and two single 20-mm guns. She also retained her two sets of quadruple torpedo tubes, four depth charge throwers and two sets of depth charge rails with an outfit of 70 depth charges. She was fitted with a lattice foremast. The refit completed February 1945.

After a work up at Scapa Flow and further repairs on the Tyne, she proceeded to the East Indies, arriving on 10 August 1945. Shortly after wards she sailed with the battleship *Nelson* and other ships for Penang for Operation Zipper, landing troops to recover Malaya. She was in the force that took the surrender of the Japanese at Penang and at Sabang, the formal ceremonies being on 2 and 3 September.

She remained in the East Indies until May 1946, when she returned to the UK and was placed in reserve at Harwich and later at Chatham. In May 1953 she arrived at Belfast to be converted to a Type 16 anti-submarine frigate at Harland and Wolff, the last of the Type 16 limited conversion of fleet destroyers to fast anti-submarine frigates. After this conversion, which completed on 15 December 1955, she carried a twin 4-inch gun in B position, one twin and three single 40-mm guns and four torpedo tubes, and also two squid anti-submarine mortars aft. She then displaced 1825 tons

(2,400 tons full load). After trials she was put into preservation at Southampton and then towed to Devonport to be placed in reserve. She was commissioned in September 1960 to replace *Ulysses* in the local Plymouth Squadron. In September 1961 she refitted in Chatham and in June 1962 was towed to Devonport, where she remained in reserve until she was sold on 18 May 1967 to P.W. MacLellan. She was towed to Bo'ness on 2 June 1967 to be broken up, the last of the RN Type 16s.

She had gained the Battle Honours Mediterranean 1942-43, Sicily 1943, Salerno 1943, Aegean 1943 and East Indies 1944 for her name.

HMS Petard was one of the fleet destroyers given a limited conversion to become an anti-submarine frigate. She was armed with Squid anti-submarine mortars aft and retained her twin 4-inch gun forward.
(Syd Goodman Collection)